In His Footsteps

Volume II

Shri Ram Chandraji Maharaj of Shahjahanpur
Founder President
Shri Ram Chandra Mission

In His Footsteps

The Diaries of
Shri Parthasarathi Rajagopalachari
[1972 to 1976]
Volume II

Shri Ram Chandra Mission
USA

First Edition: 1993 — 1,000 copies

All rights reserved

© Shri Ram Chandra Mission
North American Publishing Committee
Pacific Grove, CA, USA, 1993

No part of this book may be reproduced in any form or by any means without permission in writing from Shri Ram Chandra Mission.

Printed in U.S.A.

ISBN 0-945242-17-4 (Vol. II)
ISBN 0-945242-04-2 (Set)

Contents

The Heart's Adventure	vi
1972	1
1973	165
1974	189
1975	245
1976	283
Glossary	371

The Heart's Adventure

"Spirituality is the science and the art of remembrance", said my Master, Shri Ram Chandraji, President of Shri Ram Chandra Mission, when I met him for the first time. This meeting took place at his home in Shahjahanpur, in the north Indian state of Uttar Pradesh, where he had lived all his life. At the time of that first meeting in 1964, he was already quite an old person, being in his 66th year. Nevertheless he was very active, and ever busy with his daily work which generally began at 7 A.M. in the morning, and often went on till 1 A.M. the next morning. I was fascinated by his appearance. He was a very handsome person, very fair and slim, even his ribs showing under the thin vest that he wore. He was of medium height, not exceeding 1.65m in height. His weight was around 44 Kg, and sometimes as low as 41 Kg when he was not eating well. That first meeting with him will always remain etched in my memory, for I went as somewhat of a sceptic, and three days or so later left Shahjahanpur a totally changed person

I was intrigued by his first definition of spirituality. I had acquired some familiarity with the religious and yogic texts, though I can claim no scholarship because I lacked a knowledge of the Sanskrit language without which scholarship is virtually impossible. Nevertheless I had an easy, if somewhat faltering, familiarity with these subjects, having become interested in their study when I was around 16 years old. I had never come across such a definition for the subject. Therefore I asked him to clarify his remark, his definition. He obliged instantly, as was his wont when he wished to answer a question. When he did not wish to give an answer, then his eyes would assume a far-away look, and there would only be silence. But if he could not answer a question, then he would instantly say that he did not have the answer, but that he would consult his own Master, Lalaji Maharaj, and give the reply later if he got one himself.

To my question he said, "Look here! We have forgotten our original home from where we have descended to this world in which we are living now. We have become so addicted to material life and values that we no longer remember that original home, the home of our father whom people call God, or by any other name. Now before we can return to that home, there must be something that will make us remember that home. How can someone go to a place of which he knows nothing? And how can he go if he does not remember it? People talk of amnesia, but I am telling you that here we have a permanent amnesia. Therefore I told you that spirituality is the science and the art of remembrance". I could not see anything in this to argue with! This was my very first lesson in spirituality, and I believe that with it I got not merely a definition, but I was also awakened to a sense of the crippling loss that I had suffered over eons of time. It also awakened me to a sense of purpose to return to that original home. For after that first discussion with Shri Ram Chandraji my life was not to be the same again.

The death of my mother when I was just five years old must have touched off something in me, for it made me turn inwards. I became somewhat of a lonely and withdrawn person. This tendency strengthened as I went through school and a University course, but fortunately became oriented into some sort of search, though I knew not what I was looking for. It was a vague longing for inner peace, for inner happiness, for tranquillity.

The average Hindu child begins learning the prayers by heart by being taught them by his parents. My father personally introduced me to such prayers, since he performed puja daily in a small and sacred puja room where the gods of his choice had been earlier solemnly installed with holy chants. We were also told the stories from the famous epics of the Hindus, the Ramayana and the Mahabharatha, to implant in our growing minds an idea of the Hindu religion and its gods and goddesses. This process went on for a long period spread over many years, concurrently with such other disciplines that I evolved for myself from time to time.

My formal initiation into the mysteries of a religious education and search began rather providentially with a compulsory dose of Christianity administered at school. From 1936 to the end of 1943 I studied at the Christ Church Boys' High School in Jubbulpore, in central India. The school belonged to what the English called a public school — very English and thoroughly Protestant in character. A study of the Bible was compulsory, as also was attendance at the school's church. At the end of the school curriculum, and before appearing for the Cambridge School Certificate examination, a student had to compulsorily pass an examination on the Gospel according to St.Mark conducted by the Diocese of Nagpur. Thus I had a thorough exposure to Christianity according to the Protestant church.

I was very impressed by the teachings of Jesus the Christ, especially the emphasis on love and compassion which he preached and practiced all his life upon this earth, and for which he eventually laid down his own life. My younger brother was so very deeply impressed that later on, when he went to a school in Calcutta, a time came when he wanted to embrace the Christian religion! There he met a really dedicated and gifted teacher who honestly tried to live by these very principles. My brother was so profoundly moved by the personal example that Mr.C.Hicks, the teacher, set that he wanted to be converted to his teacher's faith. Fortunately for him we had an understanding father who was able to dissuade him from such a conversion, for we have never really believed that one must change one's religion to evolve in the religious life.

The Hindus believe that one has to grow within one's own religion, the religion into which one has been born, and to eventually evolve out of that religion into spirituality. "Where religion ends, spirituality begins" says my Master. Changing one's religion was neither desirable nor indeed necessary, for all religions offered the same package, using the twin instruments of fear and temptation, as my Master was to explain to me much later in my life. I liked the services at church, and was generally happy to attend the weekly Sunday service. I did not feel oppressed by this compulsion to participate in the practice of another religion, and this perhaps gave me a catholicity of outlook, and a tolerance for the religious beliefs of others, which I might otherwise never have had. This was to serve me well in later life.

I shall always remember that wonderfully wise saying of Swami Vivekananda that while it was good to be born in a religion, it was bad to die in a religion! When I first came across this statement, I did not really understand it, but the clarification that I later received from my Master made it transparently clear. To my Master, changing one's religion was no more effective than changing one's cell in prison. Such a change did not bring about one's liberation, in any case, but only superficially changed the conditions of one's incarceration! My Master used to say that it mattered not a whit whether one was in a bamboo cage or in a golden one! The bird was in the cage, and could never escape.

I was enraptured by the writings of Swami Vivekananda. He was truly a lion, and could roar forth his message in direct and unambiguous language. His message was ever compelling and invigorating, and his language was exceptionally powerful. As the well known German philosopher Schopenhauer has said, few could remain unmoved after reading Vivekananda. I have read deeply of his works, and they have affected my life profoundly. I have often been moved to tears by the profundity of his thought, the depth and beauty of his expression, and the enormous power that his language had to move one out of this world into a different world of wisdom, longing and aspiration. Swami Vivekananda laid, as it were, the foundation for my future spiritual life with my Master, Shri Ram Chandraji.

I had already commenced the practice of meditation on my own without any guidance even before I came to my Master. I had cultivated the habit of meditating upon the Gayathri mantra, mixing the meditation with concurrent practice of pranayama, using the inhalation, retention, and exhalation of breath as specified in the 1:4:2 ratio. Often when I was troubled in mind, I would go to a centre of the Ramakrishna Mission and meditate there. They had generally a congregational approach to their public prayers and chanted mantras intermingled with the recital of the sayings of Shri Ramakrishna Paramahamsa in musical and hymnal form. I could go into deep meditation even while the din of their worship was going on. I had even then trained myself to meditate in all situations. I could slip into a state of meditation even when up in the air, travelling from one city to another — and this has often helped me to travel unaffected by even the worst possible weather conditions, as for instance in a thunderstorm raging outside the plane, which kept most passengers extremely anxious, and some even quite air-sick. Even when I was abroad, there were occasions when I was disturbed in my mind, and extremely lonely. I have often gone to a church to meditate, and derived much solace from it.

It was at Benares while I was a student at the University that I had my first and very gentle exposure to the teachings of Gautama, the Buddha. In a nearby hostel I used to meet a Buddhist monk, Bhikku Sangaratna, who very unassumingly and gently introduced me to that great body of teaching, and this again moved me profoundly. Bhikku Sangaratna hailed from Ceylon, as Sri Lanka was known then. He also gave me some insight into the Sinhalese language. I used to spend many a free hour with that kind and loving savant, and I have profited from his mild and profound character, as much as from his unassuming teaching of the Buddha's message to the world delivered more than 3000 years ago.

Thereafter I started reading books dealing with inner peace, inner harmony and similar subjects. I had always been a voracious reader, but now my pace of reading doubled and trebled, till I was reading a book almost every day. I was fascinated by W.Y.Evans-Wentz's "Tibetan Book of the Dead". My Master was talking about liberation of the human being, and he said, "It is easiest to liberate a person at the moment of death. All that I have to do is to take the soul and lift it up from here to the Brighter world. Later on it becomes more and more difficult as time passes on. And if the soul has taken another birth, then of course it has to go through that existence completely until it becomes worthy of liberation". This is what the Tibetan Book of the Dead also says!

I came across the Sufi mystic, Rumi, and read not only his famous works but went on to literally consume the well known works of other great Sufis, until I had a select collection of books on Sufism. I read books about the Jewish religion, and was amazed at the similarity, in many respects, between its teachings and that of the Sanatana Dharma, as well as some similarity with Buddhism. I read, or rather consumed, the literature from Gurdjeef, and his famous disciple, Ouspensky. I liked Ouspensky's writings very much, and felt that in comparison Gurdjeef's style was obscure and heavy — and rather difficult to understand. Further, the feeling that many have expressed that Gurdjeef was in reality a man without character, and a charlatan, perhaps influenced my opinion.

Many years later when I met my Master, I was quite surprised to find that he was familiar with Ouspensky's name, and had obviously some acquaintance with his book, "In Search of the Miraculous". To my chagrin, I discovered that my Master did not believe in reading books. He told me that at one time he had felt impelled to read some books on philosophy, and had sent for a copy of Mill"s "Utilitarianism". He laughed and said, "I read a few pages of that book because I wanted to know something of philosophy. But look here! The thought came to me after I had read a few pages that if I read that book, or any other book, then I would only repeat their thoughts like a parrot, and I would not be able to bring out my original thinking. So I closed the book and kept it away from me. It is good to read some books, but one must learn to depend upon one's own inner resources for original thinking."

This was something of a blow to me, for as I have said I am a voracious reader. But I derived some satisfaction from the fact that I had not read much my by way of philosophy. I had gone through the works of Plato, whose writings gave me a great joy. I had read one or two of C.E.M. Joad's books. William James fascinated me, and I have been delighted to read his "Essays" again and again, for he has a sublime way of expression, and a profundity of thought, that impressed me deeply. Ralph Waldo Emerson has been one of my all-time favourite authors. I had some familiarity with Schopenhauer. But that was about all. I am somewhat ashamed to say that I had virtually no feeling for poetry. In my effort to read and to understand poetry, I have bought quite a few books and ploughed through them laboriously, but all to no effect. I thought something must be lacking in me. But to my great relief and satisfaction, I found that Babuji Maharaj had no regard or love for poetry, for he felt that poets used their imagination, and were therefore "away from reality" as he put it!.

There is however one genre of literature that has continued to fascinate me throughout my life, and to which I am addicted even now. And that is Fantasy. I have read widely of such books, and my permanent companion is Tolkien's "Lord of the Rings", which I read with great interest year after year. The fascination that those books have for me does not seem to abate, but on the contrary seems to increase with every reading! I also read books on Parapsychology, and the new class of literature which tries to bring the world of matter and the world of the mind into a synthesis.

I was also impressed by the traditions of the Mayas and the Incas. The philosophy of the Chinese was of course a major aspect of my reading, its similarity with the Indian philosophies being really striking. I was also wonderstruck with the novels of certain authors such as Marie Corelli, who revealed through their writings glimpses of their own understanding of the higher truths and values of life. I built up quite a good personal collection of books for, fortunately, I had an income which made it possible for me to indulge myself.

I have been a voracious reader of good science fiction, for I believed that the better writers were endowed with some intuition, and could write about things which were yet not, but which would come later. I remember reading in one of Arthur Clarke's books, for example, about the presence of Oxygen on the moon, and also of a magnetic anamoly. This was later reflected in the findings of the Apollo astronauts which has become history! Why I refer to this here is because my Master had once, perhaps in 1944 or 1945, 'taken' an abhyasi on a spiritual tour, as it were, of the moon, and she gave her report on her findings. The astonishing thing was that what she found tallied exactly with what scientists who landed on the moon discovered several decades later. She has recorded her findings in a note book. Unfortunately, science would never accept her findings revealed to her through my Master's spiritual help, since such spiritual discoveries are not, in their opinion, reproducible - and therefore not scientific! In my Master's major work, Reality at Dawn, which is to Sahaj Marg what the Bible is to the Christian religion, my Master has made several predictions about the future of the world. That too was written in 1944. It is remarkable, or perhaps not so remarkable, that many of those predictions have taken place in actual life decades later.

A fortunate meeting with the famous Indian philosopher-statesman Dr.S.Radhakrishnan led me to a study of the Bhagavad Gita. Dr.Radhakrishnan was then at Oxford as Spalding Professor of Eastern Religions, but later came to the Benares Hindu University as its Vice Chancellor. I was then studying for a Bachelor's degree in Science in the Science college of that University. Dr.Radhakrishnan used to frequently deliver lectures on the Gita, once a month or so, if my memory serves me accurately. We were forced to attend those lectures and to listen to them carefully as we were expected to write a paper on Hindu philosophy as part of our Graduate course studies. It was in any case easier to listen to his enthralling lectures and to write that paper than to have to read through enormous tomes on Indian Philosophy. Those lectures were widely attended, persons often coming from as far away as several hundred miles from Benares to listen to the great man. He was a great speaker, and an erudite scholar and Sanskrit pundit, but I have no doubt that it was his powerful oratory that impressed me so deeply for, not knowing Sanskrit, it was always a problem to understand the quotations that he used. Nevertheless he turned my attention towards the Gita.

As soon as I had completed my degree course at Benares and returned to Bombay I bought a copy of the Gita and read it faithfully at the rate of one chapter every morning. Some chapters were extremely short, while some were quite long, but I would wade through the 18 chapters in eighteen days, and begin the next cycle of reading all over again. That particular edition had the text in Sanskrit together with a word-by-word translation in English. By reading the Gita in that way I managed to get a very limited acquaintance with the profound message of Lord Krishna. As something in the nature of a bonus, I also acquired a somewhat faltering familiarity with the Sanskrit language. I have always regretted not having learnt Sanskrit while at the Benares Hindu University. There were sufficient opportunities for it, but a preoccupation with body-building exercises in the gymnasium, as well as a military training programme in the University Officers' Training Corps, took up a substantial chunk of time available to me.

From the references to other texts in the Bhagavad Gita, such as references to the various Upanishads, I was inspired to read them one by one, and thus I was able to lay down for myself a foundation of the fundamental teachings of the Sanatana Dharma, loosely called Hinduism. The Upanishads were utterly fascinating, and often left me breathless with their grandeur of vision, and their generosity of approach to the human condition, while at the same time offering the Ultimate, and nothing less, as the prize for a proper approach to self-development. At this stage of my fumbling search, I commenced the practice of yogic exercises - both asanas and pranayama - as taught through books which I got from the Kaivalyadhama Yoga Institute in Bombay. Unable to find a proper guide, and not even knowing where to look for one, I did all this entirely by myself, and some disastrous consequences were to follow. But nevertheless I was fairly well established in the aspiration for a different life, somewhat removed from the merely material existence that I was compelled to lead to earn a decent living, for I was married in 1955.

Marriage, with a natural commitment to the family life, inevitably brought about a shift in the focus of my life, but I was able to preserve my longing for the higher life even as I entered the Grihastha existence, and fathered a son in 1957. Since I was employed in a business organization, and especially since I was in the sales force of the company, there inevitably followed what can only be termed as a grossening in some aspects of my life. This was of course to be deplored, but I was able to swim over those temporary temptations and deviations with the strength of the inner longing for the higher life, and so escaped a diversion from the main purpose of my life. The life of a travelling salesman is always fraught with such possibilities of deviation because of the essential loneliness of the traveller who has to be away from home and family for long periods — often as long as three to four weeks at a stretch in my case.

I continued with the practice of yoga but only in a very superficial and desultory manner, and gradually even the practice of asanas stopped. I had abandoned the pranayama exercises as soon as I was married, for I had been warned repeatedly that it could be quite dangerous to do them without the guidance of a Guru. A frightening experience confirmed this. This occurred one morning just as I was preparing to go out of Madras on tour. I was shaving, and suddenly for no reason at all, I was terrified of looking at myself in the mirror. It was a peak experience of terror, at 4 o'clock in the morning! I just wiped my face dry without looking in the mirror and went back to bed. That experience confirmed that I had to stop pranayama, and so that was the end of that. For the practice of asanas there was literally no time as my daily schedule varied almost from day to day, and in any case it was not possible to practice them on my travels. So all that remained by the time I was 29 years old was a fierce longing in my heart without the support of any practical attempt to realize whatever goal lay hidden in my heart — for of the goal too I had no clear concept.

After graduating from the Benares Hindu University in 1948, I had to move to Bombay where my father had a job. I had to search for employment, and found a decent job which gave me some free time too. I was attracted to the teachings of the Theosophical Society, and used to attend their monthly meetings to listen to readings from their literature. I was curious to read the bulky books of Mme. Blavatsky, as well as those of Olcott and Mrs. Annie Besant. There was much room for thought, but after reading them I was left with the feeling that they dealt more with Esoteric and Occult subjects, and had no real practical approach to a higher life to offer to an aspirant.

At this stage I turned to religion and to religious studies, and commenced what is called Veda Parayana - the study of the Vedas by recitation in the prescribed manner with the help of a qualified Vedic pundit in an effort to memorize them. I did this for approximately three or four years, and was able to progress to the satisfaction of my teachers. Our home in Madras frequently resounded and reverberated with the holy chant of the Vedas rendered by a scholarly group of pundits, for we became quite addicted to their sonorous and hypnotic chant. There was then no substitute available to this, and so I went on with it. I was often perturbed by the sundry deviations from the so-called religious life that my life as a company executive imposed upon me, but there was no help for it. I tried to solve this by accepting initiation from our traditional Vaishnavite acharya, who at first refused to initiate me on the ground that my father had not yet been thus initiated. This upset me, for I rightly felt that my father had nothing to do with it, the need for initiation being a personal inner demand that could not be refused. This abrupt refusal by him was to eventually lead me away from the path of Brahminism, and religion altogether.

It was a time of agonizing inner struggle coupled with apparent external success, for I was rising fast in my company. But the inner feelings of turmoil were ever present until a chance meeting with a new friend of my father's brought Sahaj Marg into my life in February 1964. Thus the divine presence of the person who was to become my spiritual Master — Shri Ram Chandraji Maharaj — came into my life, almost as if by the back door! The miracle that I had been awaiting for three decades had become a reality, and my journey towards that Reality commenced. The journey, I was to discover with something of a shock, was never to end, for my Master aptly called it "Towards Infinity".

It was by this apparently fortuitous circumstance that my life acquired a definite and positive orientation towards the life of spiritual pursuit. I had assumed that this meeting had occurred by 'accident', but my Master later clarified that what a human being thought of as an accident was really part of the Divine plan, and that there were really no such things as accidents except those that occurred due to human foolishness, greed or error. The time had come to bid good bye to religion and to ritual practices such as *parayana, puja, nithya upasana* etc., strictly enjoined upon the pious Hindu. I was able to do this without much regret. I was never a temple-goer, my rare visits to temples being in the company of visiting friends or officials whom I had to escort for one reason or another. It was fortunate for me that even though I had been deeply involved with the Vedas for some years, it was not a problem for me to drop the daily Veda *parayana*, though it saddened my teachers who had hoped to see me emerge from their hands as perhaps some sort of a minor teacher to follow them. I was sad for them, but that too did not trouble me in any way, for after all I had to satisfy my inner longing which was thirsting for fulfillment.

When I met my Master for the first time there was an element of disappointment for I made the asinine mistake of looking at his physical person to evaluate and judge him whom I was seeing. I could not have done otherwise as I did not have the ability to look 'inside' him to perceive or experience the inner being of resplendent luminosity that was seated there in harmony, silence and eternal bliss. For a few moments I was sorely disappointed with what I saw, for I had travelled a long way from Madras to Shahjahanpur to meet him. I had imagined his home as an enormous ashram teeming with devoted spiritual practicants, the whole place humming with activity and resounding with the chanting of the holy hymns of the Vedas. I had also fantasized and imagined him in some mysteriously divine form with divine attributes and so on.

He was not there for me to see. There was only one person present, and he led me inside the small and rather musty old house to a room where Babuji Maharaj, as he was generally called, was sleeping on a frail bamboo-and-ropes contraption which people in the north of India use as cots. What I saw lying on that charpoy, as those cots are called, was a small man, very delicately built, not tall at all, lying with his knees drawn up almost to his chin, so that he was really a tiny bundle of human presence. He had a beard which I saw as soon as he turned in his bed towards me, and became awake perhaps sensing the presence of a visitor near his bed. He sat up and looked at me with a keenness that was extremely disturbing, for he seemed to look right through me, and to see instantly all that was there to be seen. It was a moment of intense embarrassment for me, and there was an element of fear in it too, for I had just arrived from Bareilly, a town near Shahjahanpur, after a hearty company lunch there, with all the paraphernalia of such lunches.

He had such penetrating and keen eyes, deep gray in colour, with the central part, the pupil, almost totally transparently blue-gray, so that as I looked into them I seemed to be looking into something endless, something that was as profound as eternity, with no beginning and no end to it. I have never seen such a pair of eyes in any human being before, nor have I seen any since then! While he was thus inspecting my inside, and all it took was but a moment of time, I could sense in him an utter gentleness and a love that surpassed all that I had ever experienced in my life till then. I understood that there was absolutely no need for fear, and the fact that I was embarrassed and mildly anxious with his inspection was due to my own feelings of guilt rather than to anything in his keen gaze.

He finished his inspection of my inner self in a brief few moments and then, with a gentle and somewhat shy smile, he asked me where I was from. I told him that I had come from Madras. He was the perfect host, going to the extent of asking for my luggage to be brought into the house from my car, and even pumping vigorously away at the handle of a primitive hand pump to pump water into a bucket for me to wash with. I was extremely embarrassed by this attention, for in the Indian tradition a disciple is supposed to serve the Guru, and not vice versa! I had also come with the intention of returning to Bareilly after a few hours with him, but he gave me no choice, and my stay with him eventually extended itself to a couple of days — an extremely fortunate thing for me, for it created from the very first moment an easy intimacy with him which I was to treasure and cherish for ever. Apart from that, this friendly intimacy made it possible for me to establish a relationship with him in which guilt played no part, and where consequently there was no fear of him, except on one or two later occasions.

The only way I can describe my discipleship under my Master, with the growing intimacy between us, is to call it a spiritual love affair. It might sound quite absurd to say that I had a deeply fulfilling love affair with him, and some may even think this to be puerile, a juvenile crush or some silly thing like that. But it would not be wrong to say that I fell in love with him again and again as my spiritual life progressed under his care. I wrote to him once to tell him about the sense of wonder that I was then experiencing. I asked him how it was possible for love to grow and grow, seemingly without any limit, and would not the human heart simply burst with the pressure of such love? My Master wrote back very simply and said, "I too love you, and this I must not repeat." He was probably giving me a silent but potent lecture on the ethics of love for, in the Indian cultural and moral tradition, one does not speak openly of one's love for another, since love is a sacred matter, a matter for silent communication between the persons concerned!

It seemed to me that this association with him was a predetermined affair, an affair of destiny. There was such a naturalness to it from the very beginning that I felt that he and I had been together several times in our past lives, and that in the present life we were but renewing an old and long established relationship in which, time and again, He had been the Master and I his disciple. Some years later, after our relationship had become one of loving friendship between a Master and his disciple, he revealed that this had in fact been the case, and that I had been his disciple at least in two previous existences!

It is true that for the first year or so I kept a little distance between us, for he had with him a devoted older disciple who looked after him with a fierce and somewhat possessive protectiveness. This person looked with suspicion upon all who ventured to approach the Master too closely, and he also had some notions of his own about how a disciple should behave with the Master. If I had approached the Master too closely, I would have been accused of lack of respect towards him — and in India that would have been a serious accusation. But as if to offset this attitude my Master drew me closer and closer to himself all the time, and a time soon came when even Mr Ishwar Sahai, for that was his name, could no longer come between my Master and myself. My closeness with Babuji

Maharaj created a great deal of problems for me, human nature being what it is. It was not all smooth sailing, but his love and affection made even the most obnoxious circumstance bearable, if not acceptable. It was a training in one of his most often repeated statements, "Only he who is happy under all circumstances is the really happy person!" By his grace and with his blessings it is possible to approximate to this state of being, as I have discovered for myself with joy, and with increasing confidence in myself.

To say that my spiritual life was all smooth sailing would be to indulge in a gross understatement. But there were never any serious problems for, from the very beginning, I had not gone to my Master with any expectations, even for spiritual progress such as liberation etc. There was therefore never any question of my expecting any reward from him. I think that he was delighted by this attitude, though he never publicly remarked upon it. Nevertheless he told me quite often that it was difficult to get a disciple who left everything to the Master without making any demands upon him. In fact he has often gently admonished persons who came to him with such demands, saying that if the Master were to be given total freedom to do what he thought necessary in each case, the abhyasis, as spiritual practicants are called under the Sahaj Marg system, would marvel at what they could become in a short time.

Being a busy company executive with duties involving a great deal of travel throughout India, as well as visits to Europe and the U.K., someone had suggested to Babuji Maharaj that I would make an ideal preceptor as I had the possibility of travelling freely almost at will. Once when I was in Shahjahanpur, Master called me into his room and asked me to sit before him in meditation. I sat as ordered, and the sitting, as we call them, lasted about forty minutes. Midway through the sitting my Master mumbled something in Hindi which I could not hear. I opened my eyes to see what he wanted. He gestured to me to continue with the sitting. Later on I asked him what he had been saying. He laughed and said, "I was giving you permission to do the spiritual work of the Mission. I have just made you a preceptor, and I know that you will do good work by the Master's grace". I was taken aback because he had not asked me whether I was willing to take up the work, but he brushed aside my unspoken objection, saying, "I did it under the instructions of my Master, Lalaji Maharaj." And to that of course I had no comment to offer, for who could override the wishes of the Grand Master, as Lalaji was called!

It was in memory of Lalaji Maharaj that my Master had created the organization which bears his name — Shri Ram Chandra Mission. This was in 1945. I joined the Mission in February 1964. When I attended the annual celebration of Lalaji's birth anniversary at Shahjahanpur for the first time in 1965, there were no more than forty abhyasis present for this holy and auspicious event. I was made a preceptor in 1967, and found that by then numbers had increased considerably. By 1970 it had become necessary to hire premises for the visiting abhyasis because by then the number of participants at the celebration touched 700.

I was appointed as the Secretary of the Mission in January, 1970. The Mission was still operating only within India, but the organization had now to be properly structured and made an effective one. The Mission had been functioning from my master's home ever since it had been founded in 1945, but there was very little correspondence, and visitors to his home were few and far between. In those years even up to 1967, I have seldom found more than two or three persons in residence. Now it became necessary to cater to ever increasing numbers of abhyasis who all had to stay in his home. The organization had also to be strengthened to take on bigger and bigger loads of correspondence. This formidable task fell to my lot. I was quite apprehensive of my being able to perform my duties to Master's satisfaction, but he brushed aside all my fears, saying with a sweet and loving smile on his face, "By Lalaji's grace you will do good work. The Mission will grow, and you will also grow with it. So don't have any negative thoughts about it. And of course my help is always there".

I now had two very demanding responsibilities to fulfill. On one side there was my job, and already in 1968 I had been given a position on the Board of Directors of one company, and placed in sole charge of it. On the other side there was the Mission, and my responsibilities as its Secretary, with the whole organization in India as my responsibility, and some 1500 abhyasis to serve. But I had no choice at all. I was being pushed by my destiny into something which was far beyond my capacity, but when the Master trusted me I could hardly refuse. Thanks to my job, I had the possibility of travelling all over India, and so could meet abhyasis almost everywhere, and spend time at the centres of the Mission giving talks and conducting meditation sessions. All this kept me extremely busy, but I found the work very satisfying and fulfilling, and I began slowly to actually enjoy what I had to do. It became possible to streamline the working of the Mission, and I am happy that my work invariably found favour with my Master.

The Mission's work brought me closer and closer to my Master in all ways, and his confidence in me grew so fast that soon I was handling practically all the administrative work of the Mission from my home in Madras, thus relieving him to concentrate more and more on his spiritual work of 'overhauling nature' as he put it. I had visited

France and Germany in 1970 and brought some promising aspirants to the Mission. In 1971 my father went to Europe on a private visit, and was able to establish centres of the Mission in Rome and Copenhagen. Thus the Mission's work went beyond the shores of India. On a subsequent visit I was able to establish centres of the Mission in France and in England. Encouraged by this activity, Babuji decided to visit Egypt, Europe and the U.S.A. during the three months of the second quarter of 1972, and chose me to accompany him. I urged him to take someone who could help him more than I could, but he calmly said that if I refused to accompany him he would cancel his plans to travel abroad. That was the first of several overseas travels, and it was on these journeys outside India that our association became very close and intimate, since we, just the two of us, were together for 24 hours a day for weeks or months at a time.

I have accompanied my beloved Master on six overseas voyages of discovery during the period from 1972 to 1982. The human joy and the spiritual benefit that I derived from being His devotee and His servitor cannot be described. They were indeed voyages of discovery, discovery of myself more than of anything else. On those wonder-and-ecstasy-filled voyages the Master too revealed Himself to me progressively in all His glory and transcendence. It was my greatest good fortune that he selected me for this work, and I shall always cherish the blissful memories of those long months spent in intimate association with him — months full of work when we could hardly rest for more than a couple of hours every day; months of profound and deep instruction; months of the most inspiring discussions; and for good measure those long months were filled to the brim with his delightful but meaningful jokes, and his sharp wit and brilliant humour, all punctuated by His blissful and charming smiles and innocent laughter, which made all the abhyasis gathered around him roar with laughter. Often he would move us to tears, for he had the capacity to make everyone plunge into the very depths of his being, and none escaped those moments of raw emotion when the very soul of the person was bared for all to see.

I slowly imbibed the teaching that he imparted to me both through subtle discussion as well as during meditation sittings with him. He made me give sittings to other abhyasis in his presence, and thus trained me by commenting on my work, teaching me the various techniques of cleaning and transmission that were necessary for the work. Eventually a day came when he permitted me to prepare preceptors — a work exclusively his own till then. He had also made me a full preceptor in January 1970, thus making it possible for me to do what he called "higher work on the cosmic plane" under his definite orders. Such higher work could of course be undertaken only upon orders from the Master himself. It is perhaps a feature unique to Sahaj Marg that preceptors were 'permitted' to work, and there was no such thing as being qualified to work. When permission to do some higher work was given by the Master, the ability to perform that work was automatically bestowed upon him. Therefore however elevated a preceptor might be, nothing could be done except under the specific orders and instructions of the Master. In course of time I was even assigned certain specific cosmic work which I carried out to his satisfaction, as he personally confirmed to me.

In 1974 Babuji Maharaj went into a coma from which he fortunately recovered after a month's sojourn in a hospital in Lucknow. When he became conscious again, he called sister Kasturi, the abhyasi I have referred to earlier in regard to her experience upon the surface of the moon, and told her that the time had come for him to nominate his spiritual successor, as the future of the Mission had to be ensured and put in capable hands. He had told a few of us that he would live on the earthly plane till 2006 or 2007. When sister Kasturi reminded him of this, and asked him what was the urgency to nominate his representative, he answered gravely, "Life and death are in God's hands, and none can say when the call to go back to Him will come. I am no longer confident of living so long. So it is imperative that I appoint my successor, and I have decided to do it immediately". He then revealed to her that he had chosen me to be His successor, and had been preparing me for the work over a period of many years. I had been with him in Lucknow, and accompanied him back to Shahjahanpur. It was there the next morning that he revealed to me my future destiny, and this intention he executed some time later in the form of a nomination, after he had recovered almost fully from his grave illness.

I had wanted to do, and to be, many things in life. I loved music, and I had become quite a capable flutist too. As a matter of fact I had almost decided to become a professional musician. Music continues to haunt me to this day, and whenever possible I still listen to the music of my choice — though I love all music. I had wanted to be a geologist, for geology fascinated me, and I had studied the subject for my B.Sc degree in Benares. I was also drawn to the discipline of the army, and had participated in a two year training course in the University Officers' Training Corps while at Benares. I had even appeared for selection into the armed forces, but my bad eyesight prevented that. None of these desires were childish day dreams or merely juvenile desires for the future. They had been serious choices at different stages of my life. To be a spiritual guide had never featured in my scheme of things, for I had strayed quite innocently into the field. Given a choice, the job of spiritual trainer would not have featured on my list at all.

In India I was considered to be above average in intelligence. I had also acquired a good education, and my wide travels in India had given me a broad outlook on life, as well as an ability to manage adequately in many of the Indian languages without embarrassment. My frequent visits to Europe, the U.K., the middle east, and to certain of the African countries had brought many changes in my outlook, and earned for me a reputation of being somewhat westernized! Therefore most of my relatives and acquaintances were puzzled when I took to the spiritual life like a duck takes to water. There was a great deal of criticism when I was made a preceptor before my father was. This was a typical manifestation of the general Indian attitude to such situations. Why I say all this is to show that I had no desire whatever for the job my Master eventually bestowed upon me. I do not know even now why my Master chose me to succeed him. But when I asked him this question once, he replied with a most disarming smile, "Lalaji chose you, and of course you are my choice too. You will do good work. You will achieve all that I have not been able to do, and the Mission will shine under your leadership." He had stated a great number of times that the ideal human being should have an Indian heart and a European mind. Perhaps in this lies the clue to my dilemma, and to that of many others.

My Master emphasized that one who wanted to achieve the highest goal open to mankind must work for it. A practical approach under a capable guide was essential for this. And the guide must be one who has traversed the path himself, and be so familiar with it that he could guide other seekers over it again and again. In a sense the Guru, for that is how we call the spiritual guide in the Indian tradition, is the bridge from here to the hereafter; from this human life into the eternal spiritual existence; from this mundane world to the Brighter world. I also prefer to think of him as a tunnel which leads us from here to the destination. It may be dark and even frightening at times, but the circle of light at the far end of the tunnel guides us surely and certainly to the destination, into a world illumined with the light of truth and immortality. For the adventure, the spiritual quest, the spiritual journey, is from one's own heart to His divine heart, and this is the way that such an adventurer must travel. Such a tunnel or such a bridge is the Master.

My Master thus guided me into Himself with enormous patience, compassion and his divine love. I shall be eternally grateful to him for his timely assistance and his eternal love. And for the faith and confidence that he has reposed in me to carry on His work, I can do nothing better than to pray to him to guide me from the Brighter world as He has been doing from the earthly plane till my work is completed, and the light is bequeathed to the destined heart awaiting to take over the responsibility from my hands, once again, and so on, in unending succession.

Bangalore
31st December, 1991
P. Rajagopalachari

Beloved Babuji with Parthasarathi
Copenhagen, 1972

1972

I attended Basant Panchami at Shahjahanpur on 20, 21 and 22nd January. Mr. B. Ramachandran, W/M, ITPT Ltd., and R. Swaminathan, were both with me. Mr. M.A. Sayeed of Hyderabad turned up direct. Record attendance. There were also the Danish abhyasis Vibe, Thomas, Ole Larsen, Bjorn and his wife Kirsten.

11 Feb. 72 - Friday

Revered Master accompanied by Sister Kasturi arrived at Madras by air from Delhi at 18:35. I met them at the airport and drove them to Umesh's house at Besant Nagar. Spent some time there with Master. He said, among other things:

"Destroy your own creation ... God comes! For everything there is a base. If you destroy this base then the Divine base comes."

"Satisfaction is your own production, and Peace is the production of God! Restlessness is pregnant with Rest."

12 Feb. 72 - Saturday

Some of Master's sayings:

"A *gnani* is one who does not lament over the past, and is grateful for the present."

"An intellectual is inwardly talented. Intelligence is inward tangibility."

13 Feb. 72 - Sunday

Satsangh at Ashram taken by Master. After satsangh Master went to Shri S. Narayanaswamy's house and then came to Gayathri by 9:15 A.M. Mr. Fred Weinstock of U.S.A. was granted Provisional Permission by Master at 11 A.M.

At 12:30, I accompanied Master, K.C. Narayana, Kasturi and Miss Spencer Kimball of U.S.A. to receive Mrs. Grace Kimball and two others. Then we all came back to Gayathri.

At 3:30 P.M. Master gave an individual sitting to Dr. V. Parthasarathy and his wife. At 5 P.M. took Master back to Besant Nagar while Kasturi remained at Gayathri.

While we were returning from the airport to Gayathri, Master told Kasturi, "Look here, Kasturi. For this person (meaning me) I am thinking of doing something for him but I am not able to do it. Just now Lalaji Maharaj told me, 'Whatever you are thinking of doing for this person it will be done in 24 hours.' Lalaji Saheb is very happy with him." Kasturi, addressing me, said, "See Brother, now your work is already over."

14 Feb. 72 - Monday

Went to Besant Nagar at 12:30 P.M. to see Master. He came to Gayathri and stayed till 3:15 P.M. He told Kasturi, "Now you try and tell me his condition." Kasturi said, "Whatever was locked up in his heart has now been released and there is now light in his face." Master said, "Yes, and look here. Lalaji Saheb told me at exactly 12:30 P.M., 'Here you are brother. He is your case.'" Master went on to say, "Now look here, there is still something I want to do." Then he asked me, "I think your super-conscious has been opened up to this point?" (pointing to *brahmanda mandal*) I said, "No Master, only the heart." Then Master told Kasturi, "Now I want to take up his *kundalini* and side by side also the super-consciousness. I have been thinking about this from the beginning but two months ago he was not ready for it. Now his intelligence will increase very much."

The whole day I felt very light and gay. After 8 P.M. I felt **LOST** and some sort of deep sleep coming over me.

15 Feb. 72 - Tuesday

Sat for meditation in the morning by myself as usual. I felt that while I was sitting still, things like walls, roads, all moved towards me, into me, and through me, and finally it was as if the world itself was moving into and through me. I told Kasturi of this experience. She said, "Very good. It is the condition of *hiranya garbha* but your present condition is far far ahead of this." Then she told me that after we had all gone to bed last night, she was in the downstairs room as usual. She saw me entering her room, and it was so real an experience that she sat up in bed to greet me — and found I was not there at all! She feels that it must have been my *sookshma sharir*. Then I told her about Master's letter to me, where he says that due to the *annamaya kosha* having been broken, I can develop certain *siddhis*, and that I can be in two places at the same time.

Later, at 2 P.M., I asked Master about my morning experience during meditation. He said, "The experience no doubt is good, that the world has gone in through you is very good. The meaning of this is that hitherto you were going after the world but now the world is running after you."

16 Feb. 72 - Wednesday

Master was with us at Gayathri the whole day. Master took satsangh at the ashram in the evening. Record number of overseas abhyasis in attendance: Vibe, Thomas, Ole, Bjorn, Kirsten and a sixth Dane, Leif Larsen, then Mrs. Grace Kimball of USA, her daughter Spencer and two other ladies of the USA.

I asked Master about something I have experienced for quite long — when meditation is deepest, when devotion is almost complete, one corner of my own mind seems to throw up doubts asking questions such as, "How do you know your Master is not deceiving you? How do you know what you are feeling and experiencing is real? Perhaps the old man is using you for his own purposes, and all this is sheer humbug," and so on.

Master answered, "When there is much devotion then emotion also begins to be there. And Lalaji Saheb has said that emotion instead of being associated with the *atma* keeps a connection with the self, and then such ideas are born."

17 Feb. 72 - Thursday

Came across a French proverb 'Le meilleur moyen d'eliminer est de remplacer,' i.e., the best way to eliminate is to substitute! Very apt for concentration.

"An idea is a Being incorporeal, which has no subsistence of itself but gives figure and form unto shapeless matter and becomes the cause of the manifestation." (Plutarch: *De Placit Philos*.)

Master spent the whole day at Gayathri — deep in his work of correcting the manuscript of "At the Feet of the Master", the 1st part of his Autobiography. In the evening

Master sent Kasturi to the ashram to take the satsangh, Sulochana and I alone remaining with him at Gayathri.

Suddenly at 19:03 Master said, "Look here, I wanted to give you both a sitting. But Lalaji is saying, 'Send them to me.'" So we went inside (we were sitting out) and Master put a fresh cover on his bed. We meditated for about 10 minutes. As I entered Master's room I felt an electric flash going through me — but nothing significant during the meditation itself. But when Master came into the room after about ten minutes (he had gone out after asking us to sit before Lalaji) and said, "That's all!", again an electric flash went through me.

Master told me, "You are already full but whatever was inside was not coming out. I was thinking about this only when Lalaji completed the work for me."

Later, when accompanying Master to Besant Nagar, he spoke about dreams being true indicators of a man's condition. Then I told him about the dream I had regarding Mr. B — on the hill top where I felt a murder had been committed, and that Mr. B was the murderer. I reminded Master I had written to him about this dream but he had not replied. Master said at first that he could not know what it was about. Then suddenly he said, "Now I have received a reply from above. Mr. B killed himself — the real meaning of this is that he had not developed to the extent that was possible in him. There was a great deal of ego in him and this was the reason that he could not develop further!" Addressing sister Kasturi, he said, "Do you remember Kasturi how much excitement there was in him at the time of his death and how, only after I was able to remove it, his work was done?"

Miss Kathryn Paul of USA, a student learning the flute under Shri N. Ramani, and her sister Deborah, both took their first sitting from Kasturi.

19 Feb. 72 - Saturday

Master and Kasturi left for Bangalore en route Channapatna, by Brindavan Express.

I left by car with T.K. Narasimhan and R. Swaminathan for Bangalore.

20 Feb. 72 - Sunday

To Channapatna in the morning. Master took over a property donated to the Mission — big gathering — meditation in the new place. After the function I left for Mysore and Nanjangud and on to Bhavanisagar.

23 Feb. 72 - Wednesday

I returned to Madras from Bhavanisagar. Master had arrived from Bangalore yesterday. He was at Gayathri when I arrived at 4:15 P.M. He explained a few points he had been thinking over for some time.

1) Why abhyasis who have attained high spiritual levels fall? He explained that when they rise, a way is created for them to ascend by. Later, when they have reached the height, the way is still open, and it is by this they fall, if they do fall. So the way is to forget the way after one has gone up.

2) What is the activity of nature? It is inactivity — but nature lays the **base**.

24 Feb. 72 - Thursday

Master called me to Besant Nagar for a special sitting of 35 minutes from 7:40 to 8:15 A.M. Sister Kasturi was observing. As soon as transmission commenced I felt that something was turned in me in the vertical plane, making some sort of inner adjustment. Thereafter I felt I was soaring away upwards at rocket speed, and the whole world fell away beneath me. At a particular point the upward movement stopped and I felt a great expansion. When this ended the upward movement began again. Great white billowing clouds, glowing brilliantly white, appeared to float into me. I felt my chest and abdominal viscera were all carved out of me leaving only the spine, head and lower skeletal frame. I felt I was a room or box which went on being filled up — and at one stage I found that the filled vessel had melted away and the inside and outside were all one. At this point Master ended the sitting.

Master told Kasturi, "Every point of his is now glowing. I have done a lot of work on his heart, and I have also opened the super-consciousness at this point — pointing to the *brahmanda mandal* — now see, how every point is glowing."

Took Master at 3:30 P.M., to T.K. Narasimhan's office — there till 5:30. We then went to the beach for some time — then to Gayathri till 8:15 P.M., after which I took Master back to Besant Nagar.

The whole day I felt that I was asleep with my eyes open.

25 Feb. 72 - Friday

Master called me to Besant Nagar at 7:30 A.M. for a special sitting. When transmission commenced, I felt tension in my forehead and some slight pain also. Later it became deep. Master stopped the sitting after about 15 minutes. When I told him of the tension and slight pain Master said, "I have increased the power." Later after 15 minutes rest he again gave me a sitting for about seven minutes. Kasturi said she saw a snake. Master answered, "Yes, it is correct. I have also touched the *kundalini*. Now look here you already know that there are three sets of points — referring to the points in the lumbar region of the spine. I have just touched the middle set of those points." Kasturi said, "But it is not yet awakened." Master answered, "No, for that three touches are necessary — but it shall be done." Then he continued, "Now I should have my reward for it." Then to Kasturi, he added, "I also wish that I could give him two slaps because in between he also creates some problems."

26 Feb. 72 - Saturday

I went to Besant Nagar at 7 A.M. Master was talking to Kasturi and me generally about the *kundalini* and its power. He said that when the *kundalini* is awakened:

a) Nature becomes an open book — you can read nature.

b) Power of concentration increases.

c) Work can be done in higher worlds.

At 7:30 A.M. Master gave me a special sitting for about seven minutes. I felt as if my head had been cleaned out and a vacuum created inside, and into which Master was pouring in something.

Master told Kasturi, "Do you remember that his 4th point was swollen up. It was because of some worries. Maybe worries connected with the office or maybe connected with his home. Too much power has been put in it. I have withdrawn that power and in its place I have filled it with Divinity — now he is all right." At this point I related my own experience and Master was very pleased. He got up from his seat, patted me on the shoulders and said, "Sabaash! You have told me your correct condition."

Then suddenly after about 10 minutes he asked me to sit again saying, "Sit in front of Lalaji Saheb." It lasted only two minutes. Master said Lalaji had adjusted something. I can't remember exactly what. Master said all points were still glowing.

27 Feb. 72 - Sunday

Master told me not to join the general satsangh. But after Master completed 30 minute satsangh I gave an extempore talk on 'Sadhana' for about 15 minutes, much appreciated by Master, who wanted me to speak only so that he could study me and see if anything was necessary to be done before going abroad. After satsangh Master came to Gayathri.

At 9:45 A.M. Master took me upstairs for a sitting — about 15 minutes. I felt as if a snake were rising out of a dark ocean. The movement of the snake was a spiral movement, and where the head of the snake should have been was a lotus flower. As the lotus emerged out of the ocean — the surface of the ocean seemed to coincide with the level where the sternum ends — it opened up and power flowed out of it upwards like a fountain spray, coming down to spread all over the system. Some heat was also produced. When the sitting ended at 10 A.M. Master said, "Now your *kundalini* has been awakened." I asked him whether this was temporary or permanent. Master said it was permanent and nothing could change it back.

Master discussed with Kasturi this difference in the *kundalini* in his system from all other systems — that it does not go up by the spine but in front, and said, "I don't know what the *rishis* saw. But brother, this is my experience."

29 Feb. 72 - Tuesday

While we were sitting in Besant Nagar, Master suddenly started laughing amusedly — I asked him what was the matter. Master said, "Look here, Lalaji Saheb is saying that I should take that poor girl also — do you understand? And he is referring to my daughter-in-law, Sulochana." Later he gave a special sitting to Sulochana. He told me privately that there was some grossness which he was not sure whether it was due to some disease or just due to grossness. He said there was some enlargement in the heart area but was positive there was no enlargement of the heart itself. He however, seemed worried and went on to relate several instances where he had foreseen a future heart attack many years earlier — 15 years earlier in the case of Mr. Hari Gopal Agarwal who has had a heart attack about 4 months ago. He seemed worried whether in Sulochana's case there was some such complication. He asked Kasturi to take her pulse — Kasturi said it was normal, just two beats faster. Master said he would examine Sulochana again tomorrow.

1 Mar. 72 - Wednesday

Master gave Sulochana a special sitting. As soon as I came home from the office Master told me, "I have examined my daughter-in-law again — now she is cleaned. Brother, I was a bit worried that it may not be any disease of the heart and that she may not have a heart attack. But there is no such thing. It was only heaviness, and that has now been cleared away." Then he asked me, "And how are you feeling today?" I told him I had been feeling so light the whole day that my heart is singing. Master said, "Yes, there will of course be lightness. What lightness there was originally is not there now. But greyness has been born. Lalaji Saheb is saying that this means that the *kundalini* has been awakened and this is of course a fact, but now there has come into it a naturalness. From tomorrow you will not feel anything. Look here! What I have done for you the same thing I have done for Dr. K.C. Varadachari also. But he didn't feel anything, and he was not prepared to accept it. I had even written to him but what can I do? Whether he had accepted it or not whatever work was done was in fact done. This is all that I can say. Brother, if one who is looking cannot see, what can I do about it? I am also in need of encouragement and if somebody can encourage me then let him see what all I can do for him. By Lalaji's grace everything is possible, and so far there has not been any failure in my work. All that is necessary is that people should strive for growth, and see what is going on. And suppose they do not see anything, at least they should accept what I am saying — but instead of that when they begin to doubt me then brother I become weak. Because, after all, I am also a human being."

General satsangh at Ashram at 7 P.M. About 10 minutes after commencement I felt as if someone was massaging my spine upwards, by holding it in the closed fist and squeezing it, then putting the fist of the other hand above the first one and squeezing that part of the spine, and so on — three times only. I also felt that the transmission was in two bands — one band brilliant and dazzling, the other, grey.

2 Mar. 72 - Thursday

Master, accompanied by Sister Kasturi, left for New Delhi by plane, en route Shahjahanpur.

Master's Overseas Tour 1972

18 Apr. 72 - Tuesday

I left Madras by Indian Airlines evening Boeing 737 on Flight 439 for Delhi to meet Master and accompany him abroad. Quite a fair-sized group saw me off at Meenambakkam. Master is staying with Sethuratnam at Jor Bagh. This time he did not stay with the Sundaras as their son and daughter, Vivek and Kalpana, are preparing for their examinations, and his presence would be a disturbance.

On arrival at Palam at 9:30 P.M., I was met by K.T.V. Santhanam, T.T. Jagannathan and A. Ganesh Viswanathan of our Delhi office. I drove straight to Jor Bagh where Master was anxiously awaiting my arrival. Sister Kasturi and Shashi Tandon had already arrived and were with Master.

19 Apr. 72 - Wednesday (Delhi)

Dr. Harnam Singh came in the morning to see about Master's requirements. All visas had already been obtained, the only thing left being to obtain foreign exchange. We left at 10 A.M., went to the State Bank of India and in two hours managed to get the U.S. $100/- to which Master is entitled. Master went back home. I went with Sethu to see about Air India reservations for Delhi/Bombay and Bombay/Cairo seats for tomorrow — and found they, AI (Air India), had not even received the Madras AI request for these reservations. Anyway by running up and down between IAC and AI, I got everything done by 3 P.M., bought a pair of shoes for myself and came back to Jor Bagh.

At 4 P.M., Mr. Sundara gave a tea party at his residence in Sundar Nagar for a small group of invitees with Master. Sethu, Shri Raman Lal Mimani, who came in from Calcutta to see Master, Shri S.K. Rajagopalan and I were part of the group.

At 7 P.M. a large group of invitees numbering more than thirty gathered at the nearby residence of Shri Rajeshwar Prasad. Mr. S.K. Rajagopalan spoke in English on Sahaj Marg, then I spoke, and finally Sister Kasturi spoke in Hindi. Then there was group meditation for 20 minutes and finally dinner for the whole gathering.

20 Apr. 72 - Thursday (Delhi)

People started coming in to see the Master from about 9:30 A.M. onwards. When we left Sethu's house in Jor Bagh for the airport at 4:30 P.M., nearly 30 people were assembled to bid goodbye to Master. At the airport we had nearly 45 minutes to wait. A large number of people had assembled at Palam airport including Shri Rohan Lal Chaturvedi and his wife, Mr. and Mrs. Sundara, Dr. Harnam Singh and his Canadian wife, Helen, Shri S.K. Rajagopalan, Sethu, the TTK group staff and many others including Sister Kasturi.

We boarded IAC Boeing 737 Aircraft on Flight 405, which took off at 17:55 hrs. and landed at Santa Cruz airport, Bombay, at 19:35 hours. It was still virtually daylight when we got out of the aircraft, and we were pleasantly surprised to see Seth Vallabhdas K. Tank, Bapubhai Desai, and a police officer waiting at the plane to receive Master. The police officer took our baggage checks and retrieved our luggage. When we came in to the arrival lounge we found about 30 abhyasis gathered to welcome Master — this being his first visit to Bombay! The gathering included C.A. Gupta, my uncle Vijai,

Moralwar, Mr. and Mrs. Sirikar, K. Ramu of Voltas, R. Swaminathan and P.S. Vasu who have come over from Madras on duty. We were driven to Seth Tank's house 'Yogodaya'. There my real duty commenced by the first formal filling of the hookah! Master rested for about an hour. Then he took group satsangh on the lawn of 'Yogodaya' with some 30 abhyasis — who dispersed after satsangh so as to be able to reach Santa Cruz airport in time to see Master off.

Master and I had dinner, a very fine one, and then left for the airport. At the airport there were over 30 persons to bid good-bye to Master, including our Navsari preceptor Devram Chavda, and two abhyasis from Hyderabad and Ratnagiri. Sethji's police friend completed all formalities in a matter of minutes and I also collected the $9.00 each to which we are entitled. We said good-bye, and the police officer escorted us into the departure lounge where we had to wait for about 45 minutes due to a slight delay in departure. At 1:00 A.M. we finally boarded Air India Boeing 707 aircraft "Annapurna" and flight AI-101 took off at IST 00:20, only 20 minutes behind schedule. The plane was full. Master went to sleep, comfortably curled up with his knees drawn up to his chin, and slept all the way through to Cairo. Only occasionally was he disturbed by the slightest of bumps when we hit a stray patch of cloud, and then he would uncover his head (for he was sleeping totally enclosed in a blanket as he always does) and anxiously ask, "What has happened? What, have we arrived?" The flight was very smooth and comfortable and we covered the 2650 miles from Bombay to Cairo in six hours 20 minutes, arriving at Cairo at 4:10 local time (3 1/2 hours behind IST).

Reverend Babuji Maharaj with abhyasis prior to departure for tour of western countries at Bombay - April, 1972

Parthasarathi and Babuji Maharaj, Copenhagen, 1972

21 Apr. 72 - Friday (Cairo)

At Cairo airport we cleared immigration in seconds, but customs held us up over a dozen mangoes in a small basket which Master had brought to present to Madame Dina. After a great deal of argument we had to abandon the fruit as customs refused to allow it to be imported into Egypt because the mango is a protected crop! Fortunately this diverted attention from the hookah basket containing nearly 6 kg. of tobacco, which if they had opened they might not have allowed!

We emerged out of customs at 5:10 A.M. and found Nicola Joannides waiting to receive Master. He was looking happy, and apologised to Master for his wife Madame Dina being unable to personally receive Master at the airport. We drove to Midan El Giza by a circular desert road, avoiding Cairo city completely, and reached Dina's residence at just before 6 A.M. Dina was at the door of their second floor residence, very happy and in tears, and welcomed Master. She was very moved to see her own Master for the first time ever. Their own large Master bedroom had been prepared for our stay — a nice and comfortable room. I prepared Master's hookah and Master lay down to enjoy it.

At 6:40 A.M. the door bell rang, and Dina opened it and came back to say there was someone to see Master. I was somewhat mystified by this, but when I went to the door whom should I see but a beaming, though tired, Rakotondrainibe, our Tananarive preceptor. He had just arrived from Tananarive via Nairobi — a longer journey than our own — and had found his way to Dina's residence. Rako will be with Master till Master leaves France. Master was very pleased to see Rako. Rako moved into the bedroom assigned to us — a spare bed being produced by Dina.

At 10 A.M. Antoine Kreidi came, followed by Husein Altawargy, and later by Renee Astrinos, sister of Henri G. Astrinos. Henri's absence was much felt — he has migrated to Australia last November. Master gave a group sitting to them — Dina, Rako, Antoine, Husein and Renee. After this Master rested.

At 4 P.M. Antoine Kreidi came back, and took Master, Dina, Rako and me in his car to see the Pyramids at Giza. Master was anxious to see some of the important sights, only for one reason. "Dear Brother, when we return people will ask whether you have seen this and that, and if I didn't see anything then the people will think I am a fool. Therefore we have to see something." But all the same he enjoyed his walk at Giza. He asked Antoine quite a few questions about the Pyramids too. From there Kreidi drove us back through Midan El Giza to the centre of Cairo, to the Cairo Tower on the banks of the Nile. There he left us as he had work to attend to. The four of us went up the tower and sat in the rather shabby and unclean restaurant, and had a look at Cairo. The view was bad because the window panes were very very dirty. Master couldn't see much because he had not brought his spectacles. We had a cold drink each and I pointed out to Master the Nile Hilton, just across the river, where I had stayed when I was in Cairo last September. We left the tower by 6:30 P.M., caught a taxi and came back to Midan El Giza.

I cooked some dinner for Master, some chapatis and potato curry — which Master ate. Master was not happy with Kreidi who asked him several foolish questions.

Q: You are a spiritual Master, but smoke?

Master: Yes. I smoke. Why do you worry? I may take poison myself but if I can give you nectar you should take it.

Q: You are married and you have children?

Master: Yes.

Q: If you are persecuted and put in jail what will you do?

Master: Well, I am telling you — you should correct your own thinking first. Why should you think of bad things when you can think of good things?

This exchange was in the afternoon before we left for Giza. At 10 P.M. there was a phone call for Master, and it was Kreidi. He wanted to ask Master a few questions.

Q: You are so far away from your home. Do you feel homesick?

Master: Wherever I am, that is my home.

Q: But what about your children? They will worry and maybe they have problems without you.

Master: When I am not there, they have to solve their problems. It is their problem and they must solve it.

Later Master told me, "Look, what a fool he is — he is trying to entangle me. If I say I am worried he will say what sort of a saint are you. I have understood his mentality now."

Dina was with Master, sitting on his bed, till about midnight, talking to him at very great length about herself. We finally went to bed well past midnight.

22 Apr. 72 - Saturday (Cairo)

Received a letter from Vera Davies and one from Andre Poray, welcoming Master to foreign soil. Wrote to Vera, Sulochana and Krishna Murari.

At 10 A.M. two sisters, Arab women, friends of Dina, came to see Master. They are: Mrs. Mounir Aziz and Mrs. Amenophis Acer.

They spoke to me for over one hour, during which I explained to them our basic teaching and practice. They were keen listeners, and intelligent questioners, knowing English but not too well. When in difficulty they spoke to Dina in French and she translated for me. They both took their first sitting from Master. Master later told me that both of them had very good hearts, and Mrs. Amenophis Acer was very good and the better of the two. He seemed to be very impressed with her.

Later Mrs. Namet Mohammed Abbas came with her five year old daughter. She knows only Arabic. She had her first sitting with Master. Her daughter was on Master's lap for hours, stroking his beard lovingly, and Master seemed to be thoroughly enjoying it. Later Master presented the girl with a Channapatna wooden figure of a bearded old man. Husein Altawargy and Kreidi came for sittings. In the evening the two sisters also came for their second sittings.

Dina was agitated that Nicola refused to come to Master. Finally at 9:30 P.M. he was persuaded to be alone with Master for some time. He finally emerged at 11:15 P.M., having spoken to Master and also having had a sitting with him!

23 Apr. 72 - Sunday (Cairo)

Dina was speaking to Master till 1 A.M. Then we had an hour's rest in bed. We left Dina's residence, Master, Rako and I with Nicola, at 2:30 A.M. and drove to the airport. Nicola said good-bye when we entered customs. But Husein Altawargy was on duty at the bank counter, and he asked a colleague of his to look after his work, and went in with us to the departure lounge and spent over one hour with Master. Rako had no seat but managed to get a seat on the same plane with us at the last minute. We all boarded Air India's Boeing 707 'Gouri Shankar' and AI-115 took off from Cairo at 4:11 hours local time. The plane was again full. The flight of 1350 miles to Rome over the Mediterranean was very comfortable and pleasant. The weather was just lovely and with the early sunrise in those latitudes the view was beautiful. But as we came near the southern tip of Italy, the sky became completely overcast with heavy clouds. It became bumpy, and there was some rain too. The distance of 1350 miles was covered in 3 hours 15 minutes and we touched down at Rome at 8:27 A.M. local time — European time being one hour behind Cairo time.

Rome

When we came out of the aircraft there was a fairly heavy drizzle. Master attempted a run to the rather steep stepless ramp leading up to the arrival enclosure of Fiumicino airport. The ramp was a bit slippery, and Master had to be helped up. I was surprised to see Mr. G.L. Saravanamuttu, our preceptor, standing just behind the glass doors at the head of the ramp. I was even more surprised to see nearly a dozen people with him, forming a sort of reception committee. They all greeted Master, most of them with joined palms and a murmured "Namaste" and were introduced to Master. They were Prof. Andrea Scandurra, Mr. Giorgio Furlan, Signorina Luciana Suberni, Sig. Maria Pia, an official of the Italian Finance Ministry and also the Italian Prime Minister's Secretary. I didn't get the names of the last two. They had obviously come at Sara's invitation to meet Master, and to help with entry formalities. In fact they took our passports and baggage checks and disappeared. We were escorted out through immigration into the customs enclosure, where our baggage having arrived, we only had to identify our luggage. They were picked out and taken out of the enclosure. When we emerged into the public lounge we found about twenty more persons waiting to receive Master. They had been unable to go into the forbidden section. This group included our errant preceptor Paolo Passaquindici, abject and apologetic, Josita Della Rocca, another Maria Pia, and some others whose names I was unable to get. Master was allowed just two minutes with them before Sara bundled us into his car and drove us to his residence in Casal Palocco, in Ostia.

On the way Sara informed us that his wife had been ill for the past ten days, and was in fact in hospital with an attack of meningitis. She has been unconscious ever since she was admitted into hospital. Sara was unhappy that his wife's absence may prevent Master from having all the conveniences and refinements of cooking which she would have provided. Master was concerned to hear of her ill health. Sara also said his two sons had come over from England, where they are schooling and, along with his daughter, the house was a bit crowded. Rako came along with us and will stay with us at Casal Palocco. We reached home at about 10 A.M. A large basement bedroom had been set apart for our use. Master first had his hookah — Sara had thoughtfully arranged for a large bag of fine French charcoal — and went to bed. I had a bath, had breakfast and hung around. Master has stood his long plane journeys very well and **that** is something. He was not particularly tired even though he had no sleep worth mentioning last night.

From 3 o'clock in the afternoon people started coming in one by one, and from 3 to 5 P.M. there was an informal session of questions and answers, Master personally answering most of the questions. Most of the questions were of a general nature.

At 5 P.M. Master transmitted to all those present, and after that there were again some questions and answers.

I gave first sitting to Mr. Antonio Siniscalco, a self-employed dealer in high quality Persian carpets. I then gave first sitting to Cosma Filme.

24 Apr. 72 - Monday (Rome)

Yesterday was cloudy, chilly and windy the whole day with occasional rain. Today continues to be the same.

After 9 A.M. some abhyasis came and kept Master company. There was not much active conversation as most of the callers knew Italian only. Being a working day no one was available to translate. Sara had taken the whole week off, but had to go to the hospital at 9 A.M. and did not get back till 3 P.M. Those who had come, however, appeared to immensely enjoy just sitting in Master's presence and gazing at him, drinking him in as it were, all the time chatting among themselves.

Gave first sitting to Sandra Montenegro and Lino Montenegro, a young couple living quite nearby.

25 Apr. 72 - Tuesday (Rome)

Rather desultory the whole day. Still cloudy, windy, rainy and cold. People kept dropping in and out much of the day.

I gave first sitting to Mrs. Gilda Tissino, a very pretty, young, hatha yoga teacher. She speaks no English and is a good friend of Luciana Suberni.

During the day Master gave several sittings as people kept coming in throughout the day. No organized schedule had been established for either visits or for sittings. A loose arrangement had more or less evolved itself that

Master would rest between the hours of noon and 3 P.M. — and this everybody scrupulously respected.

Paolo Passaquindici came in the morning and spent over an hour with Master, discussing the future of the Rome centre of the Mission. He pointed out that most of our existing abhyasis were members of Prof. Andrea Scandurra's 'Centro Yoga'. Prof. Scandurra has been very co-operative, but the breaking away of Giorgio Furlan, one of his own students, and the setting up by Giorgio of his own 'Accademia Yoga' had created a certain amount of tension. Paolo seemed inclined to favour Giorgio if we are to think of any active collaboration with either of these rivals. Paolo felt Prof. Scandurra would be more interested in his own development — that is the 'Centro Yoga' developing — rather than in aiding or actively participating in the growth of our Mission. Paolo's advice was that we should steer clear of both and try to establish our own centre and stand on our own legs. If collaboration became necessary, he would prefer Giorgio's 'Accademia Yoga'.

I had spoken to Luciana Suberni yesterday, asking her whether she would like to become actively associated with Master and the Mission as a preceptor. She wanted time to think it over. Today she came and said she would be greatly honoured if she were chosen for Master's work. I informed Master. She spent some time with him. Others who came included Josita Della Rocca, a constant and very voluble companion of Lucy, Antonio Siniscalco, Taddea Szezimoth, and a Danish girl with her Italian partner Francesco, and Gilda.

At 2 P.M. Master, Gilda and Josita left in Lucy's car, with Paolo, Rako and me in Antonio's car. We did a short tour of Rome, very brief and mainly from the car. Master was uncomfortable as it was windy and cold, but no colder than Shahjahanpur in December. Perhaps he felt it cold, having expected it to be warm, sunny and spring! After this abbreviated sightseeing we went to Luciana's house. We spent nearly one hour there, and Master also gave a sitting to those present.

From there we went to Josita's house where her husband Antonio Della Rocca welcomed Master. Master gave a short individual sitting to his mother Signora Massara Maria Luiza. While the sitting was going on Josita played for us on the piano. She plays remarkably well and sings very well too.

From Josita's house we drove to Antonio Siniscalco's house for a brief visit. Then on to Accademia Yoga at 7:30 P.M. for the first formal engagement in Rome. Paolo spoke in Italian on Sahaj Marg for about 20 minutes. Then Master conducted group meditation for about 50 persons who had gathered there, many of them already followers of Sahaj Marg. At 9 P.M. Sara called for us and drove us out to his home. Lucy and Josita also came, I going with them in their car. Later Antonio Della Rocca also came to Casal Palocco and the three stayed till midnight.

Received a letter from Andre Poray giving the outline of the programme of visits in France.

26 Apr. 72 - Wednesday (Rome)

I telephoned Vera Davies at her French residence in La Cadiere D'Azur to confirm Andre's programme. This was at 8:45 A.M.

At 9 A.M. Master called me and gave me a sitting for about 5 minutes. When the sitting was over he suddenly moved over to my side on the carpet, and said, "Lalaji Saheb has come. See how He comes down for the higher work! It is all a question of adjustment — what is to be done and how much power is to be given. Brother, it is all His work. Now sit in meditation."

During the five minute sitting I felt as if I was glowing with a mild, pleasing heat as if warm water was being poured over me. Then I saw something like sunrise, but the sun was black, and radiating out of it was light, expanding all around. It was a very deep sitting.

Master asked how I felt and I related my experience. He said, "Look here, the limitations have now been broken. I have broken Raghavendra Rao's and now I have broken yours. I have not removed Kasturi's limitations. Now you can work upon the whole world."

I continued to feel expansion, and after 10 minutes I felt some pressure on the top of the head. I told Master about this. He said, "See, there is more expansion going on, and this is of course Lalaji's work." This calmed down after 15 minutes.

At 10 A.M. Luciana and Gilda came to see Master. Master took Lucy's case separately to prepare her for permission. I gave a sitting to Antonio Siniscalco, Gilda and Rako. Later Rako gave first sitting to Mrs. Vera Drancali Buzzdroglio of Rome. Master gave first sitting to Armado Bianchi and his wife Anna Maria Bianchi, of Rome.

In the evening the Accademia Del Meditteraneo gave a dinner to Master at Roxy Hall, presided over by Onerevole Principe Giovanni Batista Alliata. The meeting began at 8:30 P.M. I spoke for 20 minutes on Sahaj Marg, Prince Alliata translating as I spoke. Then Andrea Scandurra spoke briefly. Then we had dinner, after which I had to speak again. The meeting looked like going on for ever. At 11:30 I told Prince Alliata that Master was very tired and we would like to leave with his permission. He reluctantly agreed and we parted, Sara driving us home.

I got the impression that Prince Alliata had rigged the whole dinner solely to get us to look with favour on Andrea Scandurra, whom he referred to as his 'Guru' — and possibly ensure our formal and *pucca* collaboration with Scandurra's Centro Yoga. He was quite open in his suggestions that we could do nothing without Andrea's active help and participation.

27 Apr. 72 - Thursday (Rome)

At 7:30 A.M. Master gave provisional permission to Luciana Suberni Dalla Torre of Rome and later at 8 A.M. to Madam Antonietta Bernardi Correnti of Rome.

The latter is a fine woman, wife of Mr. Lino Bernardi. She works in some chemical company and the Bernardi's are great friends of Sara, and seem to spend all their free time at Casal Palocco. Toni has been taking much interest in Mission work — much more than Sara or Paolo — and laughingly said she had appointed herself secretary of this centre! She speaks English very well, and is very sincere.

At 9 A.M. Master told me Lalaji would transmit to me. I had a sitting with Lalaji for about 12 minutes. I felt a bright beam of light playing inside my head from the *brahma randhra* to the central region. I felt a lot of expansion. Then the brightness disappeared and I felt as if two halves of something which had been separate were becoming joined together. Then I went into deep meditation. At this stage Master terminated the sitting. He asked me what I had felt and I told him.

Master congratulated me for the experience of two separate halves being joined together and said, "Brother, the work of a very high order has been completed due to Lalaji's grace. I had made a request to Him. Do you know what it means? Today your will has been very nearly connected with the Divine Will, and your will has now become like the Divine Will. Now dear Brother, you have been rewarded much more than you deserve for the work you have done."

Later there were some questions asked.

Q: What is surrender?

A: Suppose you have surrendered to God, how do you know you have really surrendered? If the surrender is real there will be surrender to the whole of humanity. Absence of 'I' is surrender. First thing is devotion to God. Second, always feel dependence.

Talking of satisfaction Master said, "Satisfaction is your production, peace is the production of God. Peace can give satisfaction, but satisfaction cannot give peace."

We left in Lucy's car at about 9:20 A.M. and drove to Prof. Scandurra's Centro Yoga. I gave a talk on Sahaj Marg for about 20 minutes, and then Master gave group sitting to about 25 persons assembled there.

Irene Imperiali arrived from Naples and met us at Centro Yoga. From Centro Yoga we all drove to Antonietta's home for lunch — invitees were Sara, Paolo, Lucy, Josita, and Irene. Master rested for some time. Irene had what must have been a mild nervous break-down. She was weeping on Toni's bed after lunch, and when it was time to go she refused to budge until I made her pull out of it. Poor thing, she has a history of family strife, lack of love and being unwanted, and broke down on seeing Master.

Master gave Irene a special sitting for half an hour. At 3 P.M. we went to Marc Ben Mayer's house. Paolo was there. Master gave a sitting to nine people.

At 7 P.M. we went back to Centro Yoga for group meditation with nearly 35 in attendance. A very good sitting.

28 Apr. 72 - Friday (Rome)

At 9:15 Master, Rako and I left in Lucy's car for Giorgio's Accademia Yoga. There was a sitting for eight persons at 11 A.M. I gave first sitting to Dr. Vincenzo Giorgio, Guy Candidi and Rossi Maura all of Rome. Master gave a special sitting to Irene Imperiali. At 3:30 P.M. we all went to Gilda Tissino's house and met her husband too. Lucy, Josita, Paolo, Taddea, and Irene were there.

At 5 P.M. Master granted provisional permission in Gilda's house to Irene Imperiali of Napoli.

Master was feeling tired after this, so he decided to rest in Gilda's house. Paolo and I, in Maura Rossi's car, drove to the Accademia Yoga, where I conducted the evening satsangh at 7 P.M., spoke briefly and returned to Gilda's house at 8:30 P.M. We left at 9 P.M. in Sara's car, I in Toni's car, and we all went back to Casal Palocco.

29 Apr. 72 - Saturday (Marseille)

At 7:30 A.M. Luciana and Josita arrived, followed by Toni around 8:00 A.M. A little later Paolo and Antonio Della Rocca also came.

Sara drove us to the Fiumicino airport at 11 A.M. We had planned to leave for Marseilles by Alitalia flight at 12:10 but that flight was cancelled. Instead, we had to take Alitalia flight 338, operated by a Caravelle aircraft, and fly to Nice. Sara, his daughter Lakshmi, Toni, Paolo, Lucy, Josita, her husband Antonio Della Rocca were all at the airport to see Master off. Most were moved to emotion at the parting. Even though in Master's tour programme there is no provision for a return visit to Italy, he promised to come here again on the way back to India at the end of the tour, particularly in view of Irene having been made a preceptor for Naples, and there existing the possibility of work commencing there. Master reiterated his promise of coming back to Italy and this, to some extent, lightened the hearts of those present.

We left at 1:00 P.M. and flew west along the coast and arrived at Nice at 2:00 P.M. The flight was very smooth, the day being nice and sunny, after a whole week of bad weather in Rome. It was unfortunate that while our destination was Marseille we had to fly to Nice. We had tickets, but the connection from Nice to Marseille was available only at 6 P.M., and flying would have entailed a four hour wait at Nice, so we chose to terminate at Nice itself.

When we landed at Nice, along with Rako, Andre Poray was at the airport with his car. Rako had to take a train from Nice to Marseille as Andre felt that with the luggage of all three of us it might be an uncomfortable squeeze in his Citroen. It would not have been so, but clearly Andre preferred that Rako make his own way to Marseille, and we let it go at that — even though Master was not happy, and would have liked Rako to continue to accompany us.

Andre drove us expertly to Marseille, covering the 220 km in about 3 1/2 hours, with two halts en route for refreshments. At Marseille arrangement had been made for us to stay at the Catholic Monastery of Nuns at Cenacle, a modern, well-built, comfortable monastery atop a hill commanding a magnificent view of Marseille and the bay. Andre stayed with us at the monastery. We arrived at the monastery at about 6 P.M. We had light refreshments, rested a little, and then Andre and I had dinner at 7:30 P.M., Master not eating as he felt a little queasy after the long car drive.

At 8:30 P.M. a meeting had been organised in the main hall of the monastery, attended by all the nuns as well as by a few outside invitees. Andre spoke in French and also screened a film show. After this Master transmitted to the whole gathering for 25 minutes, all the nuns also sitting in meditation.

30 Apr. 72 - Sunday (Marseille)

Today is Master's birthday. At 10 A.M. Rako and his son Francis came with flowers to greet Master. Master was pleased to see Rako again. I gave first sitting to Mr. Francis Rakotondrainibe of Marseille. Master gave first sitting to Madame Galinir Heidy of Marseille. Master later gave first sitting to Madame Monique Egger of Marseille.

Today again was a lovely day. Master had lunch with us. Soon after lunch Vera and Elidir Davies came over, having driven from La Cadiere D'Azur, to meet Master. Master was very happy to see them again.

At 2:00 P.M., just after lunch at Cenacle, Master gave me a special sitting for about 10 minutes. I felt bright light inside my head. About midway through the sitting I felt as if a hammer had been struck on stone and a spark flew off — a single spark — then almost unconscious condition. I told Master. He said, "Lalaji Saheb came for two minutes. But I am unable to understand what has been going on!!"

Earlier, Andre had a special sitting at noon, as also Vera and Elidir when they arrived.

At 3:45 P.M. the nuns of Cenacle had a special service in their chapel for Master. We attended it and heard some delightful church music. At the end of the service the mother superior offered up a special prayer for "Master and for India and the Indians."

We left the monastery of Cenacle at 4:00 P.M. and went to the Societe Theosophique of Marseille for a public meeting. Andre had received just this morning 300 copies of *L'Aube De La Realite*, a French translation of selected chapters of Master's *Reality at Dawn*. For his lecture Andre read out three selected chapters from this publication. His talk lasted about 25 minutes. After this Master conducted group meditation for the 80 odd assembled members for 15 minutes. When this was terminated, all the members said they had felt so good they wanted to continue. So Master gave a second sitting for a further 15 minutes.

After this I answered a few questions. Copies of *L'Aube De La Realite* were sold at 10 Fr. each — very successfully. Rako, his son Francis, Vera and Elidir all attended the meeting.

We left Marseille at 5:30 P.M., Vera and Elidir going off to La Cadiere D'Azur, Rako staying on in Marseille. Andre drove Master and me in his Citroen to his country house 'Le Chenes Vert' at Le Beausset. The drive was pleasant and Master was quite relaxed and comfortable. He missed his hookah which he naturally could not smoke at the Cenacle Monastery. When we left Cenacle somehow I felt much lighter, a lightening of the heart, and after we left the Societe Theosophique, I felt even more light.

We arrived at Le Beausset at 7 P.M. Madame Blanche and Poray's daughter Martine welcomed the Master on arrival. They gave us an excellent dinner and then mother and daughter drove off to their permanent home, L'Hippocampe, at Sanary, about 18 miles away on the seashore.

After dinner when Mrs. Blanche Poray and Martine had departed for Sanary, Andre wanted to know about the aura. Master explained that almost all that was written about the human aura projected an inaccurate picture. The important points to be noted are:

a) The aura is inside, not outside the body.

b) There are only three colours in the human aura, red, black and what Master called "brilliancy". The black is very bad and shows vice, misconduct, etc. Red shows a short-tempered person, one who is wrathful. Brilliancy shows spirituality.

c) The colours appear along the facial outline, along the cheeks, etc.

How to read the aura? Just peep into the condition of the person. Then the aura, the real one inside, will be revealed.

I told Master that I saw these colours only on the surface of the facial skin. Master confirmed that this was correct and this is how these colours should appear. Andre remarked that he had often seen a blue colour, whereas this colour, according to Master, did not exist in the aura. He wanted clarification. Master answered that each centre of the heart region had its own colour and when reading an abhyasi's condition the colour of a particular centre may appear, and be mistaken for the auric colour. Master told us the story, a dream he had, in which a sannyasi appeared and told Master about the science of chromotherapy, or effecting cures by using light of different colours. The sannyasi had suggested in the dream that if a sick person needed a particular colour for his treatment, then Master could transmit from the centre which had that particular colour, and a cure would surely result.

1 May 72 - Monday (Le Beausset)

Four youngsters noted below came at about 10:00 A.M. to Le Beausset. Master gave them group sitting (Andreine Bel, Bernard Bel, Chantal Tarteret, Jean Claude Jacques).

We had a quiet lunch by ourselves, Madame Blanche and Martine having come in at 8:00 A.M. to cook it.

At 3:00 P.M. a Catholic abbot, Mayer Michel, came with a group of boys and girls, all between 19 and 23 years, the group numbering about 30 persons. The abbot, having found the Christian Catholic church unable to give him the spiritual guidance he needs for his spiritual growth, has broken away from it and is looking for a source of real, living inspiration. The youths with him are also involved in a search to fulfill their deep inner needs. They came to see Master. Andre spoke to them on Sahaj Marg for over an hour in French. They were rapt and attentive, and wanted to meditate. Master gave them a sitting for 20 minutes. Even after the meditation was over they did not disperse but hung around talking to Andre for quite some time.

Michel Mayer, Anne Innocenti, Olivier Ferand, Brigitte Mayer, Jean-Jacques Fourn, Andre Carbonnel, Genevieve Mayer, Annie Venaut, Roger Guillon, Marie-Therese Ferrais, Sylvie Pasquet, Jean Mayer, Eric Baret: this group will come to India later this year. They will write to Master well in advance.

At 5:30 P.M. Vera and Elidir came and drove us to their home in La Cadiere D'Azur, about 18 km away. Met Mme. Jourdan their neighbour. I gave her a first sitting while Master gave Vera, Elidir and another neighbour a separate sitting. This other neighbour had her first sitting with me when I was here last September.

Madame Jourdan asked several questions and was impressed with answers given by me. We went back to Le Beausset at 7:00 P.M. As soon as we returned to Le Beausset, I first filled Master's hookah. When I washed my hands and came into the drawing room Master said,

"Dear brother, you have become very keen. I have made some comments against you to Lalaji Saheb, but do you know why? Because the opposite would happen! I was talking to Lalaji Saheb about you and He has started praising you, and said, 'You have prepared a very good person.' Then I told Lalaji, 'I have already prepared two or three persons by your grace but nothing has come out of it.' Do you know what Lalaji Saheb said, 'Oh! Do you think every one will turn out to be an utterly useless person? Now give this person full work!' Now look here, there is one thing. Lalaji Saheb has said that you need not meditate any more because it is not necessary. But you should be immersed in remembrance. Meditation is no more necessary. Lalaji Saheb has said, 'Tell him that his time has been saved and this should be applied to the work.'" Then Master added, "Brother, you have been now given so much power as cannot be obtained in thousands of years, and the limitations have also been broken. Do you think this is an ordinary thing? Brother you have become a very keen person," saying this he laughed happily like a baby! "Now take the whole world for your work. Apply power and spread it throughout," he said.

At 8:30 P.M. Dr. Andre Felissier, wife Christiana Felissier and a cousin, an old lady, all came to see Master. They had meditation with Master for 20 minutes.

After meditation there was some discussion on faith. I explained to them how we were required only to start with trust, and when our experience in meditation ripened, trust would become faith. This faith would make us steadfast on the way, the practice, and increasing internal development and spiritual growth would ripen faith into surrender and lead us to the goal. Therefore, Trust — Faith — Way — Surrender — Goal!

2 May 72 - Tuesday (Le Beausset)

Practically as soon as Master got up at 8:00 A.M. and started smoking his hookah he called me and said, "Don't tell this to everyone but Lalaji was saying that I should get good food and eat butter and cheese because in raja yoga a great deal of energy is consumed. In hatha yoga, etc., much food is not necessary. But brother, in raja yoga one has to take a lot of nourishing food."

Later he told me, "Now Lalaji Saheb has just told me something about you. It is natural that everyone becomes angry, and I also become angry and you also too. But now you have been given so much power that if you should become angry you should not go into the depth of it, because if in deep anger you say something, that something will happen. Do you understand this? Now look here, by Lalaji's grace he has also created safeguards for this. He says that he has not yet given you the connection, and when you would have moulded yourself completely as necessary, then he will make the connection. Brother, Lalaji is very very happy with you."

I asked Master what this connection was, to which Lalaji referred. Master said, "It is the connection with Reality. Look here, there are few persons in regions higher than you, like Seshadri and your father, who are in the central region. But see! They have not got the powers that you have got. The real thing is that if there is no interest in the work then what is the use of giving them power?"

At 10:00 A.M. we were driven by Mr. Poray in his car to his seaside home L'Hippocampe at Sanary — a distance of about 18 km. But the road was full of twists and turns, and even halfway through Master began to feel giddy and nauseous. Andre drove very slowly during the latter half but it made little difference to Master's suffering — once he begins to complain of nausea and giddiness then nothing seems to stop it. When we reached L'Hippocampe he was feeling quite bad, and the last ten minutes of the car ride became almost unbearable. On reaching Andre's home he went straight to bed.

From 11:00 A.M. people began to come in to see Master. They included: M. Laven La Noira of Sanary, who has been a follower of J. Krishnamurthi for the past 24 years; Eric Baret who was at Le Beausset yesterday; Aimec Andre of Nice; Christine Lazarides of Cannes; Denise Bonjour of Nice — this lady will be our hostess when we go to Nice — and Jean-Michel Piquemal of Nice. All of them had a sitting with Master and later had lunch with us. After lunch this group continued to talk to Master for well over two hours — Master was back in form by then. At about 3:00 P.M. Rako arrived from Marseille to see Master. A bit later Rako's son Francis turned up with two of his friends, all from Marseille. Rako talked to these youngsters and then gave them a sitting in which, I found later, Andre's daughter Martine had also joined. By this time Vera and Elidir also joined us at Andre's place, having driven over from La Cadiere D'Azur.

Master gave Vera an individual sitting while I gave Elidir a sitting. It was a jolly gathering and all were happy. Master was not very pleased with the arrangement to segregate Rako, poor fellow, who has come all the way from Madagascar. At Marseille, under my persuasion, Rako agreed to prolong his journey and be with Master till we leave London for the U.S.A. He has changed his tickets also accordingly — and after all this to be separated from Master in France, where he perhaps thought he would be closest to Master, is a bit too much.

When we were in Italy, Master had suggested that Rako could be requested to speak in French wherever possible, and I had written to Andre informing him of Master's wish. When we landed at Nice almost the first thing Andre did was to take me aside and say that this would not be a good idea or an acceptable one. I asked him why not. He shilly shallied a bit and then came out with the comment, "Madagascar was a colony of France, and people here may not like to be lectured to by a Malagasy." So at last it was out — this business of colour and race and what not. I of course reported this to Master, and he was quite disturbed that such ideas should prevail in the minds of members of this Mission. Thereafter every time Rako met him and had to leave, Master became more sad and annoyed. He constantly remarked, "For hospitality, one will not get a country like ours."

At 5:30 P.M. all said good-bye to Master, going their several ways. Andre took Master and me and drove us out to see a garden-cum-zoo, the Jardin Exotique. We spent about half an hour seeing mainly tropical birds, plants etc., and met the proprietor and his wife, friends of Andre. Then we drove on to Le Beausset, arriving there around 7:30 P.M. We had a quiet dinner.

At 11:00 P.M. Master suddenly asked me to sit in meditation and I had a sitting again with Grand Master. It lasted 20 minutes. I felt it to be a routine general transmission, and also felt that some slight readjustment was done in my system.

3 May 72 - Wednesday (Le Beausset)

Woke up at 6:00 A.M. as usual. By now my own daily routine has crystallised into a definite pattern. I wake up at 6:00 A.M., have my wash, bath, and simultaneously clean Master's dentures. I am ready, dressed, by 7:00 A.M. generally. At 7:15 A.M. or so I prepare Master's 'chillum' and when it is ready, at about 7:45 A.M., I wake Master up.

Because on waking up the first thing he looks for is his hookah, which he generally smokes while still supine in bed. Generally at 8:00 A.M. or 8:30 I have my breakfast. Master does not generally eat anything in the morning. After I finish my breakfast, preparation has to be made for Master's bath. He is generally through with his hookah by then. He starts oiling his head, ears, all the while commenting on something or other. He then goes to the toilet. After the toilet is over, I have to mix his bath water for him, i.e., the hot and cold taps to be correctly blended to deliver water of desired warmth. Notwithstanding a daily drill to teach Master this simple business, he has not been able to 'master' it! Generally I get the taps going as needed. Then he asks to be shown how it is done. I close the taps and turn them on again, adjusting the warmth. Then he asks to be permitted to do it himself. I say go ahead. He does — and finds he doesn't know which is the hot tap and which the cold, nor how to turn them on and off. Then he instructs me to demonstrate this again, which I do — after which he generally has another go at it, but abandons it half-way through with the remark, "Brother, you may do this work because I cannot do it." Then I have to finally mix the water, and carefully instruct him how to close the taps when he has finished his bath. Another fear of Master is about locking himself into the bathroom — and so he generally refuses to turn any keys — some doors are provided with keys — and if the locking arrangement is anything different from the simple tower bolt common in India, Master will have nothing to do with it. In such cases I have the additional duty of standing guard outside the bathroom to see no one goes in while he is in his bath! When he has completed his bath I have to get his glass of milk for him. Then usually a second hookah is smoked, and by 10:00 A.M. Master is generally ready for the day.

Thereafter begins the official day with visitors coming to see Master from 10:30 or 11:00 A.M. onwards till after lunch is over, say 2:30 P.M. Then Master goes to bed, generally, and rests a couple of hours while I handle any visitors. Generally we have a group satsangh at 11:00 A.M. for those present and one at 7:00 P.M. or so. Generally also by 5:00 P.M. Master would have smoked on an average three more hookahs. By 5 o'clock he is ready for the fray again, and then his day really begins, because, all said and done, Master is a night bird. From 5:00 P.M. he becomes jolly, witty and very very talkative, whereas in the mornings he is generally withdrawn and taciturn, and tends to sit leaning back in an easy-chair with his knees drawn up, gazing at the ceiling.

The evenings are generally the times when question-answer sessions are held. After satsangh we generally have dinner by 8:00 P.M. and then Master comes into his own, aided by anything up to three more 'chillums' by midnight. By midnight his 'chillum' count generally averages a minimum of nine!! Generally we hit the hay at midnight, but that does not by any means mean that we sleep. Generally he needs his feet and legs to be pressed for at least half an hour, and all the time he rambles on about one thing or another. When finally he says, "Very well brother, now you should go to sleep because you have got a great deal of work to do," it is generally near 1:00 A.M. On occasion, not frequent, but not infrequent either, when Master for one reason or another has been unable to sleep, a final hookah has to be prepared between 3:00 A.M. and 4:00 A.M. This last episode is not part of a 'typical' day but not unusual.

Well this morning at 10:00 A.M. a group of six people came from Marseille — all persons who had attended the public meeting at the Societe Theosophique, and had participated in the group meditation also — Mme. Darmon, Mme. Martha D'Or, Mme. Guillarme, Mme. Manson (this lady is the secretary of the Societe Theosophique), M. Manson, Mme. Desana.

They all spoke to Master and Andre for over an hour and then had group sitting, after which they left for Marseille. Then two ladies came for lunch with us. Mme. Colette Tiret is a member of a psychic research society and seems to be dabbling in all sorts of things — she has also written two books; and Mme. Allegre Leone.

After lunch Vera and Elidir also came to see Master, with a dentist Philip Demange and his wife Lisa Demange. Mme. Egger, who was with us in Marseille and had a sitting with Master, also came at 3:00 P.M. All had a sitting with the Master at 3:30 P.M.

About 4:30 P.M. a news reporter of the *Provencal Magazine* came to take photographs of Master. Andre gave him a copy of *L'Aube de la Realite* from which extracts will be published in the article they will bring out. By 6:00 P.M. all dispersed. A quiet dinner was followed by a quiet evening.

4 May 72 - Thursday (Le Beausset)

Madame Blanche and Martine came at 9:00 A.M. to Le Beausset. They have been staying at Sanary, coming in the morning to prepare our lunch for us, going back, and coming again in the evening, generally with a prepared meal for dinner, which they got ready and served, going home to Sanary after dinner. Andre has been staying with us.

Mme. Blanche commenced meditation by taking a sitting with Master — we are all so happy that she did this, though only at the last moment. Martine also sat for meditation. They have come to say good-bye to Master as we are about to leave for Nice.

Our stay here has been very comfortable. The house is a beautiful one, secluded in this little village the total population of which is about 10 families. Behind the house are nice woods mostly of pine, in rocky terrain. This part of Provence is supposed to be one of the beautiful areas of France, full of vineyards and farms. There are no cars or traffic to disturb us. We are about three km. from the nearest main road. The house has a nice orchard to the front and on the right, with woods behind. Yet all modern conveniences are available, such as telephone, frigidaire, the latest propane gas cooking range, hot and cold water laid on, just about everything. Master has enjoyed his stay here — the climate has been just wonderful, Mme. Blanche's food just wonderful and Master has, to my mind, put on about 4 lbs. since we left India.

We bid good-by to Mme. Blanche and Martine and set off with Andre in his Citroen at 10:00 A.M. for Nice, with a stop en route to visit, and have lunch with, a friend of Andre's who, he says, is very very spiritual. The road was good to this place, Roquebrunne Sur Argens, and though only about 100 km., the road was a bit twisty so that Master began to feel giddy, and when we reached the home of Madame Regis called 'Le Chevalier' at exactly noon, Master was quite upset and had to lie down on a couch. He was to be the main guest for lunch but declared himself totally unable to eat. So Andre and I had a special vegetarian lunch, very well prepared indeed, with Madame Regis, her husband and a daughter. It was a bit dull because our hosts were a rather desultory lot, the husband particularly seeming to have developed no talent of any sort except to eat stolidly — though not heavily. Madame Regis tried a little conversation with me but it was one of those occasions when we seemed to fail to find anything in common. It was, on the whole, a bit of a bore for all of us except Andre who seemed to find some pleasure and sense of accomplishment in it. I understood that Navnit Parekh and his wife have been here, and I think Andre uses this place very much like guides of conducted tours use certain historical places to fill in gaps!

We left 'Le Chevalier' at 2:45 P.M., Master being a bit better by now, and arrived at Nice at 3:30 P.M. We are guests of Madame Bonjour in her residence 'Maridis' in Parc Liserb off the Boulevard Chimiez. Madame Bonjour had visited Sanary for a pow-wow with Mme. Blanche to prepare herself to entertain Master. She is a nice person, with a husband somewhere in Africa, and apparently no children. We also found at 'Maridis' Mrs. Irene Di Marle De Richleacoff, who has arrived from Paris. She will be our hostess in Paris and she has come in advance to learn what are Master's needs. Irene speaks French, Russian and a little German and Italian, but practically no English. Mme. Bonjour speaks only French but seems to understand English, simple English, when it is spoken.

We had a room assigned to us in the ground floor, really the basement if viewed from the opposite side of the house. It was hot in Nice, compared to Le Beausset, and the room smelly with the smell of fresh paint, obviously having been prepared for Master's occupation just a day earlier.

Master was tired, and still a bit giddy, and rested after his 180 km. drive till 5:30 P.M.

At 6:00 P.M. Master went to the toilet and had an accident. I heard a crash, and minutes later he came out very agitated, saying something had been broken when he slipped and had a fall. I found that the seat and seat-cover of the Western-type WC had been smashed to pieces. Master was, very fortunately, unhurt except for a slight bruise on the right hip well above the thigh. It did pain him though. I asked Master how this happened and initially he hedged. But on tactful questioning I found that he had tried to sit on the WC, Indian fashion, and a certain unbalance had made the seat tear off from the bolt and taken him down with it. It was a very narrow room, just walls around the WC, so that Master could not really fall. If it had been a larger room with space to fall in, Master might have sustained a fracture. I took a promise from Master that in future he will use the WC in the way for which it has been designed, and even though he grumbled that he would not be able to empty his bowels, he finally agreed. He insisted on seeing Madame Bonjour at once to apologise for the breakage and to offer to pay for it. But she, good lady, was very concerned about Master, and she and Andre were relieved only when I repeatedly assured them that Master had suffered no injury. It took Master a couple of hours to get over this episode.

There was some talk — one person asked Master, "Do you enjoy your stay here?" Master answered, aiming his answer at Andre rather than at the questioner, "We should not enjoy, but people should enjoy us. Saints are not for enjoyment. As I have written somewhere, a saint is a target for the world's sorrows."

At 6:45 P.M. Master took group satsangh with Andre, Mme. Bonjour, Mme. Irene, Jean-Michel and Jean-Marie. The sitting was for 20 minutes. At 8:30 P.M., after dinner, about 15 persons assembled. Andre spoke to them till 11:00 P.M., with me clarifying from time to time. Jean-Michel Piquemal and Bertrand Jean-Marie have agreed to work for the Mission — both are young and good.

1972

5 May 72 - Friday (Nice)

Under instructions from Master I gave Irene Di Marle of Paris an individual sitting to clean and prepare her for permission.

Madame Renee Thieux of Nice came in the morning to see Master. She will come to India later this year. Many more came in the morning. At 11:00 A.M. Master conducted group meditation.

Mme. Bonjour showed us a sort of hall, all of wood, being put up behind her house on her property. A group of boys led by Jean-Michel and Jean- Marie, are doing this job on the site of a demolished building, so that they may have a gymnasium-cum-meditation hall sort of place for their own use. All the work is done by the boys themselves, and Mme. Bonjour suggested that our own afternoon meditation could be held in this place — though the building is in no sense ready, and one has to negotiate a rather steep ladder sort of stair-case to climb up to it. Master was privately very pleased with this, having seen that the place could easily accommodate up to 100 persons at a pinch. He told me, "Look, it is Lalaji's grace that we are getting persons as well as ready made places for the work. See how we are getting the co-operation of Nature."

The 3:30 P.M. group meditation was held in this wooden hall which the boys have already started calling "ashram". Master took the satsangh and nearly 30 persons attended.

At 4:00 P.M., I gave group sitting to a group of seven persons who came too late for the 3:30 P.M. session.

At 8:30 P.M. a public meeting was held at 'Maison des Jeunes et de la Culture' or the home of youth and culture. The meeting had been organised mainly through the efforts of Jean-Michel and Jean-Marie.

The Maison des Jeunes is an enormous building, and our own meeting was held in one of the rooms in the second floor. The whole building was bristling with activity.

Our meeting began with a 10 minute introductory talk by me on yoga vis-a-vis human evolution. Andre Poray translated this as I spoke. After I finished Andre read out one chapter from *l'Aube de la Realite*, and then spoke generally for another 15 minutes after that. Then the whole group sat in meditation while Master transmitted. At least 20 of the 130 present were persons who have already met Master and commenced our meditation. The last five minutes were superb. We returned to 'Maridis' at about 10:30 P.M. When we were alone in our room Master said, "Today, I have given a transmission such as I have never given in India till today. It is not a question of any deceit, but brother, as the circumstances are created so also I go on thinking of new methods for the work. Now this is Lalaji's grace that when I set out from Delhi I had of course prayed to Him and He patted my shoulder on both the sides to encourage me. Now look here! I started thinking about this and Saheb, what should I say! From where will you people get such a Master I am not able to understand! When I thought about it I could understand it. Now you may fill my hookah and then I shall speak further about this."

So the hookah was made ready, and Master commenced smoking. After a few contented puffs he continued, "Now look here, this is the method — I transmitted from all the four points of the heart region simultaneously. I didn't open up the points because that would become too high a level. I just made the thought that the transmission is coming from all the four points together, and went on applying pressure from the brain, but not continuously, just little by little I went on giving a little pressure from the brain and then I stopped, and then gave a little pressure and then stopped it. Now see I never had this thought in India. But here where it is necessary I got the technique. I want to create such a light that people should remember it forever, and for which they should search and come again and again."

After this Master was in a ruminative mood. He had a second hookah after this and we went to bed around 12:30 after midnight. Andre Poray and Irene said good-bye — they go to Paris.

6 May 72 - Saturday (Nice)

Andre and Irene left in Andre's Citroen at around 5:30 A.M. destination Paris, some 1100 kms. away. They go in advance to prepare for Master's arrival. They hope to reach Paris late this evening and Andre will meet us at Orly airport when we ourselves arrive there tomorrow. So today we are on our own, looked after mainly by Jean-Michel for Mission work and Mme. Bonjour on the domestic front.

At 9:00 A.M. Master suddenly looked at me and said, "How does this heaviness come in you? (pointing to the region along the sternum on both the sides). You have no thought at all within you, neither about your house nor about your office and it is not any question of some hidden grossness. But nevertheless even if there is the least bit of heaviness, it appears very bad to me. There is heaviness in me too, and if there is someone who can see it, he will be able to see it. I will now have to study your past life for this."

At 9:15 A.M. Jean-Michel Piquemal of Nice was granted provisional permission by Master and authorised to organise the Nice centre of the Mission, assisted by Jean-Marie Bertrand of Nice, who was granted provisional permission by Master at 9:30 A.M. Both these young gentlemen (aged 20 and 21) will organise the Nice activity, and work under the overall supervision and guidance of Andre Poray.

Master was very tired after this. He asked me to take the 11:00 A.M. group satsangh. About a dozen persons were present including Vera and Elidir who arrived earlier at 8:00 A.M.

Later I gave first sitting to Brigitte Bardet of Nice. After giving this sitting I fell ill with severe headache and went to sleep. The afternoon group meditation was taken by Master at the 'ashram' — 46 were present, most of them of course persons who have already commenced meditation under our system.

Master was busy the whole day, and after lunch I don't think he had any rest, because I was asleep with my own headache. The whole day I could hear him in the next room talking away to a group, which kept reconstituting itself as members went off, and were replaced by others, the number in the group remaining more or less constant.

In the evening Master was absorbed in discussion with a French gentleman who, several years ago, had spent a few years in Tibet under a 'living lama' and had undergone the prescribed operation for having his third eye opened. He was a tall, well-built person, a face not at all French, but more Middle Eastern, say Lebanese, Arab or something like that. He had a powerful physique and a grave visage. He rarely smiled. He claimed a high degree of evolution, also the power to transmit, the power of healing, etc. Master asked him to study him and give his finding. This gentleman said that he found that Master's Master was always with him. He found the Grand Master's power like a rainbow or something like that, from one shoulder, over the head, and down to the other shoulder. Master agreed with this. Then this person transmitted to Master, and Master told me that it was true that he could transmit. Then, because Master was still suffering a little pain on his right hip, due to the fall of a few days earlier, this person gave him a few 'passes' as done by mesmerists, to reduce his pain.

All in all, Master was very impressed with this person, his sincerity, his true regard for Master and spoke highly of him again and again. Later he tried to cure my headache too.

7 May 72 - Sunday (Paris)

Got up as usual at 6:00 A.M. Master had two quick 'chillums'. We left for the airport at 8:45 A.M. in Madame Bonjour's car, driven by Jean-Marie Bertrand, with Master next to him in the front seat, with Madame Bonjour, Jean-Michel and myself in the rear seat. The weather was fine, the chill of the first two days having gone. We reached the airport at about 9:15 A.M. At the airport Vera and Elidir Davies met us first, and a little later Rako also joined us. These three will be flying with us to Paris — in fact Vera and Elidir are something of a formal escort, taking the place of Andre Poray. Rako was originally to accompany Master up to Paris, but under my persuasion he has changed his programme and will now accompany us to London, leaving Master at London when we leave UK for the USA.

We left Nice at 10:20 A.M. by Air France Super Boeing 727 on their flight AF 408 and arrived in Paris at 11:30 A.M. The flight was very pleasant. Vera and Elidir had seats just in front of us and there was some conversation. When we landed in Paris at Orly Sud airport, Andre was already there to meet Master. Vera and Elidir went off by themselves to stay in the Hotel Belmont (where I had stayed in 1967) in Rue Bassano, while Rako left separately as he has a flat here in Paris. In fact Rako has been thinking of selling this flat if he can get a good price for it, and investing the money in a sizable property just outside Tananarive, which he wants to convert into the main Mission Ashram in Madagascar.

We were driven by Andre in his Citroen to the 4th floor flat of Mme. Irene Di Marle De Richleacoff. Paris is cloudy, and much colder than Nice. Master felt the cold as we came out to the car park, but is adequately protected against it.

After lunch Master gave Irene a special sitting, and then went off with Andre to see something of Paris, undeterred by the cloudy, chilly, rainy weather. I did not go as I had a bad headache again. I went to sleep and only woke up at about 6:30 P.M., just before Master and Andre returned. Master seemed to have enjoyed his brief outing on which he saw the Eiffel Tower — up which he did not go — and the Notre Dame, from outside — and a brief drive up and down the Champs Elysees, where he saw the Arc de Triomphe.

We had our evening meal at 7:00 P.M. and left at 8:00 P.M. to attend a public meeting organised under the auspices of the Societe Theosophique in their own huge building. The meeting began at 8:30 P.M. and was presided over by Mr. Francis Brunel, a past President (for over 10 years) of the society. He is a tall well built person, with somewhat of a Cossack attire, and a misleading demeanour — appears to be a knave but surely isn't one! He speaks English, Malagasy and, surprisingly, some Hindi too!!

I spoke for about 20 minutes on Sahaj Marg, and Mr. Brunel translated what I said into French as I went along.

Then Andre took over, reading a chapter from *L'Aube de la Realite*. After this Master conducted group satsangh for the 100 odd persons assembled in the hall. Andre has visited Paris several times in the last year, and given his talks and picture shows, and so quite a few are already practicants of our system of meditation. I saw Andre's name listed quite a few times in the Society's magazine as a speaker, among other topics, on Sahaj Marg. So in his own quiet way, talking of Buddhism, the Dalai Lama, Indian temples and so on, he has managed to rather unobtrusively introduce Master and the Mission to his audience too. I found in Marseille he had followed the same precise pattern in organising his work. He **is** rather **dependent** on these other subjects to introduce Sahaj Marg, and this perhaps indicates that he is himself unsure of where he stands vis-a-vis the Mission, and consequently the progress, for all the work he does, is slow; but Master is pleased with what he has done.

The meditation lasted about 20 minutes. I gave a closing talk for 10 minutes.

8 May 72 - Monday (Paris)

In the morning Master granted provisional permission to Madame Irene Di Marle De Richleacoff. She is an artist — Peintre (a commercial artist) — and appears to be well-to-do, having a nice flat, well furnished and very comfortable. She, in my opinion, has had a very varied background!

At 10:30 A.M., Vera and Elidir joined us, and a little later Rako also came in.

I have recommended Elidir for permission — and today Master took up his case personally and gave him a special sitting to prepare him for preceptorship. Master later took up Rako, gave him a special sitting and raised him to the *brahmanda mandal*.

At 11:30 A.M. a Mr. Pierre Faideau, government graphologist (handwriting expert) a friend of Andre, called to see Master. Andre has spoken highly of Pierre and has requested that he too be made a preceptor so that Paris could have two. Andre feels that with just one lady preceptor the work may not develop very well, as many men may be unwilling to take sittings from a lady. This suggestion was agreed to — and Master gave Pierre a special sitting to prepare him for preceptorship.

At 3:45 P.M., Master granted provisional permission to Mr. Elidir Leslie Wish Davies of London.

After this Elidir, Vera and Rako all left. Master, Irene, Andre, and I left at 4:00 P.M. to visit the Nobel Tour, a gigantic building housing modern commercial offices of the Nobel organisation. We went up, I think, to the 28th floor and had views of Paris on all sides. Master was impressed with what man has done, and what man can do, in the external world, and added that if all this attention, wisdom and effort were diverted inside, how much could man not achieve!

After this was over, by 4:30 P.M., we left in Andre's car to go to the residence of Dr. Angelo Tomatis. Normally this distance of less than 5 km. should have been covered in, say, 20 minutes at the most. But this evening it took us nearly two hours because of traffic blocks all the way on account of the French President passing that way.

When we arrived at the residence of Dr. Tomatis we found about 15 persons assembled in their large drawing room. Master took group meditation for the whole lot over a period of about 20 minutes. Master was tired by the long car ride from the Nobel Tour — slow, jerky, full of automobile fumes, hot with windows closed and unbearably stuffy, but chilly with windows down. Andre introduced all those assembled by calling out their names, but even though he included Vera and Elidir — who were present — in this ceremonial introduction, he passed over Rako who was also here. He has been deliberately and systematically cold-shouldering poor Rako. Master is very unhappy about this.

After meditation there was dinner for all — only uncooked food, divided into two sections, one side having sweet fruits with cheese, the other acid fruits and nuts. The variety of fruits was something astonishing — mangoes, avocados, bananas, pineapple, figs both fresh and dried, to name just a few. They don't eat cooked food at all — no milk, no coffee, nothing. Today they had one dish of soup only for the Master as a concession to his needs. Dr. Tomatis believes that acid and sweet fruits should not be eaten together in the same meal. Either the one or the other. By going on this regimen — a millionaire's, if they eat this way every day! — he has reduced his weight, being a very trim 155 lbs. to his former 220 lbs. — I saw his former photograph — wow! Some bulk!

Dr. Tomatis treats retarded children by sound therapy, playing sounds recorded under water, to resemble the first sounds the foetus hears in the mother's womb, where it is surrounded by the amniotic fluid. His theory is that by playing such sounds to his juvenile, retarded patients, he recreates for them the safe and secure original environment, and this helps them to get rid of tensions and they begin to be normal. It was observed that when children, in special individual cubicles, on couches, were exposed to such played back sounds, they invariably went to sleep assuming a curled-up position similar to that of the foetus in the mother's womb. Slowly the children begin to develop normally. Most of his patients are children who stutter or stammer, or who are abnormally shy, etc. We left Dr. Tomatis at 11:00 P.M. and came home.

Andre has been keeping our Paris address a secret, even from Vera and Elidir (and very naturally, for him, from Rako too) and today Master had to request Andre to call them over. Andre says he is doing this to "protect Master from crowds so that he can rest!"

9 May 72 - Tuesday (Paris)

My fourth week away from home begins today. I feel I have been away for years, but probably due to the tight daily routine, I also feel I have just come here. There are almost no thoughts of home, and but a few stray thoughts about the office.

Master was a bit lazy and languid this morning, and continued to be in bed, curled up in a rug. At 9:00 A.M. I requested Master to read my past life as he himself told me in Nice that this was necessary. He agreed to do so at once, and was apparently in the mood for it. He said, "See, you were of course a Brahmin, and you were very strict. You were not a soldier but you were an officer of some rank. You were living in a village but you were working in a city, and you used to go home once every month or two months. You were not in the army but maybe it was the police, but whatever it was your heart was very hard. You were tall and thin with a wheat complexion. You were straightforward and honest. Now let me see whether you were someone's disciple or not. No! You were not anyone's disciple, but whenever you found time you used to attend speeches or other sessions of a religious nature, which means that there was some attitude of devotion in you. In that life too, you had one son."

Then I told him about the *Nadi* reading which says I had ruined some old woman out of power-madness, and therefore in this life I would get only 1/10th of what I deserve. He looked a few minutes into me and continued, "No. This is not correct. You had taken some money from some woman, maybe hundred or two hundred rupees which she had left with you. But it was an ordinary matter and she too was not put in any difficulties because of it. The woman was wearing a dhoti. Your heart was very hard but there was, brother, nothing else the matter with you. Now I am getting some details about your father. He was not a Brahmin in his past life, but he was an honest officer."

After this Master gave me a sitting for 20 minutes to clean the impressions of the past life.

At 10:00 A.M. Andre drove Master, Irene and me to the residence of his friend Pierre Faideau in Paris. When we arrived there we found Mr. Francis Brunel had arrived there, and was wanting a private session with Master. The others retired after greeting Master, and Mr. Brunel, Master and I were alone for nearly one hour. Mr. Brunel spoke of his past work for self-development, about his travels abroad, and about his present preoccupation with world development and mass improvement of people of the world. Master explained how it would be possible only by tackling individuals and helping them to develop themselves. When individuals are so helped, then society is automatically helped because society is nothing but a large mass of individuals.

At 11:00 A.M. Master granted provisional permission to Mr. Pierre Faideau. Pierre's wife joined us for lunch — a really lovely lunch — and after lunch Master rested for an hour or so.

We left Pierre's house at 4:00 P.M. and drove straight to the residence of Mrs. Marianne Kohler in Paris. Mrs. Kohler seems to be a particularly good friend of Andre, and he obviously respects her very much. During the last two days he has been almost constantly speaking of her. She is something of a writer and journalist, the latter function being apparently more important since, according to Andre, she contributes to quite a number of journals and is well known, and a recognised figure in journalistic circles for the past several years. She has been dabbling in a serious way in yoga and mysticism, and seems to be familiar with several Eastern schools. Andre seems to have persuaded her to take up our meditation about a year ago, and apparently she has benefited by her experience of this system. Andre tells me she is planning a trip to India to see Master in Shahjahanpur, and is also thinking of writing a book on her experiences under Sahaj Marg. Now that Master is here she feels she should wait till her Indian visit is also over so that she can have more, and better authenticated, material for her proposed book. Andre perhaps, would like to see her made a preceptor too — but it is as yet premature. While Andre has certainly persuaded her and had sufficient influence over her to make her start meditating, taken all in all I think she has influenced him much more than he has influenced her. She is quite a charming woman, in her mid forties, I would say, with a quiet manner but very quick and alert. She is not the domineering type but is rather the quietly efficient type, unobtrusively assertive.

When we entered her salon nearly 15 persons were already there. Master met all of them. It was a small but very elegantly furnished drawing room. She, Marianne, is quite an art lover — she had some very valuable antiques in this room. Master met all of them, and then answered some questions for nearly one hour, mainly on subjects like *kundalini* and hatha yoga.

Then Master conducted meditation for 20 minutes — the last five minutes were just superb. Again some questions and answers followed.

Q: How would you define the world?

Master: I can say that the world is the exaggeration of Reality.

We left Marianne's home at 6:10 P.M. and returned to Irene's flat.

At 8:30 P.M. we went to the Societe Theosophique for a group meditation. About 46 persons were present. Master transmitted for about 25 minutes. I gave a short concluding talk on Sahaj Marg for 15 minutes, and we were back home by 10:00 P.M. It was very cold when we came out of the Societe Theosophique building.

10 May 72 - Wednesday (Paris)

At 10:00 A.M. Mrs. Terry Haas of Paris came to see Master alone. She is a good lady, an artist. She was with Master for over one hour. She also had a sitting and was very moved.

Andre drove us to Le Bourget airport, leaving Irene's flat at 12 noon. It is a long way to Le Bourget and the drive took us nearly one hour. It was nice and pleasant at this time of the day, though the morning had been chilly and cloudy. Master has not had his hookah in Paris as Irene's is a 4th floor flat, with wooden flooring, carpeted wall-to-wall. There was only one small balcony where it could have been managed but it was too exposed and windy. So he is looking forward to it very much now!

We were quite early at the airport. Rako joined us at about 1:30 P.M. He goes with us to Copenhagen. Master was persuaded to have some lime juice. When we were sitting in the restaurant he looked at the bar and saw all the bottles in the gleaming chromium-and-mirror bar. He wanted to know what the bottles contained. I told him they were all bottles of whiskey, brandy, wine and so on. Master was quite amazed that there were so many bottles. Suddenly he looked at Andre and Irene and said, "You see all those bottles. They contain wine, but are not drunk. We must be like that. We must have the world inside us but we must not be drunk with the world." Andre and Irene were quite moved and visibly sad at the parting.

Master, Rako and I left Le Bourget at 14:50 by Scandinavian Airlines System DC-9 aircraft on flight SK-566 and after a 90 minute flight arrived at Copenhagen at 16:20. We passed through immigration and customs, and though customs wanted to examine the hookah basket there was no trouble. When we came out of customs we found Birthe, Elsebeth, Henrik, Vibe, Thomas, Ole, Bjorn, Kirsten, Leif, Lakshminarasimhan and family, Jytte, Anne (carrying) and about 10 others waiting to welcome Master. It was a grand reception. Master spent about 20 minutes chatting to the abhyasis.

Then Birthe drove us to her home in Greve Strand about 35 kms. away. All abhyasis dispersed from the airport, wanting to allow Master to rest for the rest of the day. Rako came in another car, and after parting from us at Rome is back in residence with us again! Leif Larson and Rikke were with us during the evening. At about 7:00 P.M. Birthe's daughter Helle and her husband came to see Master and spent a brief 20 minutes, but said nothing to Master. After dinner Master sat with his hookah and started talking in a relaxed way. Rako, Birthe, Elsebeth, Leif and Rikke were the only persons present. Later we telephoned Vibe and Thomas and got them over too.

Master: Birthe, can you tell me what is transmission?

Birthe: I think Master it is the passing of the highest consciousness into the heart of the abhyasi.

Master: It is a good definition. But I will tell you what I think. Transmission is the utilisation of the Divine power for the transformation of man.

Birthe: Thank you Master.

Master then talked of the world and how he had defined it elsewhere as "exaggeration of Reality," but now he offered another definition: "The world is sensed objects." When Birthe asked Master what is Reality, Master said, "Reality is baseless Base."

Master then told Birthe of his experience in Egypt which had enabled him to "understand the Greek mentality," and added "Look here, the Greek philosopher says, 'know thyself', but I say 'forget yourself' — that is what I say. What is the use in knowing myself? I know what I am, but what I have to know is what I must be or ought to be. That is the purpose of life. Some people have taught meditation on this idea too, of knowing the self. But suppose you meditate on the idea 'who am I' — well the concentration is only on the 'I', so that egoism will grow. Look here, we meditate and egoism grows! So what is the use of this meditation? It is my view that we must forget ourselves and then only we can find Him. I may be wrong but this is my view. Now people have craving for God. He is everywhere, but people do not develop spiritually. Why? Because they do not know how to approach Him. But because they have this craving they are prepared to do anything. Look here, I met a person in Nice who was in Tibet and had an operation for opening the third eye. You must have read about this. There are many books about it. He was a very good man and I admire him greatly, because look here, who will be prepared to undergo an operation? He was prepared to bear all the pain and troubles, and therefore I admire him.

"Some people asked me in France why I had come to Europe. I told them that when Birthe was in India to see me last year she was invited to lecture to the Rotary Club at Shahjahanpur. There she was asked why she had come to India, and she answered, 'I have come to seek India in India.' I told these people I have come to put or create India in Europe."

11 May 72 - Thursday (Greve Strand)

Abhyasis of the Danish centres started coming in from 8:00 A.M. on. By 9:30 A.M. about 35 had gathered. Most of them were the old members of the Mission whom I had met last September when I was here for three days. There were a few new faces too, indicating swelling in the Mission membership since my last visit. The newer members are somewhat older than our first batch of abhyasis.

At 10:00 A.M. Master personally conducted group satsangh. The satsangh lasted for about 35 minutes. It was very good.

I have forgotten to record a conversation with Master on the SAS plane yesterday while travelling from Paris to Copenhagen. We were talking in a general way of liberation, liberated souls, the past life and so on. When talking of the past life I asked Master what could be the time interval between two births, or rather between death and rebirth. I told Master that I had read somewhere that souls with good samskaras, which have however to be reborn, are reborn almost immediately, whereas the souls with bad samskaras remain suspended in limbo, as it were. Master said this was not correct. According to Master it was the soul with bad samskaras which was reborn soon, some almost immediately too, whereas the ones who were good had usually to hang around awaiting the creation of circumstances suitable for rebirth. Also, good souls were reluctant to be reborn, and avoided this as long as possible. He then pointed to certain known examples where a soul had to wait several hundred, or even several thousand, years before taking rebirth. Master added, "Now I am going to tell you a very private matter. I have of course called some liberated souls and had talks with them. Well, this you know. Now at one time I thought that I should also have a conversation with Patanjali and see what sort of a person he had been. I also wanted to ask him for some clarifications. But look here! When I looked into the brighter world for him, I could not find him. I searched the brighter world a second time but again he was not to be found. It was an astonishing thing. Such a *rishi* he was and how could it be possible that he had not been liberated! Then I thought that I should ask Lalaji about this. I told Lalaji Saheb, 'What is the matter that he is not to be found in the brighter world?' Lalaji Saheb answered, 'He has not yet been liberated; he is being liberated in this life. Now look for him and you will find him.'" Then Babuji added, "When I searched again for him I found only myself — have you understood this? I was myself Patanjali in a previous life. Now look here! How many thousands of years have been taken for this!"

After the meditation sitting we sat out in the garden — it was sunny and pleasant, though surprisingly Master felt a little cold. Some people asked questions, which Master personally answered.

Q: Why should we meditate on the heart? For me I find it is better if I meditate on the head.

A: This is **the** method. For us it is the ONLY method.

Q: I have been doing mantra meditation. Is it better, or is your method better?

A: It all depends on your experience. If you find you are improving in your method, then continue it. If not, search for another method.

Q: Here it is beautiful sunshine, and you have come in spring, and we can't help thinking of God.

A: Well, I will tell you. It is we who spoil the world by our bad thoughts and wrong actions. Every thought leaves its impression on the atmosphere. If anyone can read it he can see that the thoughts are flowing in the atmosphere, more than the clouds. You can yourself see the difference if you go to a slaughter house, and you go to a church or temple. The difference is in the thoughts in the two places. Our duty is to leave the world a better place than we found it when we came into it. Then we are co-operating with Nature. Now we are going against Nature, and so there is destruction.

Q: How to have faith, or develop it in oneself?

A: Really speaking faith is not necessary. What we have to do is to trust in someone and begin. And then if you find you are progressing faith will automatically develop. Now I tell you, people speak so much of the conscience. Conscience should guide us, but we guide our conscience as we choose. Now what is conscience? It is really of four levels, the *manas,* the *buddhi, chit* and the ego. When these are all balanced and merge into the one original thought, then that is the real conscience.

Q: Some say the guru is inside?

A: I will tell you, God is the only guru. All the others are working under His guidance and directions. Really speaking if a man says he is a guru he is not fit to train others in spirituality. Such a person is really usurping the position of God.

Q: God is inside us?

A: God is inside everything, but the real question is, are you inside God?

Q: Are all the methods good?

A: Well, all may be good, but I tell you milk is good, but to some it gives diarrhoea. So they must avoid it!

12 May 72 - Friday (Greve Strand)

Master woke up refreshed after a good night's sleep. He was in a thoughtful mood. He started talking to me. He said, "Look here. If you want to change the world, I will tell you a method for it. When your mind is almost in a state of vacuum, then make this thought and apply your will to it that such and such a change should occur, and that same change will begin to descend. Or you may make one *paramanu* as is present in the sun, and that will descend to bring about the change. Now look here brother, I am discovering such excellent techniques that if I should ever meet the Special Personality I will also tell him these things (laughing)."

9:00 A.M. I gave Master a haircut and beard trim — it was a good job!

About 30 abhyasis collected at 11:00 A.M. for group satsangh. The sitting lasted about 25 minutes. Then Master and the whole group sat out in the brilliant sun on the lawn. The weather is just superb.

12:30 P.M. Michael and Tony, a young man and girl from the Danish radio network, came to interview Master. It being something formal, Master made me do the answering. I was able to make him say something occasionally. This interview was recorded on their equipment and lasted over half an hour. I have also recorded it on cassette, this being the first recording on my Philips mains-cum-battery model cassette recorder that I acquired this morning, Dr. A. Lakshminarasimhan helping me to buy it and pay for it in this country. It is slightly more expensive than if it had been bought in an airport duty-free shop.

12 May 72 - Friday

Verbatim Record of Radio Interview

Q: What is the purpose of a human being, of human existence?

Master: The purpose is only 'realisation', or to realise his own nature, which is divine.

PR: The purpose of human life, my Master says, is to realise the divine nature in man, and his teaching is developed to make it possible in this life itself. You see normally in yoga, we take it as a means of evolution. Now it is true that evolution goes on for millions of years, and maybe we will see the fruit or result of that evolution some day. But yoga is a short-cut to achieve what we will ultimately achieve in this life itself. This is my Master's teaching.

Q: But to realise God, or the divine nature, is that to **be** God?

PR: No. Nobody can be God. There is only God and nobody other than Him can be God. But we can be God-like.

Q: What are we supposed to do?

PR: The basic thing is that mind is itself the vehicle through which we have to develop ourselves. The mind is also the instrument of degeneration or fall. According to our system of raja yoga called Sahaj Marg, my Master says the only way to do it is to give a new direction to the mind, and orient it towards its proper goal which is the divinisation of man. That is, what is necessary is a diversion of the mind from its present trend or tendencies to its proper trend.

Q: How do you think it will all end? It may sound silly, but how do you think it will end for civilisation?

PR: Well, we find that civilisation can have many meanings. For instance you don't mean by 'civilisation' in the West what we understand by that same word in the East. In the East civilisation means culture, it means many things. It is very clear. Everybody knows about it. But civilisation as it is understood today in the West seems to mean the acquisition of material wealth, comfort, a happy life, enjoyment, sensual pleasures — things like that. Today this is what is going under the name and garb of civilisation. Whereas in terms of our understanding, my Master's understanding, civilisation should mean divinisation.

Now society is after all composed of individuals. You can't change society as a group, en masse. You can only change it by changing the individuals belonging to it. And when the bulk of the individuals are changed, we say that society has changed. So we start from the individual and try to change society. Society is not our aim. Our aim is always the individual. But when you change or transform individuals, you cannot help but change society. So in a way this system of human transformation will cross national boundaries, social boundaries, racial boundaries, and ultimately it should lead, if this is successful, to a world society which recognises the real values of life, and what civilisation should really mean.

Q: The real values of life — what are these?

PR: Well. I think there is already a change in the West away from the material values of life. There is a fumbling search to try to ascertain what are the real values of life. You know, only when people have become completely saturated with material life do they begin to realise that material values have no meaning. Why is there such a drastic change in social values and moral values? There is an effervescence of change in the whole of Europe today, and it is a negation of material life. So, the people themselves are coming to understand that these material values are not the real values. Then what are the real values? Well, we say it is divinisation; it is the possession of a balanced mind; it is the correct performance of one's duty. Or, as my Master puts it, "Saintliness is the proper functioning of all one's faculties." **Proper** functioning, mind you! No exaggeration, no suppression.

Q: And now can you tell us something about transmission?

PR: Transmission is something we believe to be unique to our system. Master defines transmission as the utilisation of Divine power or energy for the transformation of man. This is made possible by the discovery of his own Master that a human being **can** transmit to another, provided he is in contact with the Ultimate source of all energy. And my Master is doing this work. And, apart from his doing it himself, he has made it possible for people, called preceptors, teachers, trainers, to also transmit this same energy under his control, under his guidance and directions.

Q: Is it physical, this energy which is transmitted?

PR: It is not physical energy. We believe it to be the Ultimate energy which is not physical, which is not chemical — in short we don't believe it is matter at all. Of course science recognises matter and energy as two divisions, but in energy you can have grosser energies and subtler energies. We believe what is transmitted to be the subtlest of all energies. You can call it divine energy, you can call it the ultimate energy, or you can call it the subtlest consciousness. It can be called by many names but my Master's own words are, "Using the divine power for the transformation of man."

Q: How does this transmission work on you? Can you explain it a little?

Master: It brings out the divine energy into you, and then it works. When divine energy of that nature is coming into you it will function.

Q: But how does it work on **you**?

Master: You mean on myself?

Q: Yes.

Master: Well, in myself it brings me to the balanced state of mind. Unbalanced character is lost. These are the effects of the transmission.

Q: Can you feel it?

Master: Yes, if we are sensitive we can feel it. And suppose you do not feel it, the changes that occur will convince you of the effects of the transmission.

Q: Yes. I understand. And now may I ask you another question? It may be a silly question too, but can you explain who you are?

Master: I am what I ought to be! (laughter)

Q: Yes, but can't you say something more?

Master: More and more, and less and less, these things have no value.

Q: Are you a guru, for example?

Master: I don't think like that. I think myself to be only one of the associates of my own associates.

Q: But I think that many people regard you as the guru or the Master.

Master: Well, they will have to use some word. They prefer this word, which I don't like.

PR: I will clarify this. My Master once said that suppose you are the president of a corporation. You are a president to all the other employees, but to yourself you are not the president. To yourself you are Michael. Isn't it? So, no man is to himself what he is to others. So to us my Master is a guru of course. But what is he to himself? (laughter) I mean this seriously. It is a serious subject.

Q: Do you recognise him as a master?

PR: Yes. We recognise him as a master. But one of my Master's important teachings is that the Ultimate guru or Master is only God. But there are people who function under the direct guidance of God, using the power of God. So they function in His capacity, but they don't function **as** God. Like, for instance, we preceptors function on behalf of our Master, but I cannot say I am a Master. But certainly the work goes on. And maybe there are people to whom we are preceptors, but for myself I am a disciple of my Master, and for himself he is himself, and as my Master himself told you, he himself is what he ought to be.

Q: But I am what I am, how is it different?

PR: It is a good question. As you correctly said, we are what we are, but we are not yet what we ought to be. That is the difference.

Q: Is your Master an authority on yoga?

PR: On this particular yoga, yes. We consider him to be the authority. This system of raja yoga, called Sahaj Marg, which means the natural way of Realisation, was discovered by his Master, also called Shri Ram Chandraji, but belonging to a different place, Fatehgarh. He rediscovered — I say rediscovered because this power of transmission was there many many centuries ago according to my Master, but this faculty of transmission was lost — he rediscovered the possibility of transmitting the divine energy into the hearts of persons so that they grow not by their own power, which is after all limited however strong or powerful a person may be, but by the divine energy which is poured into them. And my Master is now following this tradition, this practice. This is unique. And therefore it is correct to say my Master is an authority on this yoga. It is a practical yoga. It is not philosophical or metaphysical. It does not need these foundations.

Q: The words 'Freedom', and 'to be free', what do they mean?

Master: Freedom — when you are free from freedom, then that is the real freedom.

Q: Free from freedom?

Master: Yes. That is the real freedom — when you are free from freedom.

PR: It can be explained like this. Real freedom is that state when you are not conscious of either freedom or bondage. Because when we say we are free, we associate it or compare it with a previous state of bondage. So it is a comparative state. But the absolute state knows neither freedom nor bondage.

Q: Master, why have you come to Denmark?

Master: To give a good thing to my associates here. They are also human beings. Otherwise we have a good field in India itself. But since this is a good thing, and the people here are also human beings, they should also partake of it. So I have come to Denmark.

Q: What do you feel about Denmark — I mean in relation to the rest of Europe?

Master: Every country is good provided the people follow the natural laws. If the people of Denmark follow the natural laws, then Denmark will be a better country than others.

Q: Yes, but haven't you got any predictions about Denmark?

Master: No. I don't think of it. If it comes automatically then it is correct. I do not think of it. This is not my work.

Q: No? But I have read some record of your visions in your book.

Master: Yes. When I was in that state I wrote about them. Or when the things come down direct to me, then I write about them. I do not try for visions or predictions.

PR: You know those were written when Master was in a state of super-consciousness, which he does not normally like to call, or bring down upon himself, for this sort of work. Because there is the danger that it may degenerate into cheap forms of astrology or prediction. His fundamental work is the regeneration, the transformation, of man. While in the process of doing his work sometimes he gets the superconscious state coming on, and then he writes these things. It is not that he seeks for things to predict, or for ideas of the future. That is not done.

Q: But haven't you got any visions about Denmark?

Master: Well, now you have given me the idea. After some time you may ask me about it. (laughter)

Q: How did you begin this work that you are doing now?

Master: My Master ordered me to do it, and so I started it.

Q: Your Master? Who was it?

PR: His Master was also called Shri Ram Chandraji, and this Mission is named after him. It is a coincidence that both my Master and his own Master are called by the same name. Now in India, we have a system of offering fees to the teacher or guru when the course of study is completed. We call it the *guru dakshina*. Our Grand Master, we call him Grand Master, told my Master that his *guru dakshina* would be the propagation of this yoga throughout the world for the benefit of mankind. So that is why my Master is travelling over half the world, in his old age too. Originally this yoga was restricted to India, but as my Master has said again and again, yoga is not the monopoly of the Indians but is the birthright of all humanity. So he is now trying to help those who seek it. We offer it only to those who seek it — we don't thrust it on anybody.

Q: But how was your own origin with the Grand old Master? How was the beginning, I mean? How did you meet him?

Master: It was accidental. I had the idea that I must get a good Master, and I prayed for it, and I got my Master.

Q: When did you meet him?

Master: I think about 45 years ago.

PR: About 50 years ago, when my Master was 22 years old, he came in contact with his Master.

Q: And what did he teach you all?

Master: What we are doing here now, that is what he taught me.

Q: But it is not every human being who can be a Master. Isn't it?

PR: No. But my Master was selected from among all the disciples the Grand Master had as the proper person to carry on this work. He was given the necessary power to do it. This is true of any hierarchy. For instance if you are a king your son becomes a king. It is by birth. Some things come by birth, by inheritance. Certain things come by transfer of power. Certain things come by endowment. I endow upon you property, and immediately you become a propertied man. In spiritual life or in spiritual hierarchies it is not necessary that the son becomes the spiritual descendant — I mean the blood son. There may be spiritual sons who carry on the tradition entrusted to them by their own Master.

Q: And what about karma, the laws of karma, reincarnation. How does that work?

PR: You can see from all the books that are published that karma is a very well discussed, and much written about subject. Simply put, karma means the effect of the past on the present. I don't think we can dispute it. The dispute comes only when we talk of a past life or a future life. Certain religions don't believe in a future life. Certain religions believe in reincarnation.

Now there may be room for a certain logic to make it necessary that there was a past life. And once you accept a past life logically, a future life seems to follow, also logically. And karma really means the effect of past impressions arising out of our own actions. We do something, and that action leaves an impression upon us. This impression governs or conditions our future action. And the sum total of all such impressions put together is grouped under one word 'karma'. In our Mission we call karma by another word 'samskara'. And it is not only the bad actions which lead to karma, it is also good actions. Good actions give rise to a good future, whereas bad actions give rise to a bad future. But our idea of spiritual development is to have no future life at all. I mean this sort of life, in the physical plane of existence, we don't want it at all. Nor do we seek to live in other planes. The idea is to be liberated.

Q: But what is good action, and what is bad action?

PR: Well, as traditionally understood. You know the general norms. For instance, charity is considered to be a good action. But we can take the meaning as traditionally understood. It doesn't make any difference.

Q: It doesn't make any difference? How? Does it not depend on the feeling you have of what is good and what is bad?

PR: I am telling you what karma really means. Karma means all actions put together — the impressions of such actions. Some people misunderstand karma as applying only to the effect of evil actions. Let us say murder, robbery, rape, etc. But in India we believe that the sum total of all impressions constitutes karma. A particular act or action may be good according to you, it may be bad according to me — it does not matter. There is always a sum total of impressions.

Q: Yes, but an evil action can just as well be a good action.

PR: Well, that is something you can't debate here you know. It all depends upon circumstances. For instance you kill an enemy soldier in war. Under moral law it is bad, but under national and patriotic laws it is good. So it depends on from which level of human existence you are looking at a particular thing.

Q: Yes, but how does it work?

PR: The law always works from its absolute level, the highest level. The rest are our interpretations. For instance take the case of conscientious objectors in the last war, people who refused to fight because it is evil. They were put in jail. So you can say that if you refuse to kill the enemy, you will go to jail. At least that would appear to have been the cause-and- effect relationship for those particular people.

Q: I was told that when you are trying to receive this transmission, you have to meditate on the heart. Is that right?

PR: Yes. We meditate on light in the heart. My Master says that the heart is the most suitable for meditation because it is the heart that is the seat of life. It is also the seat of emotion. And, traditionally, in all religions, God is supposed to be seated in the heart. There are other points for meditation but my Master says they have only limited effect, mainly psychical, as against the total spiritual effect of human transformation that we seek in our Sahaj Marg yoga.

Q: But isn't the point between the eyes more suitable?

PR: Well, it is certainly more popular and well known because even in the *Bhagavad Gita* that point is mentioned — the *ajna chakra*. But according to my Master the *ajna chakra* is the point of distribution of power to the human system. So by meditation on that point we may acquire power, but not spiritual growth. There is also another interpretation, that the *ajna chakra* is a point suited and meant for the *sannyasi* — the ascetics who renounce life — but it is not suited for the householder.

Q: Master, what is your opinion about *sannyasa*?

Master: *Sannyasa* is not necessary.

Q: Why not?

Master: Because when they go to the forest they often think of their families, their children and so on. Then why should we go there? We should remain here, disregarding what is happening, discarding attachment. There is no need to run away. When we can get God cheaply why should I go to all these troubles?

PR: There is another aspect to be considered. God cannot be **only** for those who renounce life. If God is in everybody, in everything, then surely God is for all of us. So if there is a way for the *sannyasi*, surely there must be as effective a way for the householder too! Once somebody questioned my Master about celibacy. Is celibacy a necessity for spiritual progress? That is what he wanted to know. Very bluntly my Master said, "God is not a fool to create two sexes if one was enough." (laughter)

Q: Are you able to see in a human being how far he has developed?

Master: Yes, as much as my work needs, that much I can see.

Q: Do you have any more incarnations left?

Master: Well. That I cannot answer. Only one who is not willing to take an incarnation can reply to that.

PR: What my Master implies is this. He has no objection to being incarnated again, or to not being incarnated again, as the Divine plan may need.

Q: But when a human being reaches a certain point, is it not an end?

PR: You see, there are two ways of looking at this. We recognise two ways of rebirth. One is the karma tradition where you are reborn under the compulsion of your karma. You have no choice in the matter. You are reborn at a specific time, in a specific environment, under specific conditions, so that the future is worked out according to the foundation laid in the past. The others are the so-called liberated souls, as masters, who descend into the physical plane of their own free will to help humanity to develop from time to time. Now, I believe we are all compulsive reincarnations. But if my Master should reincarnate again it will be purely voluntary, it becomes something on which karma has no bearing. So it is not possible to say whether he will reincarnate again or not. Because it will depend on

Cosmic circumstances, and if they need his presence on the physical plane he may descend again, otherwise not.

Q: How do you select preceptors?

Master: When there are four or five things before you, how do you select one from them?

Q: Yes, I see. But why do you prefer one person to another?

Master: For qualities. If a man has good qualities he is preferred. A man can also be made to have good qualities.

Q: What kind of qualities do you mean?

Master: Sympathy, charity, service, thinking of good thoughts — these are some.

PR: I will explain one thing to you Michael. There are people in our Mission who are very highly developed, but who are not preceptors. And there are preceptors who are practically on the first rung of the ladder of spiritual development. So a person's spiritual level has no direct bearing on his qualification to be a preceptor. What I personally believe — you have heard what the Master has said — to be really necessary in a preceptor is dedication to the spiritual cause. If this is there, Master can create the other qualities by his power. I believe this dedication to be a fundamental quality in a preceptor.

Q: Do you feel any contact with the Grand old Master?

Master: There is contact always.

Q: How?

Master: In the way in which it should be!

PR: That is, spiritual contact. The Grand Master is no longer in the physical plane. He passed away into *maha samadhi* in 1932. But there is continuous contact between him and my Master. We have seen it. My Master seems to receive guidance from him from time to time. He tells us about it. What the relationship is I don't know, because it is from one plane of existence to another.

Q: Have you any visions of how the Western civilisation shall end?

Master: The base will be changed. The base will become highly spiritual.

Q: But how shall it change?

Master: By following the method. By having good thoughts. I am telling you it is the work of the Divine. Some Divine hand is working for this change because some 10 or 15 years ago this was not the case. But I am feeling it here now, in Europe. Some change is taking place. The people are fed up with the life of materialism. So they naturally cling to that which has the base as spirituality.

Q: Is it all to be destroyed — I mean the West?

PR: No. No. It is not like that. In any endeavour those who co-operate are taken along, while those who oppose or do not co-operate are not taken along on the path. You may call this destruction, but it may be that they are transferred to another plane. So that which does not co-operate with the Divine plan changes until it co-operates. This change you may call destruction, you may call it conversion. When you split an atom, is the atom destroyed or is it converted? Both are correct. So what we normally call destruction may be conversion for its own good. A child is converted into a man. Is it destruction of the child? It is a transition from one phase of human existence into another. And when the man becomes old, his youth is destroyed, in a sense. But we don't consider this to be destruction because we see the transition from stage to stage. When you don't see, or cannot see, the successive stages in a transitory continuum, we perceive the end of each phase as destruction of that phase.

(End of Interview)

The radio interview lasted about 40 minutes. They had many more questions to ask, but unfortunately their tape in the recorder was completed, and so the interview came to somewhat of an abrupt termination.

Michael and Tony, the interviewers of Danish Radio, both took their first sittings.

Master went up to rest, and rested till 3:00 P.M.

I gave first sitting to Mr. Kristen Bjorg, a psychologist interested in conducting research on our system of yoga, and on yoga generally.

From 3:00 to 4:30 P.M. Master was on the lawn, in an absolutely hilarious mood. He kept the audience roaring. One of his pronouncements "Man is the hallucination of Being."

Fred Weinstock, our USA preceptor, is here.

In today's newspapers — three of them — notices have appeared regarding tomorrow's public meeting in Copenhagen. The notices include Master's photo. Apart from this Vibe has arranged for printed posters about 9" x 16", to be pasted all over the city. The poster has nothing but Master's picture — about 8" x 12", and a notice below giving place and time of meeting.

8:00 P.M. Master conducted group satsangh again — over 40 present. The meditation lasted one hour and three minutes. Most of the abhyasis stayed on till 11:00 P.M. talking to Master. Vibe and Thomas were asked to stay the night at Birthe's house by Master.

At 6:00 P.M. earlier in the evening, we had a Preceptors' meeting, presided over by Master, at which were present Birthe Haugaard, Vibe Erstad, A. Rakotondrainibe, Fred Weinstock, and Dr. A. Lakshminarasimhan. I gave a short introductory talk on what Master desired by way of organisation, and the need for such meetings periodically. I also conveyed to those present Master's desire to have the Mission registered as a permanent body in Denmark under Danish law, and requested Vibe to take the necessary steps to have this done so that by the time Master returns to Denmark again, after visiting the UK and the USA, all the formalities should be over.

Rako gave a long talk on the way he proposed to organise Mission activity in Madagascar, and of how he proposed to expand the work into Mauritius and Kenya etc., in Africa, if Master approved of his plans. His idea was to open additional centres in Madagascar itself, and also to strengthen the Tananarive organisation. He mentioned the immediate possibility of two more centres at two coastal towns, and possibly three in Tananarive itself. Thereafter he would try to open a centre in Mauritius. Later perhaps Nairobi would be worth entering. Master was pleased with Rako's enthusiasm. Rako has already picked out a couple of youngsters as prospective workers of the Mission. Master told Rako that he would try to make a one week visit to Madagascar in 1973 after the Centenary Celebrations in Madras are over in February/March. If that visit materialised then he could study the candidates proposed for preceptorship and grant permission.

Fred felt that we should not make harsh and definite pronouncements against the drug habit. He said that particularly in America he was familiar with repression and also police terroristic activities, and felt that if we in the Mission adopted a negative attitude, the Mission might very well be identified with such governmental repression and harassment.

13 May 72 - Saturday (Greve Strand)

At 8:30 A.M. Master granted provisional permission to Miss Elsebeth Haugaard, daughter of Mrs. Birthe Haugaard. At 19 she is probably the youngest preceptor in the Mission today.

Later Mr. Paul Warwick, popularly known as Shri Paul, came to see Master. He is head of the Ramana Movement in Denmark, has a wife and two children, and seems to have a large number of 'chelas'. Shri Paul has heard about Master and wanted to meet him alone — but Master's difficulty in understanding English with an accent, and the reciprocal disability on the part of his questioner to understand Master's accented English, generally makes my presence at even so called 'confidential' discussions unavoidable. Shri Paul was keen to work for the welfare of humanity. Master advised him that he should commence meditation and then study this aspect of service. Shri Paul wanted to know what precisely Master meant when he spoke of Realisation. Master answered, "You know what you are, but you don't know what He is. When you know, or feel in yourself what He is, that is Realisation." He had a short sitting with Master.

At 10:30 A.M. Master took group meditation with about 25 abhyasis present.

At 1:00 P.M. Master, Rako and I left in Birthe's car for the city of Copenhagen. We, or rather Birthe, managed to locate the nursing home in which Anne has been confined, and we all called on her at 2:00 P.M., with special permission, to see her baby. The boy was born just a few hours after Master's arrival in Copenhagen. Anne was at the airport to greet him on arrival on the 10th of May and that same night she was confined, and delivered of this baby early next morning. The baby has been named Chandra in honour of Master. There is already a baby girl named Kasturi, daughter of Jytte Gravesen. As a matter of fact quite a few babies have been born in our group here, and a few more are expected, and there is a general feeling that Sahaj Marg is good for babies! And the more serious and happy thought that Denmark will have a bright spiritual future with such blessed children born in it! Anne was of course extremely pleased, and moved too, by Master's visit — and Master seemed to enjoy seeing this girl devotee in his own quiet way. We were with Anne for about half an hour and then left.

Birthe then drove us around a little, including a drive on the Langelinie, but omitting to take us to the famous statue of Andersen's 'Little Mermaid'. Finally she took us to the Exhibition Hall of the Academy of Arts — the Festsalen in the Kunstakademiet — for a public meeting scheduled to commence at 3:00 P.M. It is a large and well-ventilated hall, and apart from practically our whole Danish group, the hall was nearly full when we entered it. Vibe and Thomas and Jens had made ready a large number of handouts, — one photo of Master, and a Danish translation of *Outlines of Sahaj Marg*, copies of which were given to persons as they entered the hall. By the time the meeting was to begin, the available seating capacity of 300 was filled up, and many had to stand.

Birthe opened the meeting by giving a short introductory talk in Danish and English for about 10 minutes. After this I spoke on Sahaj Marg as the main speaker of the evening for about 20 minutes. Most people seemed to be able to understand my English, though I was told later that my delivery was too fast — something I could well believe when I heard the speech played back to me later from a tape-recording! Bjorn Juvik spoke in Danish after me — very very well it seemed, judging from audience reaction. He speaks wonderfully, with a slow and measured delivery, every word well pronounced and accented, and with an admirable lack of self-consciousness. It was indeed a very good speech and I could see he was quoting from the famous and well-loved Danish philosopher Soren Kirkegaard. Later he told me he had found some references to meditation and similar spiritual practices, and this he had quoted to the audience. Bjorn was followed by Jytte Gravesen, also speaking in Danish. She also spoke very well. I gathered that she was telling the audience about her own personal experience under Sahaj Marg. I could feel that what she said carried conviction. After this Rako spoke in French — remarkably well I must say — and his speech was translated, sentence by sentence, into Danish by Vibe. Rako gave the assembled people an idea of the response to this system in his own native Madagascar, and exhorted the Danes to give this system a whole-hearted trial. The lectures concluded with a short concluding talk in English by Dr. Lakshminarasimhan. But we had to face a 20 minute question-and-answer session after this! Some excellent questions were asked, and to my regret these went unrecorded.

After this Master transmitted to the whole audience for 25 minutes. Before we started meditating the routine announcement was made that those who did not wish to participate were at liberty to leave and, surprisingly, about a dozen left. Surprisingly because on no earlier occasion had a single person ever left the hall! But one significant fact was that when the hall was empty we found that every single person had taken away the printed handouts which they had received earlier — not one sheet was left behind by anyone! This, to us, was something really remarkable.

The Danish group were jubilant at the wonderful success of the meeting. They have taken great trouble and effort in organizing this meeting and had every cause for joy at its more-than-successful conclusion.

We left the hall, and as there was a light drizzle, and also quite dark even though it was only about 5:30 P.M., we got into Birthe's car to be driven back to Greve Strand — Elsebeth joining us in the car for the return journey. Master was in a mischievously jubilant mood, very very hilarious, and kept saying some outlandish things — keeping us all virtually roaring with laughter. Talking of God, and power, Master said, "Look here, God may be great but the power is mine. I have never asked for power from God. When I wanted any power I took it!"

Birthe asked why it was that sometimes she felt happy, but very often sad and despondent. Then Master answered, rather cryptically, "The water is buoyant, not you." I suppose it means that we must learn to float on the water of the ocean of Bliss, and thus be buoyant.

When we reached home Master told me, "Look here, I am now giving you some work. I thought I should give you some big work and just now Lalaji Saheb told me, 'Start taking work from him. Why are you hesitating?' Now you may take up the work of America and make the thought that the minds of all the persons have become like one mind and, giving that mind transmission, pull it towards the Mission. But don't give it connection with the Mission, because then they will get the benefit of the transmission, but they will not come to me. Transmit with the thought that they are coming towards the Mission, but do not give the connection."

At about 8:00 P.M. about 10 abhyasis came to Birthe's house to be with Master — Vibe, Thomas and Jens, and one other remained over night. Master was a bit tired and went up to bed immediately after we returned from Copenhagen. He came down for dinner at 9:30 P.M. and went up almost immediately after he had eaten. Surprisingly, he came down again at about 10:15 P.M. and spent nearly 45 minutes with the abhyasis present, before finally going to bed around 11:00 P.M. The rest of us were talking till 1:00 A.M.

14 May 72 - Sunday (Greve Strand)

The morning found Master rather dull and listless. He stayed in bed rather late too — and seemed to be preoccupied with Mission matters at home in India. He was obviously thinking of problems of organisation because suddenly He started speaking to me and said, "One person asked me, why do you want a large number of disciples? If you have six or seven disciples is it not enough? Then I told him, 'Look here, I have come from Infinity and the seed of Infinity is within me. Therefore whatever I may do, dear brother, I shall only desire that that Infinity should be with me, and I shall wish for the same Infinity for all of them.'" Then laughingly he said, "Even the thieves want the same thing that they also may have many accomplices with them, and this is also the effect of that very same Infinity, but in the wrong direction. And look, I want to tell you one more thing. We should not use the part power of God but we should use the full power of God. But when the 'I' is there, full power does not come, so drop the 'I' and the full power comes, but it must be used under control. There is also the danger in utilising the power, and we have to be very alert."

Master went on to speak of gratitude, how gratitude must develop in the heart of an abhyasi for what he is receiving, and how selfishness must not be present, even as a tinge. I asked Master how exactly he would define selfishness. Master answered, "If your heart does not acknowledge the service that one does to you, then that is selfishness."

Later in the morning Master came into his own normal mood. Elsebeth was busy giving sittings to abhyasis. She has taken to this spiritual work like a duck to water. A number of abhyasis came in in the morning, and Master sat out on the lawn with them and by his merry conversation kept them roaring with laughter. One of his sallies was, "I praise myself, but look here, I also tell everybody my foolishness, so that they neutralize themselves."

Later when we were alone Master told me, "Now this thing has disappeared (referring to the grossness of my past life); but when I thought there may be yet something, then Lalaji told me that there is now no longer anything like that. But he told me that I should remove the tendency to create further grossness which is present. Now look here! For each and every thing guidance from above is coming. Such a person is fit to be called the Master. And see, this is an absolutely new finding that while grossness is no doubt there, and something which can be removed, yet there is also the tendency towards making grossness. This idea of the tendency is a totally new thing which please make a note of."

There was no general satsangh this morning as we had to leave for Copenhagen to stay the night in Dr. Lakshminarasimhan's house, since Birthe leaves for London this evening to be with Master there. We left in Vibe's car at 12 noon, all packed up as we ourselves leave for London tomorrow, Vibe and Master in front, Birthe, Rako and I in the back. We arrived about half an hour later and had lunch in Lakshminarasimhan's house. After lunch nearly 50 people gathered, and about 36 new members joined the

Mission by commencing the practice of meditation. Birthe, Vibe, Elsebeth, Lakshminarasimhan and I were all kept busy, giving individual sittings to the new entrants. Most of them are persons who came to the public meeting held here yesterday evening.

About 3:30 P.M. a young person, Hans Jorgen Hvid came to see Master. He is from Viborg and wanted to serve Master in Viborg if a centre could be established there. Master was impressed with his sincerity and simplicity, and under his instructions I gave Hans a special sitting to prepare him for permission. Later Master gave him two individual sittings so that today in the brief period of about 6 hours, he has had three sittings in all.

Later I gave individual sittings to Birthe, Jens, Thomas, and Jytte. Birthe left for the airport at 6:45 P.M. to catch her chartered group flight to London.

Master was exhausted and slept from 6:30 P.M. to 9 P.M., but after dinner, he was back in form and kept us in tears of laughter till 11:00 P.M. Thomas, particularly, was often compelled to fall flat on his back, unable to control his glee and joy.

15 May 72 - Monday (Copenhagen)

Master had a restful night, and woke up fresh in the morning. At 8:00 A.M. Master granted provisional permission to Hans Jorgen Hvid and authorised him to organise a centre at Viborg. From 7:00 A.M to 9:00 A.M. I gave individual sittings to Ole, Bjorn, Kirsten, Jens, and Edith.

After breakfast, at 10:30 A.M., we left Dr. Lakshminarasimhan's house for the airport. About 15 abhyasis were gathered at the airport to bid farewell to Master. Rako goes with us to London. We left Copenhagen at 12:05 by

BEA Trident aircraft on their flight No. BE-741, on a 90 minute flight to London. The flight was smooth, comfortable and enjoyable. Master gave me a three minute transmission while we waited to board the plane at Gate No. 21.

We touched down at 13:35 hours. Immigration formalities involved a 20 minute wait — a card to be filled up by the officer on duty himself, then stamped, then our entry permit to be stamped all over again — all this took over 20 minutes. Master had to stand patiently all the time. It seemed to me that Commonwealth queues — at special Commonwealth counters — had the longest waiting to do — preferred treatment indeed! When we finally emerged after claiming our luggage and passing through customs, Vera and Elidir were found waiting in the arrival lounge to greet Master and take him home.

Rako went off by himself to Cromwell Road to contact Birthe who has promised to arrange accommodation for him too. We drove in a big car that Elidir had obtained for the occasion, and reached Marlborough Place after approximately 35 minutes driving. It was a fine sunny day and a real summer day as the British understand it. On arrival we had a fine lunch prepared by a 'help' — a young woman acquaintance of Vera's who has agreed to help with the cooking for the whole week that Master will be in London. It was her husband John who drove us out from Heathrow airport.

At 3:30 P.M. an Indian gentleman, Mr. Shorey Kapoor, settled in England for many years, came to see Master. Fred Weinstock came in at 4:00 P.M., followed by Ose of Copenhagen and her English husband John Wadlow, both of whom had come to India some months ago. They were followed, at 5:00 P.M., by Andre Poray, who has arrived from France for a proposed stay of three days staying at a hotel within walking distance of where we are. At 5:30 P.M. Birthe and Rako arrived from their hotel in Cromwell Road, and Ron Mendelsohn's arrival completed the group for the day. Master gave group sitting to all of them at 6:00 P.M. The group dispersed at 8:00 P.M., leaving us to have a fine dinner, after which Master sat with Vera and Elidir in their drawing room till nearly 10:30 P.M.

16 May 72 - Tuesday (London)

Rako, Birthe and Andre came in at about 10:00 A.M. Master is not very well this morning. He is complaining of muscular pain near the lumbar region, and had some difficulty coming down the staircase from our first floor bedroom. Ose came in at 10:30 A.M., and revealed herself to be an expert physiotherapist. She gave Master a massage and also prescribed some infrared exposure. She put him under a hot electric blanket for some time. All this gave much comfort to Master.

Birthe, Rako and I went out for a walk, and we had lunch at the 'Star of Bengal' restaurant, about 10 minutes walk from Vera's residence.

In the afternoon Mr. Shorey Kapoor came again for a sitting. Mr. N.L. Sardhana of the Indian Embassy and his wife, together with another Mr. Sardhana and his wife, all came in the afternoon followed by Ose and John, Fred — all of whom remained with Master for most of the day. John and Fred introduced three new members to the Mission, friends of theirs. Ron Mendelsohn came in the evening. There was a short group satsangh in the evening taken by me. The group dispersed at 8:00 P.M., Vera asking Rako, Birthe and Andre to stay to dinner with us. Master is still having his back trouble but managing all right.

At 10:00 P.M. Dr. Rajendra Pal Singh telephoned from Hyattsville, USA to discuss Master's US programme. He wanted to know if we could fly to Boston direct, instead of to New York, so that a meeting could be arranged at Boston on the 22nd evening itself. I pointed out to Dr. Singh that Master would certainly be very tired after a seven hour transatlantic flight, and therefore an evening of rest would be necessary. Also, only this morning I had been to Air India and confirmed our flights to New York and I did not want to change the travel plans now. Dr. Singh agreed very kindly. We went to bed at 11:00 P.M., Master with an electric blanket under him, grinning happily at this unusual comfort.

17 May 72 - Wednesday

Master said he had a very comfortable night though he did not sleep much. He is fascinated with the electric blanket and has enjoyed using it right through the night. He came down to the drawing room at 8:30 A.M. I was reading a letter I had received in the morning post. Master suddenly said, "Brother, you be attentive to your condition. Look, I was studying your condition and I found that when you were reading your letter you had to come down from that condition to read it. I congratulate you! This is a real thing that I want, that one should remain in his own condition, and when it is necessary for the work then only he should come down to a lower condition for it. I only wish that 5 or 6 persons may be prepared like you, and then see what work can be done."

People kept drifting in the whole day, and we had to have several satsanghs for small groups as they formed. Those present included Andre, Birthe, Rako, John and Ose, an actor Murray Head and his girl friend Sue, Nicholas Roditi a young banker, and others.

Master was speaking to people the whole day but I was busy giving sittings and so could record only a few of his sayings.

"A yogi's aim is to get command over the powers of Nature. It is very easy because there there is no resistance, while in human beings there is natural resistance."

"God laughs when we weep. Do you know why? He laughs at our folly in weeping!"

"What is yoga? It is the perception of Reality."

"What is soul? It is the sport of Reality."

Andre, Birthe and Rako stayed for dinner. After dinner Andre said goodbye to Master and to all of us as he leaves early tomorrow morning for Paris. All of us were sorry to see him go and wished he could have stayed the rest of the week with us. He has been worried about his health and is obviously suffering pain, which he has concealed from all of us. He should have had treatment ere now, but has planned it for late July so that Master's European visit would be over by then. Even now he goes home so soon only to complete some business in Northern France before getting back to Sanary. A second reason is that Master has already been in France for 10 days, and Andre feels that if he stays in London he may prevent English abhyasis from obtaining the full benefit of Master's stay in London.

In the night Vera and Elidir had a long talk with me after Master retired to bed. Vera was very despondent and seemed to feel that Master's visit to London will be a waste as she doesn't expect much response. Elidir seemed to agree, and both wanted me to cut short the London visit and go to the USA where they feel the response would be much better. I told them that the USA programme was fixed and it is now too late to ask them to make changes. Vera was quite unhappy — she doesn't get on with crowds of people, being very nervous and highly excitable, and this was another reason for her asking us to go soon. She doesn't feel she can bear exposure to humanity in the mass! I told her Master's Will will prevail and we have only to see we don't impede its working — that is all that is necessary from us. They agreed ultimately that results concern only the Master, while requisite effort is our share of the job. Vera has also been annoyed that Birthe has come over for a whole week. When I was in Le Beausset I had received a letter from Birthe enclosing a letter she had received from Vera — in which Vera had made it very very plain that she does not want Birthe in London when Master is there. In her letter to me Birthe wrote that she had cancelled her London visit. I wrote to her not to be silly and upset and Birthe wrote again — and in the meanwhile Vera wrote to Birthe asking her to come. Yet, in spite of this, Vera is annoyed!

18 May 72 - Thursday (London)

There were several group sittings during the day. Master has been having his lumbago-like pain, and Ose has been giving him a massage practically every morning.

19 May 72 - Friday (London)

A very active day. People kept coming in the whole day — Ose, John, Rako, Birthe, the Sardhanas, the second Sardhana family, a Mr. Patel and a Mr. Purshottam of Malavi, Ron Mendelsohn, his friend Pauline, all were there.

Rako said good-bye to Master in the evening. He leaves tomorrow after almost a continuous month with the Master. He goes to Paris and then on to Madagascar. His presence has been of benefit to me, and Master has enjoyed having him with him. In spite of his high position and social standing he is very humble, and has served Master personally with great personal devotion and love. I am personally sorry to see him go as he has shared in many of my own tasks so far, and now that we are going to the United States, where I don't know anyone, Rako's presence as a tried and trusted friend and devotee of the Master would have been of great help.

Elidir and Vera presented me a gold 'Half-Hunter' pocket watch made in Exeter in 1835!

20 May 72 - Saturday (London)

Meditation in the morning. Birthe, John, Ose all came. In the afternoon Vera, Elidir, Master and I went to see the Westminster Abbey. Master went through it very carefully and in considerable detail, putting on his spectacles time and again to read inscriptions, and often asking Elidir to locate the place where certain individuals were buried. We spent nearly two hours inside, and Master, with his passion for, and knowledge of, history was evidently enjoying the visit, arranged entirely at his request. We were all reluctant to have this excursion because on Tuesday last Master went out on a short tour of London and came back in almost a collapsed condition. On that occasion he could hardly climb up the stairs to his bedroom, and went to bed at once. Later on he told me that the atmosphere of London had been so heavy he had almost suffocated. When repeating this to Vera she asked him, "But Master, why did you not clean it?" Master said, "I cleaned it just enough so that I could live in it."

Vera: Master, is the London atmosphere as bad as that over Paris? We have always been told that there is so much that is bad in Paris, and so we feel that the atmosphere there must be very bad indeed.

Master: No. In Paris it was quite good, I had no trouble there. I find that the atmosphere over London is the worst of all I have seen.

Vera: Oh Master! Could you clean this, if it is so bad? It would be wonderful if you could.

Master: Yes. I told you I have already cleaned it a little — maybe five percent — but more I will not do. If people want then they must pray for that.

In the evening Ose and John came and stayed for dinner.

21 May 72 - Sunday (London)

In the morning Mr. John Pierre-Higgins came for a short sitting with Master. He is a very nice person, seriously interested in yoga, religion and healing (faith-healing). He came again in the evening bringing with him two professional healers, but they were not interested in Master's teaching. But Mr. John took to this seriously, and even though he has had short sessions with Master, they were primarily for physical betterment. Now he took a formal sitting as a beginning in spiritual sadhana.

At 5:30 P.M. Elidir and I accompanied Birthe to drop her at her hotel in Cromwell Road. She leaves this evening for Denmark.

Q: Why do some people not get the deep feeling of peace in meditation?

Master: Because even though they are doing meditation properly, they are behind Being.

Ron Mendelsohn and Pauline stayed for dinner.

Mr. A had corresponded with Master and Master had written to him some of the longest letters he has ever written. Master had answered many questions he had raised, and in fact Master was both very keen on meeting him and also somewhat apprehensive. He came once, asked some questions and then failed to turn up!

Fred Weinstock left a couple of days ago for U.S.A. He will probably meet us in Stonington. I have asked him to get in touch with Dr. Singh and fix his programme in consultation with him. Originally Master was to come back to London for a day's rest, on his way back from USA to Denmark. But on learning that SAS had a direct flight from New York to Copenhagen, which took only just a little longer than the New York-London flight, I decided to cut out London. Another major difficulty is the need for a British entry permit. When we landed at Heathrow, British immigration told me that a new one would have to be obtained in New York. This is too big a problem. A third reason is that 19, Marlborough Place has been sold as Vera and Elidir are going to live in the country, and they have the problem of shifting. So all things considered we have decided to cut out London on the return trip. Vera and Elidir will meet Master in Europe, most probably in Switzerland.

22 May 72 - Monday (London)

Master woke up quite early at 6:00 A.M. He is better and his back ache has almost disappeared. It was a bit chilly, and there was a slight drizzle when we got up, but by 7:00 A.M. it was better. I had an early breakfast, and Master had a glass of milk.

Ose and John came at 9:00 A.M. We were all talking till 11:00 A.M., rather desultorily as Vera was quite subdued, feeling the impending separation from Master.

At 11:00 A.M. Master got into Vera's car while I got in with Ose and John into theirs, and we left for Heathrow airport. There was no one else to say 'Bon Voyage' to

Master. We checked in, said good-bye to the Davies and to Ose and John and passed through immigration to the departure lounge. We had a rather long time to wait as we came in very early to Heathrow, and being early there was no crowd at the Air India checking-in counter, and so we were early all along the line. Master sat on a comfortable sofa, but was thoughtful, and obviously far away.

We boarded Air India's jumbo jet Boeing 747 'Emperor Ashoka' on their flight AI-101 and took off at 13:30 GMT. This is our first jumbo jet flight, and Master was struck with wonder at its enormity, and kept exclaiming again and again at the luxury of the decor, the comfort of the seats, and also expressed wonder at the five channel music heard through a set of ear-worn speakers, and in every way enjoyed himself. Lunch was served soon after we took off. Master first said he would not eat at all, but later agreed to try some of it, and finally ate the complete lunch. This is the first time, ever, to my knowledge, that Master has eaten solid food aboard an aeroplane! After lunch, which he expressed to have been excellent, he listened to Indian music and also watched the film show for some time. He was awake and entirely active, and did not feel the need for any rest. After three hours some snacks were served and, wonder of wonders, Master ate this too.

The 7 hours 10 minutes trans-atlantic flight seemed to take no time at all as Master so happily enjoyed everything that happened aboard the aircraft. The flight was superb all the way, without even the slightest vibration to cause unease or discomfort. Soon we were winging our way over Boston and shortly thereafter landed on US soil, touching down at Kennedy International Airport at 15:35 local time. We passed through immigration and customs within half an hour, and when we came out we found Dr. Rajendra Pal Singh, Mrs. Caroline S. Miller, Mrs. Carola A. Miller and

Fred Weinstock assembled to lovingly welcome Master. It was windy and quite chilly — chilly enough to force us to seek shelter in a protected place while Mrs. Caroline Miller went to fetch her car from the parking lot — quite an arduous and time-consuming operation in this land of the automobile. We left Kennedy airport at about 4:45 P.M. in Caroline's car, Caroline and Master in front, while Dr. Singh, Carola, Fred and I squeezed in into the back seat. After some time Fred had to perch on Dr. Singh's lap to ease the pressure on Carola! After approximately an hour's drive we halted for a brief rest and some cold drinks at a way-side self-service store — a small one indeed but well stocked with normally needed candy, ice-cream, drinks etc. After a 15 minute halt we drove on to finally reach Stonington, in the state of Connecticut, where Mrs. Miller has her residence, at around 8:00 P.M. Master began to get tired soon after we landed at Kennedy, and even though he enjoyed his long trans-atlantic flight very much, like a young school boy on his holiday, the comparatively short car-ride of about 120 miles very definitely proved to be the last straw on the camel's back, and he was fatigued when we got to Carol's residence. This is not surprising, considering the fact that 8:00 P.M. here is really 01:30 GMT, and having woken up at London at 6:00 A.M., he has been virtually on his feet for all of 19 1/2 hours already. He went straight up to the first floor bedroom (2nd floor in American English!) and within minutes thereafter a 'chillum' was got ready which he deeply enjoyed before going to bed to rest. At 9:30 P.M. Mr. and Mrs. Anand Swaroop, abhyasis living in Storrs, drove over to have Master's *darshan*. Master was able to receive them for just a few minutes. They left later in the night for Storrs. Dr. Singh and I have a room between us. Fred stays at a nearby place arranged by Carol. Carola is the eldest daughter of Mrs. Grace Kimball, and is the daughter-in-law of Carol, having married her son Antony. Tony came in to meet Master. When we went to bed it was well past 11:00 P.M. — a long day indeed of 22 1/2 hours!

23 May 72 - Tuesday (Stonington)

The whole morning had been kept thoughtfully free to enable Master to have much needed rest. The weather is fine and sunny but somewhat chilly when the wind blows.

At 4:00 P.M. about 25 persons came to tea to meet Master. A few of them were interested in discussing our yoga.

8:00 P.M. public meeting held at the Stonington Community Centre. About 45 persons present. Mrs. Miller's son Tony first spoke briefly, introducing Master to the audience. This was followed by a short speech given by Dr. Singh. After this I spoke for about 25 minutes on Sahaj Marg. We then introduced Fred Weinstock to the gathering and he spoke for five minutes on his own experience of this system. After this there was group meditation for 15 minutes and we returned home at 9:45 P.M.

24 May 72 - Wednesday (Stonington)

At 9:30 A.M. Master granted provisional permission to Mrs. Caroline S. Miller.

A few people who attended yesterday's meeting came in to Carol's house and commenced meditation (Mr. John Barlow, Mr. Bill Mann, Mr. Mark Zajac, Mr. Tom Hahn).

Master's general condition is not very good. He is very tired and will take a few days to recover from the tiring travel indulged in so far. Considering all relevant facts, a decision was taken to omit a visit to Texas in view of the long distance involved including a time difference too. We telephoned Mr. Chiranjivi at Corsicana and conveyed this to him. He had made arrangements for three meetings and was quite disappointed, but was understanding Master's need for rest in view of the long journey and programme still ahead of him.

At 4:00 P.M. Master, Dr. Singh and I left with Carol in her car to go to Storrs to attend a public meeting in the University of Connecticut. At Norwich a car rammed into us from behind and smashed up the boot. Master, who was till then sitting forward, had just then leaned back and so did not suffer any injury. There was no injury to anyone but the car suffered a bit. We were delayed for nearly one hour completing police formalities. In the meantime Dr. Singh had telephoned Anand Swaroop at Storrs and he came over in his car. By then the formalities having been completed, and our vehicle being in running condition, we drove on to Storrs, following Anand Swaroop.

At 7:30 P.M. a public meeting was held in Room 217 of the Commons Building of the University of Connecticut. I spoke to the persons assembled on Sahaj Marg after Master had been introduced to the gathering by Anand Swaroop. After my talk Master transmitted for about 18 minutes. Later there were some questions and answers. We came back to Anand Swaroop's residence for dinner and left at 10:00 P.M., returning to Stonington at 11:20 P.M., covering the 80 miles in an hour and a quarter!

Anand Swaroop had arranged for Master to stay the night at Storrs but we had earlier decided to come back to Stonington for the night. Anand was upset and behaved rather rudely, accusing me of 'interfering' and 'upsetting' his arrangements. We went to bed at 1:00 A.M.

25 May 72 - Thursday (Stonington)

Early in the morning Master was talking about his own drowned condition. He started getting into this condition on 20th April at Delhi, where he asked me to write down the following:

"Actually I am feeling it. The God of God has started to grip. Because of this, one has to be extremely careful because power has increased enormously. It is so much power that you will not find anywhere in the history of spirituality. This is a new thing. This is the first instance."

I asked Master how much of my own self was in this state of being drowned. Master said, "About 1/3rd of you is in this condition." I asked Babuji, "Why, even after working for so many years, only so little? It should have been much more." Master laughed and said, "Aré, do you think this to be too little? It is too much — even in saints you will not find so much. One third is a great deal!". Dr. Singh wanted to know how much of his own mind was internalised. Master answered, "It has not started yet." Dr. Singh was very disappointed.

After his bath Master started talking to me, and said, "What should I give you, brother? Of course you are receiving something. Do you know that Lalaji has given you a great deal? You have got a great deal direct from Him about which He has told me Himself. One thing I am not able to understand and that is the powers that He has filled into you, how may I bring them to a state of awakening? Anyway, it will be done somehow."

Master later said, "Gnana is the perception of Reality." Master had earlier defined Yoga as the perception of Reality, but now prefers to so define Gnana.

Master, Dr. Singh and I were driven 100 miles to Boston by Carol in her car, leaving Stonington at 1:15 P.M.

and arriving at the MIT campus at 3:00 P.M. — 100 miles in 105 minutes!

At 4:30 P.M. there was a public meeting in Room 491 of the Foreign Students' Centre of the Massachussets Institute of Technology. Master was briefly introduced to the audience by Dr. Singh, and then I spoke on "Yoga as an Instrument of Evolution" for about 25 minutes. This was followed by meditation conducted by Master for about 20 minutes.

Boston was cold and windy when we arrived at 3:00 P.M., and even colder when we left the MIT campus at 6:10 P.M. Anand Swaroop, his wife, and a couple of friends had come over from Storrs to attend the meeting. Fred Weinstock came in yesterday to Boston to collect some of his friends whom he wished to introduce to Master. Fred joined us when we left Boston and we all drove 56 miles to Providence in the state of Rhode Island, arriving there at 7:10 P.M. for a public meeting in Room No. 279 of the Barns and Halley Building on George Street, housing the Division of Engineering and Department of Physics of the Brown University. Following Dr. Singh's introduction of the Master, I spoke on "Pranahuti, or Transmission of Yogic Energy" for half an hour, and this was followed by group meditation for 25 minutes. Mr. and Mrs. Anand Swaroop came over to Providence to attend this meeting too, before returning to Storrs.

We left Providence at 8:30 P.M. and returned to Stonington at 9:20 P.M., dropping Fred at Providence as he wished to go back to Boston.

26 May 72 - Friday (Stonington)

Master feeling somewhat less fatigued, and looking more cheerful and more of his usual self today.

Master gave a sitting to Carol, Tony, Carola, John Barlow and Dr. Singh.

We left Stonington in a specially hired car at 2:10 P.M. Due to Mrs. Miller's car being out of circulation, the insurance company made a car available at their cost so that she could take her Indian guests to New York, Troy etc. Carola joined us for this trip, and with Carol at the wheel we left Stonington at 2:10 P.M., arriving in New York, at the Columbia University campus at 5:00 P.M. — a total distance of 135 miles. We drove straight to the campus — no sight seeing at all!. At 6:30 P.M. we had a public meeting in the Foreign Students' Centre. Dr. Singh spoke first to introduce the Master, then I spoke on Sahaj Marg for about 25 minutes, and this was followed by meditation for 20 minutes — it was very deep and blissful. A Dr. Joseph Annichiarico and his wife, old friends of Dr. Singh, attended this meeting. They live in New Jersey, and are a nice couple. The doctor is a fine man. There was a question-and-answer session.

We left Columbia University campus at 9:00 P.M. and though we were originally to stay the night in New York and go on to Troy tomorrow morning, we found that it would be worthwhile going on to Troy straight away. Spending the night in New York would have first of all meant the group breaking up to stay separately as arrangements had been made with friends for Master and myself. So, in spite of the long drive, we decided to go on, and after about half an hour drive stopped across the river in the state of New Jersey at a road-side "Howard Johnson" restaurant for dinner. All of us had a really good and enjoyable dinner. Master enjoyed his mushroom soup with particular relish and ate a full dinner — after a long time! We left the restaurant at about 11:00 P.M. and reached Troy at 1:00 A.M. Mr. S.S. Ramakrishnan, having been informed by telephone of our changed plans, met Master on arrival. Master, Carol and Carola stay in Ramakrishnan's small flat, Ramakrishnan himself bedding with a friend of his, while Dr. Singh and I were put up with a friend Shri Indrajit Kumar. It was about 2:30 A.M. when we finally went to bed.

27 May 72 - Saturday (Troy)

From Indrajit Kumar's house we came in to Ramakrishnan's house at 10:30 A.M. Master was up and talking to Carol and Carola, who had slept on the floor, and had something of an uncomfortable night with too little sleep. Carol looked tired, having had to drive us all the way from Stonington to New York, and then on here to Troy, all in one day.

Master looked at me and said, "Do note this — Excitement, inner, observed."

Later He explained, "I observed your inner condition and found inner irritation at the base. Irritation in its outward aspect you have of course put far away from yourself. But when I observed you today I found that inside at the base there is some irritation. I shall pull it out. Perhaps it is not harmful for spirituality, but brother, to my vision, it looks bad."

Master was sitting rather quietly. Carol asked him to say something. Master laughed and said, "I am not a speaker but a silencer."

About an hour later Master told me, "I have been concentrating on your irritation and found that it is not your irritation but it is coming to you from your father — it is hereditary."

Christine Langstaff, our preceptor in Canada, came in at 11:00 A.M. from Montreal to meet Master.

At 1:00 P.M., Carol, Carola, Christine, Dr. Singh, Ramakrishnan and I had lunch at Indrajit Kumar's house. Master was to have been the chief guest, but said he was not feeling quite well and did not want to eat, so he did not come.

4:00 P.M. public meeting organised by the RPI India Club held at the Rensselaer-Newman Cultural Centre on Burdett Road. I spoke for 20 minutes on Master's teachings. After this Master transmitted to the gathering when we all sat for group meditation for nearly 20 minutes. It was superb! After this there was some discussion, the whole gathering breaking up into three groups, the main one around Master, all asking questions. This lasted till 5:45 P.M. Murray Head of London and his girl friend Sue, who flew to the U.S.A. mid last week, came to attend this meeting. Murray brought five of his friends. They are all staying on a nearby farm. Just as the meeting ended Fred Weinstock turned up from Boston, with two of his friends.

6:00 P.M. Master was the guest of the Rev. Tom Phelan at his residence just behind the Cultural Centre. Carol, Carola, Christine and I were also invited. Father Phelan had thoughtfully arranged a simple but elegant dinner wholly of vegetables and fruits. After dinner Master spent some time with Father Phelan in his study, answering questions. We returned to Ramakrishnan's home at 9:00 P.M. Some persons came to see Master, the last a Lebanese student by name Megdi, leaving at 11:30 P.M. After that Master was in a reminiscent mood and told Carol some of his experiences. It was 1:00 A.M. when we finally adjourned to bed.

28 May 72 - Sunday (Troy)

Mr. S.S. Ramakrishnan was granted provisional permission by Master, and authorised to organise a Centre of the Mission in Troy.

At 10:30 A.M. we all attended Mass in the Rensselaer-Newman Chapel on Burdett Avenue, and after Father Phelan finished the first part of the prayer, he introduced Master to the congregation saying that the time had come when humanity had once again to turn to the East for spiritual guidance, adding, "Here is a great Master of the East, a Master of Yoga, who will talk to you through his secretary Mr. P. Rajagopalachari, and tell you how to find that which we have lost sight of — true human aspiration leading to the Real Goal." I spoke on "Man and God" for ten minutes.

After this we returned to Ramakrishnan's residence. We were to have attended one more public meeting in a nearby town but that was telephonically cancelled by the sponsors.

Carol and Carola left at noon to drive to Stonington, and telephoned at 3:30 P.M. to confirm having arrived home.

4:00 P.M. to the Rensselaer-Newman Cultural Centre for a group meditation. I gave a short talk of 15 minutes to introduce the subject and the practice. Among those present were Fred Weinstock, his friends Jay Patt and Mrs., Murray and Sue, Prof. Koller, the Lebanese student Megdi. The meditation was again superb. After this Prof. Koller and Master had a private discussion meeting for over half an hour. Christine Langstaff did not attend the meeting, and on enquiry I discovered she had left for Canada at noon. Fred and the Patts left for Boston in the evening after the meeting ended.

8:00 P.M. public meeting at the RPI students Union Building sponsored by VPAC. I spoke on Raja Yoga for nearly half an hour. After this Master took group meditation for the 50 odd persons assembled for about 25 minutes. Returned home at 9:15 P.M.

29 May 72 - Monday (Troy)

A quiet morning. Joshi and Janardhan Bhat came at 11 A.M. for sitting with Master.

We left Ramakrishnan's residence at 1:00 P.M. in Indrajit Kumar's car, and were driven to Albany airport. Dr. Singh said goodbye rather sorrowfully to Master, as he goes back to Hyattsville from here. So once again Master and I are on our own.

We left Albany at 14:10 by Allegheny Airlines flight 489 and arrived in Detroit after one hour flight at 14:10 (1 hour time difference). We had to wait at Detroit airport for nearly half an hour as Charlotte O'Brien arrived that late, breathless, to meet Master. She drove us in her car 75 miles to East Lansing in the state of Michigan, arriving there at 17:20. We had something to eat at the place where Charlotte is staying, and then went on to Teri Litterell's house where Master and I will be staying. Teri is a nice young girl. After some rest, we left to attend a meeting of students organised by Charlotte at 'Synergy' at 7:30 P.M. I spoke on the Sahaj Marg system of Raja Yoga, and this was followed, as usual by group meditation for about 20 minutes. We were back at Teri's place at 9:00 P.M.

30 May 72 - Tuesday (East Lansing)

At 9:00 A.M., I accompanied Charlotte to the Union Building, Michigan State University for a meeting in the Captain's Room and I spoke to the assembled students of Yoga for nearly 45 minutes about our own system. Later

Master came at 11:30 A.M. and gave group sitting to those present.

From 12 to 2:00 P.M. about 15 young persons came to meet Master in Teri's house.

4:00 P.M. public meeting in the Green Room of the Union Building. I spoke on Sahaj Marg for the usual 25 minutes, and this was followed by a group sitting taken by Master.

Among those who came to meet Master was Mr. Armando Lara of Lansing. This person impressed Master much with his sincerity and good heart, and Master would like to consider him for Cuba. Another person who similarly impressed Master was Mr. Manuel Fontecha, a young man of Honduras, come to study at MSU. He leaves tomorrow for Tegucigalpa, his home town, after completing two years study here. He has been practising another system of meditation, Transcendental meditation, as taught by Maharishi Mahesh Yogi, for a couple of years but felt nothing. He sat for this afternoon's sitting and was electrified by what he felt, and was extremely sorry that he is meeting Master only on the eve of his own departure for Honduras. He followed us to Teri's home and had a special sitting with Master.

Another person who impressed Master is Mr. Clint Lockert, Bibliographer, MSU Library, East Lansing, Michigan.

8:30 P.M. we attended a Yoga group meeting in the Green Room of the Union Building, specially arranged for students of Yoga in the University. I talked on Yoga for 25 minutes. Master followed with a group sitting for 20 minutes. My speech was said to have been very good! Back home at 9:20 P.M. Charlotte agreed to work for the Mission.

1972

31 May 72 - Wednesday (East Lansing)

A number of young persons came in the morning and I gave them their first sittings, and also a special sitting to Charlotte O'Brien.

Master is not very well today. He has been badly constipated for four days now. However he spoke to about 20 persons who assembled to see him in Teri's house from 10 to 11:15 A.M.

At 11:15 A.M. Master and I left Teri's home in East Lansing in Charlotte's car and arrived at Toledo at 1:15 P.M. We stopped at Toledo for lunch, which Master ate with relish, and then drove on to Lakewood, a suburb of Cleveland in the state of Ohio, reaching Mrs. Grace Kimball's house at 5:15 P.M. (4:15 P.M. mid-West time). We drove 230 miles from East Lansing to get here, spending four hours on the actual journey. Charlotte, a 19 year old girl, is a very competent, safe and fast driver. She is very calm, speaks little, but is a very charming person. Mr. Craig Kimball, daughter Spencer Kimball, a preceptor of the Mission, and the youngest daughter of the family Celia, all were there to welcome Master. The evening was kept free to permit Master to rest. An enormous bedroom, the Master bedroom, was placed at Master's disposal.

1 Jun. 72 - Thursday (Lakewood)

9:30 A.M. — 11:15 A.M. Group of about 40 persons gathered in Mrs. Kimball's drawing room. I spoke to them for 25 minutes on Yoga vis-a-vis Sahaj Marg. Master then transmitted to the group for about 20 minutes. There was some discussion after this.

7:00 P.M. public meeting in the Cleveland Public Library, Cleveland. I spoke for nearly 30 minutes on yoga as an instrument of realisation. This was followed by 20 minutes meditation. After the meeting I met Terry, a girl, who is intensely interested and is thinking of coming to India.

2 Jun. 72 - Friday (Lakewood)

About 50 persons assembled in Grace's drawing room for the 10 A.M. group meditation. I had to give a short introductory talk on Sahaj Marg. My throat is bad and I have a bad head-ache.

Grace and Spencer took Master out to lunch to meet 75 women, members of the Cleveland Hospitals Board. I was to have addressed them after lunch but couldn't go due to indisposition. This is the only meeting I have missed so far, and the only occasion Master has had to go out without me.

4:00 P.M. Master granted provisional permission to Miss Charlotte O'Brien and authorised her to commence organising a Mission Centre at East Lansing.

Mr. Charles J. Nohava had a special sitting with Master. He attended yesterday evening's public meeting at the Cleveland Public Library. In my speech I had elaborated on the system of preceptors and stressed the important fact that this system made abhyasis independent of personal physical contact with the Master, as local preceptors could do the work of Transmission. Immediately after the meeting he came to Master and asked how he could become a preceptor!

7:30 P.M. public meeting at the Lakewood Public Library where over 110 were present. I spoke for over half an hour on Yoga, and this was followed by group meditation for 25 minutes. After this about 30 minutes were devoted to discussions.

10:00 P.M. Mrs. Grace O'Dare Kimball was granted provisional permission by Master.

3 Jun. 72 - Saturday

Nearly 50 persons present for the morning group meditation. Master told them, "Look here, in the past people had to be dependent on India, or the East, for spiritual development. They had to go there at considerable cost and personal difficulty, and usually had to spend years there to seek training. Now by creating preceptors here in your own town, you no longer have to look to India — I have liberated you from India." (laughter)

Master told me, "There is greed in abhyasis for approach but they have no such greed for spirituality."

Some questions were asked.

Q: Who are evil people, and what are evil ways?

Master: Doing unnatural things, that is evil. The things which make you spiritually and physically strong are good, while those which make man mentally and physically weak are bad.

Q: What is the moral of man?

Master: To think of higher things — that is the moral of man. When you think of it you will also have it. Try for it. I feel that civilization in all countries must be modified within 10 years.

Master: Can you tell me what is the greatest foolishness of man? I will tell you. We always think of the past but forget to build the future. That is our greatest foolishness.

Q: Are will and desire different?

Master: Desire at its own place is bad, but if it is properly moulded it is good. We are using desire wrongly. Will is the process to obtain the object of desire.

The rest of the day was free of any social obligations.

4 Jun. 1972 - Sunday

10:30 A.M. Mrs. Esther M. Hills of Lakewood, Ohio was granted provisional permission by Master. She will work under the instructions and guidance of Grace, who will be in charge of the centre.

Dr. Joseph Warren and his wife Mary came at 11:00 A.M. for a special sitting with Master. They are close friends of the Kimballs and followers of Maharishi Mahesh Yogi.

Charlotte left at 2:30 P.M. to drive back to East Lansing. At 4:00 P.M. about eight persons came for satsangh.

5 Jun. 72 - Monday (Washington)

We left the Kimball residence at 10:00 A.M. with Grace and Spencer, who drove us to the Hopkins airport at Cleveland for our United Airlines Flight 642 to Washington. The Boeing 737 flight took off at 12:15 P.M. and we landed at Washington National Airport at 1:10 P.M. after a good flight.

Dr. Singh, and Chiranjivi were at the airport to meet Master. It was very hot and we were sweating. Dr. Singh drove us home to Hyattsville, 12 miles away. Even the air-conditioner in Dr. Singh's car was unable to cope with the heat and humidity.

Chiranjivi, his wife Sujata, 9 year old daughter Lakshmi and 5 year old daughter Suneeta have all come by car all the way from Corsicana, Texas, having driven 1500 miles, the husband and wife sharing in the driving.

Master was a bit tired, and the practically unbearable heat — aggravated by the failure of Dr. Singh's domestic air-conditioning system — made a real rest impossible, but Master went to bed for such rest as he could get.

At 6:30 P.M. Mr. A.V. Rangarajan, Vatsala, Sukanya, Kamali, Rangamani, and Sushila came to see me. AVR has come for a conference. Rangamani and Sushila are here on an eight week holiday. They stayed till 9:30 P.M.

6 Jun. 1972 - Tuesday (Hyattsville)

Master slept well last night and had a good night. He has woken up feeling refreshed. The sky is completely overcast and it is windy and chilly, with a slight drizzle, in complete contrast to yesterday's sweltering heat. Master has a free day in front of Him. When the USA plans were originally made three days were set apart for Texas, but that had to be cancelled due to Master's fatigue. One of those three days was given as an extra day to Lakewood, and two days added to the stay here in Hyattsville. But it was then too late to change the meeting dates, so we have two free days here — necessary ones!

I left Hyattsville at 10:30 A.M. with Dr. Singh and drove into Washington D.C. to spend the day with A.V. Rangarajan and family at the Crystal City Marriott Hotel where they are staying. Dr. Singh picked me up in the evening at 8:15 P.M. and we came back to Hyattsville around 9:00 P.M. Master was well, and completely at home as usual.

In the course of after-dinner talks with Master the talk turned towards visions and experiences in meditation. Master explained that visions are unnecessary, and have really speaking no value as indicators of spiritual progress. A vision is nothing but a locked-down impression being allowed to surface by the cleaning process. Therefore all that comes out as visions are nothing but earlier impressions formed in us by our own thoughts and actions.

Master went on to tell a humorous story about his own period of early sadhana, but after he had commenced training abhyasis by transmission.

One day His mother asked Him, "Have you had the darshan of Lord Narayana?" Babuji answered, "No. I have never had the darshan of Lord Narayana." Where upon His mother remarked, "When you have yourself not had his darshan, how are you going to give all of these people his darshan? You are cheating the people." There was tremendous laughter at this, sparked off by Master's own delighted laughter.

7 Jun. 72 - Wednesday

Master had a good night's rest again and is cheerful and more his usual self this morning. Today is the second day of rest.

At 7:30 P.M. Dr. Robert Monroe (Mind Research Institute, Blue Ridge, Virginia) came to see Master. He is a well known author and researcher, and has several books to his credit. I believe S.S. Ramakrishnan, having read Dr. Monroe's books, many of which I saw in his book-shelf, established contact with him with a view to bringing him and Master together. Naturally Dr. Monroe is very deeply and widely read, and has an intimate knowledge of techniques and forms of meditation as available throughout the world. He spoke at length to Master, and spoke feelingly about his own personal experiences. After an hour's talk he had an individual sitting with Master. When he left at around 9:15 P.M. he promised Master that they would meet again before Master leaves this country.

8 Jun. 72 - Thursday

Master dictated the following to me at 10:40 A.M.

"Because there is no expansion this thing remains upon the whole universe. Even if there is a little expansion in this (world) even then much can be known. To bring about the accurate thing, this expansion must be there in the whole universe. Even a little knocking here, and it should be known there immediately!! It is difficult for this thing to happen unless the time for it comes. When a question was asked of Dr. K.C. Varadachari, his elucidation was that the expansion was only of this world, while the rest was all controlled, so that the expansion should not occur throughout the Universe and this was the need of the time. His knowledge had a great deal of confusion in it, and he retained some percentage of it with him. Therefore much that I wanted to do for him could not happen as it should have happened. From his own regime Swami Vivekananda is saying, 'Your case is somewhat different.' Lalaji Saheb said, 'I have made you an Emperor.'" Master laughed and said, "Now, you may understand what I am — you may think I am Deputy God! This thing is not possible for everybody until the time comes for it."

After this I gave Master a hair-cut and beard trim — the second one on this tour! He laughingly told me, "Brother, much of my money has been saved. Do you know they take $5 for cutting the hair?" — incredulously.

We left Hyattsville at 11:00 A.M. with Dr. Singh and his wife and baby son, the Chiranjivi family following in their car, and went to Washington to see the more important sights. Dr. Singh took Master to see the White House, but Chiranjivi and I got left out as we missed Dr. Singh's car on the way somewhere and came too late to get in. I waited on the pavement while Chiranjivi went to park his car, but he failed to turn up for more than half-an-hour after even Master had come out of the White House. Ultimately, just when we were beginning to be seriously worried about him, as he does not know Washington, he turned up. We all then went to see the Washington Monument, entry and ascent to the top involving a half-hour wait in a queue. Finally we saw the Lincoln Memorial. We were supposed to go on to Arlington but everyone was too tired by then — no lunch even, and it was 4:00 P.M. by then — and so we decided to drive back home to Hyattsville.

9:00 P.M. some Indian friends of Dr. Singh came with their wives to have darshan of Master — Dr. Verma, Mr. Kanti, their wives and one other.

9 Jun. 72 - Friday

Master completely well.

At 8:00 A.M. I left with Dr. Singh for Washington and spent a few hours with Rangarajan and family at the Crystal City Marriot Hotel. They leave for New York this afternoon. They dropped me at Hyattsville at 2:00 P.M., spent half-an-hour with Master, and drove off on their long drive to New York.

Dr. Joseph N. Annichiarico, his wife and eight year old son, came at 2:00 P.M. from Oakland, NJ to spend two days with Master. They will stay with us. This couple attended the Columbia University meeting.

At 5:00 P.M. Carol Miller arrived from Stonington. She also stays with us. Dr. Singh's home is quite full now, and except Master all the rest will have to sleep on the floor.

7:30 P.M. public meeting in the Prince George Memorial County Library. Dr. Singh commenced with a short talk introducing Master. Then I spoke for half-an-hour on "Yoga and States of Consciousness". This was followed by a 20 minute group satsangh taken by Master.

When we returned home Dr. Annichiarico was given a special sitting by Master to prepare him for permission. Master was very active after dinner and was talking till 11:30 P.M.

10 Jun. 72 - Saturday

At 9:30 A.M. Master granted provisional permission to Dr. Joseph N. Annichiarico of Oakland, New Jersey.

All those who have been made preceptors now were given their certificates as we had brought 15 with us. But these are finished, and so Dr. Joseph will have to wait for his certificate to be sent from India after we return!

My cousin B. Ranganathan who is studying here in the States came in at 3:00 P.M. from Pittsburgh when we had gone to attend a public meeting. He will also stay with us here in Dr. Singh's residence — one more in this already too crowded place.

2:00 P.M. public meeting in the Prince George Memorial Library. I spoke for 25 minutes on "Yoga, time and consciousness" followed by Master's transmission during a group sitting for 20 minutes. When this meeting ended we all got into the car to go home, but Master suddenly expressed a desire to go to Arlington. So we drove to Washington, visited J.F. Kennedy's grave in Arlington and came back to Hyattsville by 5:00 P.M.

8:00 P.M. public meeting at the First Spiritual Science Church of Washington DC in Washington. The place was packed full.

The husband and wife who run this church are both members of the clergy.

I gave my longest lecture so far at this place, speaking for 40 minutes on "Yoga and Sahaj Marg". The audience composed entirely of people interested in spiritual development, listened with rapt attention. My lecture was followed by 20 minutes group meditation. We were back home at 10:00 P.M.

11:00 P.M. about 10 people came for a sitting with Master. We went to bed at nearly 1 A.M.! A lady, Mrs. Gould of Adelphi Maryland, was very keenly interested, and Master who is very impressed with her, gave her a special sitting. I managed to do most of the packing after 10:00 P.M. as we leave the United States tomorrow, on our return journey towards home, which is however more than three weeks away.

11 Jun. 72 - Sunday

Dr. Joseph, Mrs. Annichiarico and son left at 8:20 A.M. by car to return to Oakland. Mrs. Miller decided to go with them and so she also left.

At 9:00 A.M. S.S. Ramakrishnan arrived from Troy, having travelled all night by bus to get here via New York!

At 9:30 A.M. we packed up and left Hyattsville. The Chiranjivi's took a last minute decision to go with Master to New York before getting back to Texas. We arrived at Bethesda, a Washington suburb, at 10:30 A.M. A meeting had been arranged there by the Vedic Culture Society. Dr. Singh spoke for 5 minutes and then I spoke for 20 minutes on Sahaj Marg. Master then took group meditation. Just as we were about to get into our cars to drive to New York, Mr. S. Radhakrishnan, a brother of Mr. M.S. Sundara, our Delhi preceptor, met Master and was almost in tears to learn that Master was about to leave for New York, and to leave the country this evening. Radhakrishnan is in Washington with his brother Mr. Nanjundiah, but had received no information of Master's visit to the USA. He saw a notice of this morning's meeting in 'India News' published by the Indian Embassy, and so came here. He was very

very upset and miserable at having missed the chance of being with Master for one whole week.

We left Bethesda at 11:45 A.M., stopped en route at 1:15 P.M. for a very bad lunch, insufficient in every way, and finally arrived at Kennedy International Airport, New York at 6:45 P.M. — a total of 240 miles by car today. Master was very tired.

This is the third time we came to New York, but we have seen nothing of it. In fact barring the brief excursion to Washington we have seen nothing of the U.S. except airports which we passed through, and the highways! We are also leaving the country without being able to meet Dr. Robert Monroe again. He telephoned yesterday, anxiously, trying to get Master to fly over in a friend's plane to his place, promising to put us down in New York this evening, but we did not wish to take any chance with Master's health particularly as Dr. Monroe's home is in the hills, and a car drive over twisting hill roads would be unavoidable. Dr. Monroe has promised to make a trip to India to meet Master.

At Kennedy Airport the Rangarajan family also joined us later to send off Master. Dr. Singh broke down completely and was in tears — he accused me of being 'cruel' in taking Master away from him. Poor chap he is much affected.

Master and I left New York by Boeing 747 on SAS flight SK 612, taking off at 9:35 P.M. on their non-stop flight to Copenhagen.

Our hectic three weeks tour of USA thus comes to an end. We fly 3950 miles, the longest single flight yet, before we reach our destination tomorrow, after a seven hour flight.

12 Jun. 72 - Monday (Greve Strand)

The flight from New York was quite comfortable and SAS looked after us very well. I had requested Air India Washington to arrange vegetarian food for us, but somewhere the whole thing had misfired. The purser said SAS had not received any request for special food, but nevertheless he managed to make up two trays for us from the 1st Class pantry, and we had a tasty dinner. Master did not sleep much on the flight. Mostly he was in a withdrawn and ruminative mood.

We touched down at Kastrup airport, Copenhagen, at 10:40 A.M. local time, somewhat behind schedule. A group of local abhyasis and preceptors lovingly greeted Master. Since Master was very tired, we drove away without spending much time at the airport, and went to Birthe's house in Greve Strand. During the day there were no visitors. In the evening Vibe, Thomas, Lakshminarasimhan, Leif Larson, and Josiah of Amsterdam all came to meet Master, the last named Josiah with two of his friends. Two new faces are here, one Mr. Bent Ruus, who has been following Transcendental Meditation under Mahesh Yogi for about 10 years, and the other Allen, a nice, well-behaved young man, a mathematician. Bent is also said to be one of the teachers of Mahesh Yogi's system — and well-read and acquainted with Eastern teachings. There was no meditation in the evening as Master was exhausted. He however joined the small group in Birthe's drawing room, relaxed with his hookah, and spoke to those present till 11 P.M.

There was some general talk of philosophy, and the value of philosophic studies. Some tended to argue for, and some against philosophy. Master broke into the discussion to give us his opinion.

Master: "Philosophy gives happiness without, but I give happiness within. And by talking of philosophy I also give happiness without! So look here, I give happiness both within and without!" (laughter)

Q: Master, you know the protons and the neutrons in the nucleus of the atom. Do you think they are ultimate particles or is there something else behind?

Master: "Well, I am telling you — if these particles were simple at the base and also simple at the outside, then they would be God!"

Q: What is wisdom?

Master: It is the proper utilisation of the power of God.

Q: What is egoism?

Master: Egoism is not a bad thing. Really speaking it is a pointer. It points to something. Now here is a table, and I lift it up. I can lift it because of the egoistic power in me which tells me I can lift it. So you see egoism is not bad, but the mistake is we identify the knowledge the self has — that it can lift the table — with the body. This is the mistake, that the knowledge the self has about itself is identified with the body. So egoism is really a clue to power that the self possesses. Now look here, I am against the annihilation of the self because if it is destroyed, then we cannot work at all. Now all saints, at least in India, have said that annihilation of the self is necessary but I am against it."

After this there was some general discussion on power and the use of power. This led to the subject of creation. Master explained how creation had come about because the power of God had to be used. He explained that power, if not used, would solidify and lead to what he calls power-grossness. This applies to preceptors of the Mission also — if power given to them is not used by them, this peculiar grossness develops. So power must be used. He then jokingly added, "God is clever, but man is wise. Why? Because man can utilise the cleverness of God, and that requires wisdom! So man is wise — look here! (laughing hilariously)."

Q: In Transcendental Meditation at one point I began, and at the other end there was the zero point to which I aspired. Now I came to a particular point where my progress stopped. If I had not accepted this fact I could not have developed further.

Master: "Well, a Master of the proper caliber could have prevented this block. It is the Master's business. If you know you have stopped, then do what you can about it. If you can do nothing yourself, then ask the Master. But don't try to be both the Master and the disciple yourself! That becomes the difficulty."

There was a drift in the discussion towards egoism. Master said, "Egoism? I will tell you what it is. Man takes God's work, and throws his own work on God. This is the real difficulty! We should play our part and allow God to do His work in His own way."

Yet later the discussion centred on love, Universal Love and so on. Master said the real thing was to transfer all love to God. "Remembrance of one brings remembrance of all. If I love you, I love your children also. There is a society which has been preaching Universal Love for the last 40 years, but there is no success. Why? It is because of hatred, the presence of hatred in the heart. Remove hatred and love will develop by itself. So you should not work on it, but on its base."

13 Jun. 72 - Tuesday

Master took group satsangh at 11:00 A.M.

When Master and I were here in May, a decision had then been taken to register the Mission in Denmark if this was possible under Danish law, and within the framework of the Mission's bye-laws and constitution. As a matter of fact Master wants the Mission to be registered in all countries, one after the other, and the preliminary work has been, in most cases, entrusted to certain members in each country. In Denmark Thomas had undertaken to complete the necessary formalities and, assisted by a lawyer, a set of papers had been prepared and were available today for study. I spent much of the day going through the English translation of the Danish original, and finding much written in that would not be acceptable, I finally prepared a draft independent of the lawyer's. In the evening we had a meeting including the local preceptors, and Master presided over it. One draft was read through carefully and Master approved it. It was then decided to submit this draft to the lawyer and see if it could be put in as it is.

Master took group satsangh at 8:00 P.M.

After dinner I sat down with Thomas, Vibe, Jens, Bjorn and a few others and typed out the final draft for the Danish Government, which was completed at 2:00 A.M.

14 Jun. 72 - Wednesday (Copenhagen)

I gave individual sittings to Mikala, Palle, Neils and Hans Jorgen Hvid of Viborg who came with two abhyasis to see Master.

At 9:00 A.M. Master, Birthe, Vibe, Thomas and I left for Copenhagen to meet the lawyer Mr. Preben Skviver in his office. Our draft was submitted to him. He read it through and felt that there was no major difficulty in anything it contained, except the provision that Master would be the permanent President of the Danish Mission, which might cause some difficulty as, under normal conditions, a

Danish citizen would be preferred. We explained to Mr. Preben the basics of our Mission and how Master's unique position as the spiritual head of the Indian Mission made it necessary for him to so act in other countries too. Mr. Preben promised to consult the registration authorities and telephone later in the day — which he did, confirming that everything had been accepted and also sending the requisite forms to be properly filled in and submitted.

Since we got back to Greve Strand only at 2:00 P.M. the 11:00 A.M. satsangh had to be skipped. The papers were filled and got ready for submission.

Abhyasis started gathering from 4:00 P.M. on. Evening satsangh was taken by Master as usual at 8:00 P.M.

Master was generally better today.

15 Jun. 72 - Thursday (Greve Strand)

Master was in a relaxed mood when he woke up, and quite cheerful. Some people came in at 9:00 A.M. Talking generally of skepticism, intellectual arrogance and so on, Master said, "This is the time not of Prophets but of atoms."

Q: How to define God, Master?

Master: "If all the adjectives in the world be removed, what is left is God. If you want to use vulgar language against God in anger and rage, then use as many adjectives as you like."

Master asked me to take the 11:00 A.M. satsangh as he wanted to be free of strain. About 44 abhyasis were present. Later I gave individual sittings to Vibe and Helle, and also a special sitting to Jytte Gravesen to prepare her for preceptorship. Later I gave more individual sittings to Thomas, Jens, Leif, Kirsten and Allen.

At 6:00 P.M. Mr. Raman Lal Mimani telephoned from Copenhagen City to say he has arrived in the city with two friends, and wishes to see Master. We gave him directions to come to Greve Strand, and at 8:00 P.M. we set out in Birthe's car to fetch them from the bus stand. Master was very pleased to see Raman Lalji and they were talking till 11:30 P.M.

Thomas, Vibe, Jens, Ole and I were up till 2:00 A.M. finalising the registration papers, forming a local committee, putting down minutes of the meeting etc. ready for tomorrow.

Thomas, Vibe, Jens, Leif, all these persons have been mostly sleeping in Birthe's drawing room the past few nights.

16 Jun. 72 - Friday

In the morning Master was taken to the Grevesparkasse Bank. The bank manager agreed to open an account in the name of the Mission. Birthe signed the necessary papers. Thereafter Birthe closed the old account in her own name and transferred the balance to the new account. The papers for the government were also posted.

There was no morning satsangh, but Master sat out in the garden in the sun and spoke to the abhyasis, about 25 of whom were gathered.

We left Greve Strand at 5:30 P.M. with Birthe and went to Copenhagen, to Lakshminarasimhan's house for dinner. Shri Raman Lal Mimani had been invited, and had promised to join us by 6:30 P.M. but till 7:00 P.M. he did not come — nor did he turn up later. We had dinner without him, and then drove to a building near the Kunstakademiet where a room is hired every Friday for satsangh. There nearly 80 abhyasis had already assembled. Master took group satsangh. The meditation was very good and lasted from 8:30 P.M. to 9:00 P.M. Master was repeatedly expressing his disappointment that Shri Raman Lal Mimani was absent this evening. After satsangh two films with sound-track were exhibited. One was taken at Shahjahanpur and features Vibe asking questions of Master. Almost the entire sound-track is this dialogue between the two, though the film shows, apart from the house, some farm scenes too. The film is a remarkable one for the wealth of expression and gesture Master uses in it while answering Vibe's questions — and the fluent movements of his hands is perhaps the most expressive — at times it is almost like watching the abhinaya and mudras of a talented dancer!

The second film features Sister Kasturi singing devotional songs. The scene is Madras, in "Gayathri". The films ended by 11:30 P.M. and then we drove back to Greve Strand arriving home just after mid-night.

17 Jun. 72 - Saturday

Shri Raman Lal Mimani made an unexpected appearance at Greve Strand at 9:00 A.M. He was most unhappy to have missed meeting Master yesterday evening. It was, as usual, a small misunderstanding which kept him away. He was sitting in his hotel room in Copenhagen from 6:00 P.M. awaiting a phone call from Lakshminarasimhan which never came — this apparently being the understanding between the two. Lakshminarasimhan had understood otherwise — and so Raman Lalji had to spend a lonely evening in a hotel room. Raman Lalji had come to say good-bye to Master as he intends going to London today. He was however persuaded to postpone departure for London by a day and go tomorrow. He telephoned his friends in the hotel at Copenhagen and made necessary changes in reservations.

We all left Greve Strand at 10:00 A.M. and drove to the North of Copenhagen to Vibe's house where we are to spend the whole of the day.

At 11:30 A.M. there was group satsangh for over 40 abhyasis. This was taken by Raman Lalji. Thereafter Raman Lalji was in great demand for individual sittings, and I think he was quite busy the whole day, giving sitting after sitting to eager abhyasis who joyously welcomed this opportunity.

At 1:15 P.M. Master granted provisional permission to Jytte Gravesen.

There was an excellent lunch after this for all present. I was busy the whole afternoon giving individual sittings.

6:30 P.M. — a meeting of the newly constituted Danish Working Committee was held, presided over by Master. It was attended by Birthe, Vibe, Thomas, Lakshminarasimhan, and myself. Shri Mimani was present by invitation. Among other things, Thomas Mogensen was appointed Joint Secretary to the Working Committee.

8:00 P.M. satsangh was conducted by Master. Over 50 abhyasis were present. After this the two films on Master and Sister Kasturi were screened for Raman Lalji's benefit. Shri Raman Lal bid good-bye to Master. We left Vibe's home at 10:30 P.M. or so and returned to Greve Strand around midnight. It has been a gala day, a festival day in every sense.

18 Jun. 72 - Sunday

Master was well and relaxed. He enjoys staying in Denmark surrounded by abhyasis of such great devotion. He told me that it would be quite difficult for him to leave this place.

Spoke to Mr. Robert Koch in Zarten to fix up details of Master's programme — a pointer to the impending departure from this place.

We all left Greve Strand at 10:30 A.M. and went to the city to spend the day with the Lakshminarasimhan family in their residence. During the day there were, on an average, 30 persons present at all times, touching a peak of nearly 50 in the evening. During the day I gave 16 individual sittings.

12:30 P.M. Master granted provisional permission to Mr. Bent Ruus who will work in Copenhagen under the overall guidance of Birthe. This brings the number of preceptors in Denmark to seven!

There was no group satsangh during the day. Master, after lunch, spent most of his time with the abhyasis in the drawing room. As I was occupied with individual sittings I missed all the conversations — except for the bursts of laughter which I kept hearing again and again throughout the day. Master kept the audience delighted and in tears all the time.

Master conducted group meditation at 8:00 P.M. which was attended by nearly 50 abhyasis. It was a long session of 50 minutes and was superb.

After dinner the Lakshminarasimhan family had a quiet and intimate half an hour with Master. This was followed by a preceptor's meeting at 10:00 P.M. over which Master personally presided. The meeting was attended by Birthe, Vibe, Jens, Elsebeth, Bent Ruus, Hans Jorgen Hvid and Lakshminarasimhan.

The meeting went into details of preceptors work, how they should handle their work and so on. I had earlier recorded a short talk on the role of the preceptor and the nature of his work. Master wanted this played to the preceptors assembled.

We left Lakshminarasimhan's house at 11:30 P.M. and returned to Greve Strand well after mid-night.

19 Jun. 72 - Monday

Early in the morning my aunt Mrs. Gouri Bhadran telephoned from Copenhagen railway station to say that she and my uncle had arrived by overnight train from Oslo. They wish to spend the day with Master and so we arranged to go and meet them and bring them over. Birthe and I left for Copenhagen at 10:30 A.M. and first attended to air reservations for our onward journey. After this we went to my uncle Mr. Bhadran's hotel and picked them up and drove them over to Greve Strand, arriving back home around 1 P.M.

The day sitting was taken by Bent Ruus. During the day I gave individual sittings to several abhyasis.

Mrs. Bhadran had an individual sitting with Master. The evening satsangh, which was conducted by Master, had a record attendance of 52 abhyasis.

Since the last two days a Polish student has been coming to see Master. With obvious reluctance — in view of the complexities present — Master took up his case, and the results after two sessions have been nothing short of miraculous. This boy had almost totally lost the capacity to think. He was fear-ridden and was a bundle of many mental problems. Master asked him how he felt, and the boy himself said that the power to think seems to have come back — though not yet fully. When he said this, Master said, "Now there is some hope!"

The Bhadran's left at 11:30 P.M. for the city. They leave for Poznan, Poland tomorrow.

I took a sitting from Jytte Gravesen, the new preceptor.

20 Jun. 72 - Tuesday

Master, who has been entirely well so far, suddenly took ill. He woke up with a bad stomach ache, which turned unbearably severe around 11:00 A.M. The morning satsangh has had to be cancelled. At 12 noon I consulted Master as to whether we should go to Germany this evening. He told me it is up to me to decide. I decided to cancel travel plans and inform Mr. Robert Koch accordingly. I decided to wait till 2:00 P.M. before telephoning him.

At 2:00 P.M. Master was miraculously fresh and pronounced himself fully capable of travelling. I tried to persuade him to stay for the day and reconsider tomorrow, but he was very adamant, saying, "Plans have been made and I must stick to them. Of course if the pain was so intense as to be unbearable then it is different, but now I am well enough to travel I must go on with the plan. I cannot neglect my Master's work when I am capable of undertaking it. By His Grace I am better, so we shall go."

I gave individual sittings to six abhyasis.

Master gave a special sitting to Lakshminarasimhan at 3:30 P.M.

Birthe, Vibe, Elsebeth and Leif left at 3:00 P.M. to go to Copenhagen to catch a train for Freiburg. They will go on up to Italy and be with Master till he leaves Italy for India.

Master and I left Greve Strand at 4:30 P.M. and were driven to the Kastrup airport by Hans Jorgen Hvid in his car. We arrived at the airport at 5:30 P.M. Master continues to be unwell but seems capable of bearing the pain. Palle, Mikala, Kurt, Jette, Thomas, Ole, Helle, Jens, Hendryk and his sister Halina, Dr. Lakshminarasimhan and family, all were at the airport to give Master a loving and moving farewell.

Our Lufthansa flight LH 017 operating a Boeing 727 aircraft took off only at 19:30 P.M., over 40 minutes behind time. I was very concerned at this delay because at Frankfurt where we have to change for Basel, we have just 40 minutes between planes — and if this delay continues we may very well miss the Swiss Air connection. With Master quite unwell, the prospect of a forced halt at Frankfurt with no one to turn to for assistance is quite frightening. However, the Lufthansa flight touched down at Frankfurt at 8:30 P.M. I had to literally drag Master by hand up and down a pair of staircases, and run nearly 250 yards before we came, panting, to the Swiss Air departure lounge and located our flight. Fortunately we were in time to board the DC-9 aircraft on Swiss Air flight SR-549 which took off at 9 P.M.

Master is suffering badly but not showing it. We had a comfortable 33 minute flight before touching down at Basel at 9:40 P.M. We passed through immigration formalities, but debacle of debacles, when I went to collect the baggage I found that our two suitcases had arrived but not Master's hookah basket. I spent 40 minutes trying to trace it with the cooperation of Swiss Air ground staff, but all to no avail. Obviously it had been left behind in Frankfurt. Swiss Air promised to have it within 24 hours. I filled up a claim form, and then discovered that even if the basket is recovered Swiss Air won't be able to send it to Germany as they can't send it out of the country. So reluctantly I agreed to have it sent to Mr. Krishnamurthy's address in Geneva, our next stop after Freiburg.

This episode was an eye-opener to me. When the piece of baggage was missed, I took Master out to the arrival lounge where Mrs. Ruth Koch was waiting to receive him, and then took him to the waiting car. I went back into the baggage enclosure, filed the claim, and returned to the car, all the time wondering how Master was going to receive the news that the hookah was not available — and this, by an irony of fate, at the time when it was most needed! But here came a minor revelation. When I told Master the unpleasant news, not a muscle moved, no trace of emotion showed on his face; there was no annoyance, no disappointment — nothing! To those who know Master, it is a matter of common knowledge that the hookah is almost his sole link with physical existence. His food intake is less than negligible, and people have often speculated how he subsists on such a meager intake. The late Dr. Varadachari used to joke that there is probably some hidden sustenance in the tobacco of the hookah! It was therefore a new insight into Master's whatever-you-call-it that the loss of a thing so vitally necessary to him left him completely cold.

Mrs. Ruth Koch escorted Master to her home in Zarten, a village near Freiburg, and we covered the 70 Km from Basel airport in approximately 40 minutes on Autobahn E4, arriving at Zarten just after 11:00 P.M. Mr. Robert Koch was standing at his door, and received Master with visible emotion. It was around midnight when we went to bed. Master has stood the long journey from Copenhagen very well, but the strain has told on him. His face, normally so calm and peaceful, is lined and drawn with pain. He says nothing, but an occasional grimace of a severe spasm of pain shows how much he is suffering.

21 Jun. 72 - Wednesday (Zarten)

Master slept well, and woke up only at 9:00 A.M. He has a lovely bedroom with a beautiful view of the nearby mountains, and farm land all around.

A lady, Mrs. Charlotte Mildner, an old friend of the Koch's, has come from her home near Uber Memmingen to help the Kochs while Master is here. She wanted to commence meditation and so I gave her her first sitting.

The Danish group had arrived at 6:40 A.M. and are staying at the Gasthof Zum Hirschen about 2 Km. from us. Mrs. Koch and I went over to see them at mid-day, had lunch with them, and brought them over to see Master. The group has been enlarged by Laura joining them.

Laura Conklin is an American girl who has come to Denmark and joined a group studying there. She came into our meditation group like Charlotte O'Brien of East Lansing, Michigan, who also came to Denmark and met Birthe and so came into the Mission — and is now a preceptor too!

Master brightened up when the Danish group came to see him. They seemed to have a tonic effect on him. Even though he is still in considerable pain, in spite of antacids, cold milk and so on, their arrival made him cheerful, and he became his usual talkative self. They left at 5:00 P.M. to find their way to the old University in Freiburg where a public meeting has been arranged for this evening.

8:00 P.M. public meeting in room no. 1010 of the old University Building of Freiburg. Master attended the meeting and suffered a silent hour on the dais without complaint. His deep sense of duty and commitment to his work make it imperative for him to attend the meeting. I spoke for 15 minutes in English, and then Mr. Robert Koch spoke for an hour in German. Mrs. Dachma Ludmile Petersen of Copenhagen, a Mission member, came to the meeting. We found that she had arrived just this afternoon, having driven all the way with her son Hans Hendrik in her Volkswagen. She is also staying at the Gasthof Zum Hirschen, and it was she who drove us up from Zarten to Freiburg in her car, as the Kochs went early to make necessary arrangements. She also drove us back after the meeting. Master transmitted to the audience for 20 minutes. The audience was sizeable and appeared keenly attentive.

22 Jun. 72 - Thursday

Master spent a restless, pain-filled night. Medicines seem to do no good. The only effective palliative is ice-cold milk taken in small, frequent doses. The milk gives immediate relief.

Frau Mildner had her second sitting. Master woke up around 9:30 A.M. He was dull and morose and generally very lethargic. The absence of the hookah is definitely felt, and the pipe which he smokes now is but a poor substitute, affording no relief whatsoever. At 11:00 A.M. Mrs. Rambeau and Mrs. Thron came to see Master. They had attended the meeting yesterday evening. They both took their first sitting from Master.

The Danish group came in at 11:30 A.M., and at once Master became cheerful and transformed into his normal self. He kept them roaring with laughter and was completely relaxed while they were with him. I asked Master the reason behind this. He answered simply, "They love me very much, and it gives me relief. I like to be surrounded by people who really love me; but really speaking people only want me to love them." The Danish group were not allowed to stay long as their presence was said to make the place noisy, and Mr. Koch needs undisturbed peace to prepare his lecture for this evening's public meeting. They were also told not to come back in the evening — and a very unhappy group bid sad farewell to an equally unhappy Master. After they left, Master lapsed back into his moody state.

At 4:00 P.M. a Mr. Muller, from Lugano in Switzerland, came to see Master. At 4:30 P.M. a Mr. Majer, who has spent 10 years in the Ramana Ashram at Tiruvannamalai came to see Master. He was accompanied by a Mr. Maser.

8:00 P.M. public meeting in room 1010 of the Old University Building in Freiburg. Mr. Robert Koch spoke in German.

23 Jun. 72 - Friday

Master spent another restless night, and looked haggard in the morning. The antacids are not helping him at all, and have been abandoned. Master takes only small doses of cold milk at four-hourly intervals. This is his only medicine, and his only sustenance too. He has adamantly refused to take any solid food, saying that solid food upsets him completely. I have tried my best to convince him that world-wide medical advice is to take small doses of solid frequently to absorb the acids secreted. He refuses to budge saying, "I have been suffering for 40 years and I know."

The Danish abhyasis came in at 9:30 A.M. Mr. Koch remarked to Master that he had observed even when in India that abhyasis of the Mission always had such happy eyes. "I can always recognise an abhyasi, Master, by just looking at their eyes. They always have such happy eyes." There was some talk about happiness. Someone asked Master whether He was happy. Master answered, "Really speaking I have never tested the effect of happiness. I cannot remember if I was ever happy. Of course I can define happiness. One who is happy under all circumstances is happy. But I am telling you one thing.

Happiness is heavier than tranquillity. I think pain is nearer God. That is my idea. Of course I may be wrong. But look here, sometimes when I am in great pain I also groan, 'Ah! Ah!', but there is some peculiar enjoyment in it also."

Q: Is it necessary to have pain to get closer to God?

Master: It is not necessary. It is for me alone. My Master used to suffer from great pain. He had abscess of the liver and used to suffer very much. But when he was in very great pain he used to sing! I asked him why. He told me that when a person is in great pain he has to groan or make some such noise, and so why not sing and make noise? My Master once told me that he could have easily removed this trouble in one minute. But he did not do so because he felt the pain was given by God, and who knows why God has given it? But there must be some reason for it! So that was my Master's submission to Divine Will."

Someone then asked about the nature of fear. Master said, "Fear is a hallucination of wisdom. If wisdom is right there can be no fear." He added, with a burst of his healthy laughter, "Woman is the hallucination of man." Someone wanted this explained, and Master said, "Parthasarathi, please explain this." So I said in my opinion this is true, because it is man who endowes woman with all sorts of romantic qualities, becoming poetic in the process, comparing her hair to a rain-laden cloud, eyebrows to a bow, eyes to stars and so on. Man creates all this in his imagination, and so woman is certainly a hallucination of man. Master laughed and said, "You see, he has explained very well."

Q: Master, do you think hallucination is 'maya'?

Master: "No. Maya is normally said to be illusion but I don't agree. I think maya is the power of God. When we do not know how this power works, we are confused and call it maya. But when we know how the power of God operates, then we perceive Reality. So really speaking it is our own ignorance. Intellectuals borrow knowledge, and the Divine Personality creates knowledge."

Frau Mildner told Master that she had come with a lot of questions, but now she found she had none in her mind. Master replied, "You came with questions. The questions are washed away and now YOU remain." (laughter)

At 11:00 A.M. five ladies came to see Master, and all had first sitting with him. In the afternoon Master was quite unwell, with unbearable pain in the stomach. There was a proposal to go out sight-seeing but this had to be dropped. At 2:00 P.M., I went with Frau Petersen and Mr. Koch to Freiburg to do some shopping for Master, and returned by bus. The Danish group of abhyasis had invited Master for dinner at the Gasthof Zum Hirschen, but since he was not well, Birthe kept him company in the Koch residence while the Kochs and I went to the hotel and had dinner with the rest of the group. They came back with us after dinner and stayed with Master till 11:30 P.M. I gave an individual sitting to Vibe before they left.

24 Jun. 72 - Saturday

Master is very weak. He has had nothing solid to eat since we left Denmark, and has been subsisting solely on cold milk. The severe pain has weakened him very much. He also does not get enough sleep. I have suggested that a doctor examine him, but Master's reply is that many doctors have seen him over the last forty years, but no one has been able to give relief. "It will last a few days and then go off. Don't worry about it. Sometimes it lasts 3 or 4 days, sometimes more, but generally not more than 15 days. So I will be all right in a short time," he said.

Frau Lassig and Frau Vollmer came in the morning. Master was resting, so I gave them their second sitting.

The group of abhyasis from Denmark came at 10:00 A.M. but were peremptorily ordered away from the door, as their presence is felt to be a great and noisy nuisance, apart from "depriving" local visitors of a chance of being with Master. Master was very upset when I told him about this and said, "Next time when we come we shall stay in a hotel, and people can come to see me there. What is this nonsense that people who come are turned away? They have spent a lot of money to be with me, and had taken Mr. Koch's permission to come here. I do not understand this. I tell you, nowhere will you find hospitality as you find in India."

Later in the morning Emma Tran and Amy Barlow came to see Master. A couple, Mr. and Mrs. Hoffmann, came for the first time. All the four had a sitting with Master. The Hoffmanns are from near Hannover. Mr. Gunter Hoffmann is a psychic healer and tried his art on Master. Later Mr. Hans Oloikner came for the first time and I gave him his first sitting. He was followed by Mr. Max Braun, an old friend of the Kochs. Master gave him his first sitting. After this the entire group present had a group meditation with Master.

Between 1:00 P.M. and 5:00 P.M. Master had a good rest.

At 6:00 P.M. Prof. Hans Bender, a well-known parapsychologist, reputed to be the only parapsychologist in Germany, came to see Master. He brought with him his daughter, and a young psychologist Miss Barbara Andres. Miss Andres is doing research on meditation techniques in Europe, and collecting material for her work by interviewing yogis, saints, religious priests, and eminent men in various fields, and she wanted to interview Master too. Master smiled and told Prof. Bender, "This is my secretary Mr. Chari. He knows all about this system and can answer questions well. He is my voice." Prof. Bender and Barbara Andres interviewed me for about 40 minutes, and the whole thing was recorded by Barbara. They appeared impressed with what they heard. Later all had meditation with Master. Prof. Bender has been once in India in connection with palm-leaf oracles, and had visited our home in Madras and met my father for this purpose.

At 8:00 P.M. Master suddenly decided to visit the Danish abhyasis in their hotel. Dachma (of the Danish group, but a privileged visitor to the Koch residence probably because of her German origin) was present the whole afternoon and drove us over to the hotel.

The Danes were virtually delirious with joy to see their beloved Master come to see them with all his pain and suffering. Love is indeed a many-splendoured thing, and what to speak of a Divine Love like Master's! His pure love draws people to him like a magnet attracts iron filings. On this trip many persons have remarked to me that their first exposure to Master is mostly one of shock. They see he is so small, physically so frail, and so utterly simple and absolutely devoid of self-consciousness. They wonder how such a small man can give them what he claims he **can** give. Then, if there is time, they find out how much wisdom he has, how he answers any and every question with such directness and simplicity as to be staggering; his way of answering questions, not as if he knows everything, but as if he too has discovered the answer just then! Then as the exposure to Master's presence lengthens, they begin to be drawn in, and then, as most of them often wistfully say, they cannot think of leaving him even for a moment. Master's magic is invincible.

The Danes were so happy just to gaze on their beloved Master who has graced them by his presence that they were busy adoring him, leaving nothing to be said. There was virtually no conversation during the one hour we remained there. They wanted Master to have dinner with them, but Master explained that the Koch's would be waiting for us. At 9:00 P.M. Master decided to go back and Dachma drove us back. When we returned we found that there was nothing for us to eat! The Kochs had eaten earlier and retired too, but got up to let us in. So we go hungry this evening. Fortunately there was some milk for Master, enough for the night.

When Master had retired the Kochs gave me a terrible fright by confiding to me that they had consulted two psychic healers who came to see Master, and they are very afraid for him, and hoped that Master would be able to return safely to India. "Dear Chari, we **hope** Master our dear Master will be able to see India again." was what Mr. Koch kept repeating again and again. I was annoyed with them for consulting doctors without my knowledge.

25 Jun. 72 - Sunday

Several persons called in the morning to see Master. Master slept well last night and got up rather early this morning. The pain continues.

The following meditated with Master: Mrs. Hildegaard Sosna Umananda, Mr. Klaus Sosna Shankarananda, Mr. Max Braun, Birthe Haugaard, Dachma Petersen. Mr. Krishnamurthi telephoned from Geneva to check on Master's programme.

2:45 P.M. Mrs. Koch drove Master, Mr. Koch and me in their car to Oppenau, 75 Km. away, arriving there at 4:30 P.M. The Denmark group had arrived earlier by train, Birthe and Vibe sharing a room in the Gasthaus Zum

Linde, where the Kochs, Master and I also stay. Master rested for two hours. The car drive had somewhat tired Him.

At 6:30 P.M. Master presided over a meeting organised under the auspices of "Esoterium" by Mr. Geissler. Nearly 60 members of their group were present. I spoke for 15 minutes on Sahaj Marg, followed by Mr. Koch who spoke in German. The meeting concluded with a short question-answer session. After this I was kept busy for nearly one hour by a group of teenagers, asking questions on drugs, spirituality and so on. Five of this group later started meditation.

One young man, Mr. Bernd Blunt, teacher of another system of Yoga, Transcendental meditation, came to see Master, but as Master was once again in bed with severe pain, I spoke to him for half an hour. He was deeply impressed, but troubled about having to give up another guru and adopt a new one. I explained to him how, if this became necessary out of one's inner conviction, it had to be done.

The Danes were with Master in our room till 11:00 P.M. Master did not sleep during the night, and was very restless.

26 Jun. 72 - Monday (Oppenau)

Commencing from 7:30 A.M. I gave first sittings to five new abhyasis.

Master gave special sittings to: Mr. Bernd Blunt and Wilhelm Tschaffler.

Master, Mr. and Mrs. Koch and I left Oppenau at 10:10 A.M. A moving farewell was given by over 25 members of "Esoterium" assembled at the hotel. It is a pity that we did not have more time here in Oppenau, where the response has been genuine and good. We drove 25 Km. to Offenburg, where the Danes joined us, having come in by train from Oppenau. We left Offenburg by 11:07 train and came in to Basel to change trains at 12:36. The Danes travelled with us up to Basel. But they now go on to Italy, skipping Geneva, and so we parted here. They are still in the same train with us, but in the fore part, which will separate 20 minutes from now and go to Italy, our half going in another direction to Berne. Yesterday when we picked on the 11:07 train from Offenburg we were under the impression that it was a through train to Geneva, but much to our surprise, and quite a bit of physical trouble too, we found we had to change not only at Basel but at Berne too. We arrived in Berne at 14:33, and had three minutes in hand to move 150 yards on the platform, go down to a basement sub-way, walk 100 yards down it, climb up to the departure platform and board our train — with me carrying all our baggage! Master had to run to keep up, but just as we arrived, panting, on our platform, the train came in. We boarded it and found ourselves in a luxurious compartment. When we recovered our wind, I discovered we had got into a I Class by mistake, but since these are vestibule trains, I was able to go to the next bogie and find accommodation for the two of us — and had to shift all the baggage all over again. It was a very hot and sunny day, and the travel was quite uncomfortable. We arrived at Geneva, hot and tired, at 16:23 and found Mr. Krishnamurthi, his daughter Indra and son Raju on the platform to welcome Master. Mr. Krishnamurthi is married to the eldest sister of Mr. G.S. Mani, our preceptor at Madurai, and Master stays with them in Geneva. Mr. Krishnamurthi drove us to their 5th floor apartment on Chemin Francois Lehmann, Grand Sacconex.

On arrival Master was reunited with his hookah again after an absence of nearly a week. He enjoyed his hookah and went to bed.

At 7:00 P.M. Dachma Petersen and her son turned up, she having driven over from Oppenau to be with Master! She stayed for dinner with us. Master went to bed at 11:00 P.M. after some conversation with the Krishnamurthi family.

27 Jun. 72 - Tuesday (Geneva)

Master is looking a shade better this morning. He wanted to see Switzerland very much, but now that he is here, he expressed himself happy with what he had seen. "What more is there to see? Mountains and lakes I have seen yesterday when we were coming by train. Geneva I have seen. That is enough. Now I know what Switzerland is like!"

9:15 A.M. Master said, "Look, I have been thinking for the last one week as to how to make you digest what you have got. Because as it is it can take eight months or even one year. Today I got the method for doing it and I have created the circumstances for it. I did not try to have it digested by the will so far as I normally do it, because your approach is a very high approach, but I removed whatever obstructions there were and created the circumstances necessary for digesting the powers given to you. Look here! What an experience this has been! Dear brother you are a very lucky boy and I wish to embrace you. Please observe your condition."

Later at 10:00 A.M. Master asked me about my condition. I told him that I felt lighter. Master said, "It is difficult to know it. Look here, being together with me has this benefit that I can observe you minute by minute. Kabir has written, 'Imagine that the Guru and the disciple are living in two houses separated by just one wall; even then the disciple should leave his home once a year and go and stay with his Guru for six days.'"

The whole day was left for Master to rest. I went to town with Raju to change our reservations for Rome from 29th to 28th so that Master would have one more day for rest before beginning the long journey to India.

3:00 P.M. I have been feeling intoxication since noon. Master suddenly looked at me and said, "Brother, now you should be experiencing something." I told him about the feeling of intoxication and he said, "Yes, it is correct." The feeling of intoxication was so heavy that I slept from 4 to 6 P.M.

8:30 P.M. public meeting in the YMCA John Matt Building. The meeting was organised by Mr. Krishnamurthi. About 35 persons, all top officials of UN organisations, were present. I spoke for 25 minutes on "Sahaj Marg Yoga". This was followed by 25 minutes transmission by Master. People were keen to ask questions, and some 10 minutes were devoted to this, but then Master began to feel bad again and we had to return home in a hurry.

One Mr. Alagappan, a friend of Mr. Krishnamurthi, and a New York resident, came to see Master at 10 P.M. and remained till mid-night. He seems to be impressed by Master, but did not have time to really get down to brass tacks with the system.

28 Jun. 72 - Wednesday

The Krishnamurthi family drove us to Geneva airport at 9:30 A.M. We were booked on Alitalia Flight 409 direct for Rome, but found that because Alitalia are on strike this flight has been cancelled. We discovered that ITAVIA are running a flight to Rome via Torino and Bologna, departure scheduled for 10:35, the same as the cancelled Alitalia flight. We had lost more than half an hour finding out about this, and had to scramble around madly to get seats on the ITAVIA flight and check in. It was really frustrating to find two ITAVIA men trying to handle a queue of more than 40 waiting passengers. We managed to get on, check in, and finally run across the tarmac to the waiting Fokker F-28 plane on flight IH 401. The plane took off at 10:35 A.M. and landed at Torino at 12:05 local time (one hour ahead of European time). We had to alight for customs and passport control. We left Torino at 12:45 arriving Bologna at 13:18, and left Bologna at 14:53 arriving Rome, Ciampino Airport at 15:55. Total flying time just 100 minutes from Geneva, but a five hour journey for us — extremely tiring to Master. He is dead beat and at the end of his enormous resistance. I am deeply worried. We had no snacks, no lunch, nothing to drink on this journey — a very poor show indeed.

When we came out we found no one to meet us. At Geneva I had requested Mr. Krishnamurthi to telephone Mr. Saravanamuttu and tell him of the change in travel plans. We waited more than half an hour but no one showed up. We then boarded the airline bus taking passengers to the city terminal. On the way Master was extremely bad, and shocked and frightened me to the core, saying, "I hope I shall be able to reach home safely." We arrived at the city terminal, with Master barely able to walk. I left him with the baggage, and went to change some money and to phone to Sara. The currency exchange took some time as all banks have suspended foreign exchange transactions due to the floating of the English pound. Fortunately a single travel agency counter was still doing business, and after a 30 minute wait I changed some pounds getting 1340 lire to the pound as against the normal rate of 1700 or 1720. Then I spoke to Casal Palocco getting Birthe on the line. She told me that there was utter confusion, Sara having been busy the whole day with Elsebeth's bookings for Africa. She told me three cars and several abhyasis were at Fiumicino to greet Master! But Alitalia had no information on the Itavia flight at all. They were still waiting at Fiumicino for Master! We took a taxi finally and drove 32 Kms. to Casal Palocco arriving home at 5:00 P.M.! Master was almost in a state of collapse. We have decided to have a doctor in for consultation.

Luciana Suberni came in at 7:30 P.M. Spencer Kimball arrived from Florence at 8:00 P.M. Mr. Arulpragasam, a Sinhalese friend of Sara came at 8:00 P.M. and I gave him an individual sitting. The Danes are all in residence here, with Spencer added on today. We have our old basement room. Toni and Lino Bernardi came in at 8:00 P.M. and stayed till past mid-night.

Master had a light dinner — his first bit of solid food in a week now — and was better after it.

At half-past mid-night I gave group sitting to all those present.

Master was slightly better, but spent a sleepless night.

29 Jun. 72 - Rome

Master had a setback — severe stomach ache with some nausea. We called in a doctor at 10:30 A.M. He examined Master thoroughly and certified his heart to be perfect, but blood-pressure somewhat low. He prescribed some medicines and asked us not to worry, and certified Master to be fit to undertake the long air journey back to India. He wanted him to have X-rays taken on arrival, and also have a prostate check. The doctor was surprised that Master showed no pain on his face even though he was suffering extreme pain. He wanted to know who Master was, and hearing he is a spiritual Master, was very happy to have met him.

Giorgio Furlan, Paolo, Josita, Toni Bernardi, Lucy and others came to see Master. Josita also happens to be a psychic healer. She did some work on Master, and Master felt better!

I gave individual sittings to Arulpragasam and Antonio Siniscalco.

In the evening Master was slightly worse, but had dinner and was better after it.

At 11:30 P.M. I gave group sitting to Birthe, Vibe, Laurie, Leif, Elsebeth, Josita, Lucy, Sara, and Toni.

30 Jun. 72 - Friday

Master almost normal — the rapidity with which His condition changes is astonishing! I have found him almost on the verge of collapse at one instant, and half-an-hour later roaring with laughter with a group of abhyasis. When in deepest pain I have seen him sitting on his bed and groaning — but in such a way that I felt it was not really he but someone else who was groaning. The face would be as usual, no lines of pain, no suffering reflected on it, but at regular intervals the mouth would open, a deep groan would be emitted, and the mouth closed again.

I gave him a hair-cut and beard trim, the third on this tour, after which he had a bath and relaxed with the abhyasis. He was his normal self again after an agonising week of pain.

I gave first sitting to Theresa, Sara's maid. Irene Imperiali came in from Naples at 10:00 A.M. Under Master's instructions I gave her an individual sitting.

In the afternoon Master set out for Rome for some last minute shopping. He went in Sara's car while Vibe and I went in Toni's car. We went to the Piazza Navona and then to Standa. We got back to Casal Palocco at 7:00 P.M. Elsebeth left for Africa for a three week holiday with her father.

1 Jul. 72 - Saturday

Master had a peaceful night and slept well.

At 7:30 A.M. I gave second sitting to Theresa, and an individual sitting to Vibe. Irene Imperiali brought her cousin Pio, who had his first sitting with Birthe yesterday. Pio had his second sitting this morning. They had three other friends with them and they had their first sittings with Birthe, Lucy and Vibe. At 3:30 P.M. we all left for Toni's house. We spent the rest of the day there.

At 4:45 P.M. there was a preceptors' meeting. Master opened the meeting by saying, "I am hoping that the Mission will grow here in Italy, and so I think we must now have an organisation here with office bearers etc. So I want to appoint a Working Committee as I have done in Denmark. What is your opinion?" There was some discussion on the difficulty of finding a place to hold weekly meetings in, on the difficulty of bringing together all the abhyasis and so on. Toni offered her house for this purpose till more permanent arrangements could be made, and this was accepted.

Master then appointed a Working Committee for Italy as under:

1) Master		Permanent President
2) P. Rajagopalachari		Permanent Secretary
3) Mr. C.A. Rajagopalachari		Permanent Member
4) Mr. G.L. Saravanamuttu		Preceptor-in-charge

(Italian Centres)

5) Mrs. Antonietta Bernardi	Joint Secretary
6) Mr. Paolo Passaquindici	Nominated Member
7) Mrs. Luciana Suberni	Nominated Member
8) Miss Irene Imperiali	Nominated Member

This committee will work under the guidance of the central organisation. Decisions taken by the local Working Committee will be implemented after Head Quarter's approval is obtained.

7:30 P.M. group satsangh was conducted by Master and followed by dinner. We left Toni's house at 10:00 P.M. and returned to Casal Palocco at 10:45 P.M. Vera phoned Master at 11:15 from London.

2 Jul. 72 - Sunday

Master slept well and woke up refreshed.

Many abhyasis to see Master during the whole morning. Lucy, Josita, Paolo, Taddea, Toni, all came early in the morning. Josita has been giving Master daily treatment, and today Master gave her a short sitting and said, "I have increased your power."

We left Casal Palocco in four cars for Fiumicino airport at 2:15 and reached there at 3:00 P.M. We go straight to Madras via Delhi. I have cancelled the Bombay and Navsari plan in view of Master's health.

To see Master off at the airport were Sara and daughter Lakshmi, Arulpragasam, Toni, Paolo, Lucy, Josita, Antonio Siniscalco, Birthe, Vibe, Leif, and Laurie. They were all very sad and depressed. Master was quite moved and so we went in early to the departure lounge, passing through immigration. We had a long wait as Air India's Flight 112 was delayed by air traffic control at Frankfurt, and came in nearly one hour late. The wait was unduly prolonged due to tightening of security measures — a plane ex-Rome having been hijacked a few days earlier! We finally boarded the Jumbo Jet "Emperor Rajendra Chola" and took off at 17:18 local time and arrived at Beirut at 20:40 local time — 1610 miles in 2 hours 22 minutes. We did not get out of the aircraft as the duty-free shopping area was under renovation. Master revealed to me again about Patanjali and his impending liberation! ((refer to 11 May 72))

We took off from Beirut at 21:47 local time on our direct flight to Delhi.

3 Jul. 72 - Monday (Delhi)

We arrived at Delhi at 6:05 A.M. IST, covering the 3180 miles from Beirut in 5 hours 25 minutes. Master was quite well. Mr. and Mrs. Sundara met Master on arrival, helped us complete airport formalities and drove us to their residence in Sundar Nagar. A large group of abhyasis were at the airport to pay their respects to Master, and most of them came to Mr. Sundara's residence later.

Master had a hookah and a bath and relaxed for two hours. Many abhyasis came to see him. We left Sundar Nagar at 10:15 A.M. and drove back to Palam airport, boarded Indian Airlines flight IC-459, operated by a Boeing 737, took off at 12:50 (1 hour late) and arrived Madras at 3:10 P.M.

A large gathering of abhyasis was at Meenambakkam airport to lovingly welcome Master back home on the completion of his epic spiritual journey. We drove to Master's son Umesh's house arriving there at around 4:00 P.M.

So ends Master's first foreign tour.

Statistics
Air Miles and Hours Flown

		Miles	Hours	
Bombay - Cairo	707	2650	6:20	AI
Cairo - Rome	707	1350	3:15	AI
Rome - Nice	Caravelle	480	1:00	Alitalia
Nice - Paris	727	510	1:10	AF
Paris - Copenhagen	DC-9	760	1:30	SAS
Copenhagen - London	Trident 3	750	1:30	BEA
London - New York	747	3470	7:10	AI
Albany - Detroit	737	550	1:00	Allegheny
Cleveland - Washington	737	520	0:55	UA
New York - Copenhagen	747	3950	7:05	SAS
Copenhagen - Frankfurt	727	520	1:00	LH
Frankfurt - Basel	DC-9	220	0:33	SA
Geneva - Rome	F-28	610	1:40	Itavia
Rome - Delhi	747	4800	7:47	AI
		21,140	41:55	

7 Jul. 72 - Friday (Madras)

I had a sitting with Sister Kasturi. I felt my heart had completely stopped.

8 Jul. 72 - Saturday

Completed overseas tour report, bound it and handed over one copy to Master. This will form the basis for the book "India in the West".

I gave a special sitting to K. Subramanian of Trichy to prepare him for preceptorship.

9 Jul. 72 - Sunday

Master granted provisional permission to Dr. V.S.R. Murthy of Tirupathi.

Master is still unwell, but better than when we came.

10 Jul. 72 - Monday

Master commented on my condition. He said that there was no grossness as such, but something seems to be thrown out from inside. Kasturi Jijji felt that whatever was coming out was from Reality, thrown out through points 1 and 2, but Master disagreed.

Master was taken to H.M. Hospital on St. Mary's Road for a detailed check-up by Dr. Mehta.

11 Jul. 72 - Tuesday

Master x-rayed at Doraiswamy Clinic on Edward Elliots Road. Ulcer in duodenum confirmed — but, surprisingly no gastric ulcer! Master feels that this latter may have got cured over the years!

12 Jul. 72 - Wednesday

At 4:30 P.M. Master asked me to sit in meditation, saying Lalaji was going to transmit to me.

Mr. K. Subramanian of Trichy was granted provisional permission by Master.

13 Jul. 72 - Thursday

Mr. S. Doraiswamy Iyer of Pondicherry came to see Master at Gayathri. Master gave him a 30 minute sitting, and told me he had pulled him up to Para Brahmanda Mandal. Lucky man indeed! When he came four years ago for the first time, he was nowhere. He caught hold of Master's feet and wept like a child saying, "I have wasted

30 years of my life — they have even lied to me, now you must help me. All that I want is not to be reborn again in this world." Master said, "You will not be reborn again. I promise you that." At his next visit, in 1969, Master pulled him up to the Brahmanda Mandal, and now to Parabrahmanda!

14 Jul. 72 - Friday

Master is much better today.

17 Jul. 72 - Monday

Kasturi Jijji gave me an individual sitting — about 25 minutes long. The first five minutes were confused. Then felt a piercing, or rather a pressing, on the Chit Lake. Felt that the entire mind region was being cleaned. Waves of light flowed in for about 15 minutes. Then I felt as if my mind was in two parts, 80% inner mind and 20% outer mind. Even while being totally absorbed within, I felt the outer, externalised mind active in its own sphere. I slowly came to a state of total absorption, and then suddenly came out of it, like a diver emerging out of water, and found that the inner mind was now 90%, and outer only 10%! Then once again I became totally absorbed, and emerged again — and this repeated twice more, at the end of which I felt that inner mind is now 98%, only 2% being externalised! At this stage sitting was terminated.

I told Kasturi about my experience. She told me, "Normally points are taken up in that manner. But today I felt I should take up the mind region and purify it. It is correct, all that you felt, and I too felt very good today. In the middle of the sitting I saw a serpent emerge from your umbilicus; I saw it very clearly. It was going right up to the top, and there was illumination downwards too — but I don't know what it is."

18 Jul. 72 - Tuesday

K. Mahalingam was granted provisional permission by Master for the Salem centre, at Gayathri.

22 Jul. 72 - Saturday

R. Venkata Subba Reddy of Cuddapah given initiation by Master at Gayathri.

24 Jul. 72 - Monday

Master left for Delhi by IC-440 at 18:10. Sister Kasturi stays behind with us for treatment.

29 Jul. 72 - Saturday (Madurai)

Early morning, at about 4:00 A.M., I had a bad dream. I dreamt that Appa was seated fully dressed in a woolen suit, with a woolen scarf around his neck, with his luggage packed around him, as if ready for a long journey, on which he is about to leave. I asked him when he would return, he answered, "I don't know." I woke up with a feeling of dread.

In the evening conducted group meditation at Virudhunagar.

30 Jul. 72 - Sunday

Conducted morning group satsangh at Madurai centre.

2 Aug. 72 - Wednesday (Trichy)

Attended group satsangh at Trichy centre at 6:30 P.M.

4 Aug. 72 - Friday (Madras)

I discussed my dream (the Madurai one) with Kasturi Jijji. She feels it is a bad one. Invariably it means the death of the person who is seen in the dream as ready for travel.

She felt that having his luggage with him is a good sign, indicating that there is time before this can take place.

She gave me a sitting which was very deep — she said she saw light, like the light of the rising sun, behind the heart, and the idea occured that this is "Reality at Dawn".

7 Aug. 72 - Monday

Sitting with Kasturi. It was very very deep. She said she had transmitted to my point (where I am now), but a very light transmission, and found that light spread to the whole system above, and also **below**, which latter phenomenon she claims to be very unusual.

11 Aug. 72 - Friday

Group satsangh at 6:30 P.M. was taken by Kasturi. I felt totally absorbed with the full mind, and also felt the mind with its full power to be also externalised! It was as if I was standing waist deep in a pool of water, the lower half of the body completely wet, the upper half completely dry. Later I felt as if the whole world was inside my heart, and that a search-light from inside the top of my head was playing on it, illuminating it. Towards the end there was the state of complete absorption.

Kasturi was very happy. She said, "What I did today was to suggest that there be complete expansion of the point which is your approach; I also made the suggestion that all the points of the heart region may similarly expand — it is very good."

Ever since collapse of a part of our ashram Pandal at Shri Viraraghavan's place, satsangh is being conducted here at Gayathri on Sundays as usual, and additionally on Wednesday and Friday evenings at 6:30 P.M. Attendance is very good — 40 on an average evening!

Before he left, Master said the flow of general transmission to Madras had been revived after a lapse of several years. It stopped some years ago when Master became very dissatisfied with Mr. Viraraghavan, I think in 1969, and now has commenced again.

12 Aug. 72 - Saturday

Individual sitting with Kasturi. The beginning was very dull. After some time I felt as if someone was sitting next to me, on my left. I felt lighter and lighter, and at one stage I saw Master waving his hand to me, as if asking me to advance — very much like a traffic policemen — and then the sitting ended.

Kasturi said she saw something unique today. She saw someone sitting on my left, but she didn't know, or couldn't see, who it was. But when she finished the sitting she saw this person get into my body and enter into me, and then she saw the face of the person and saw that it was Master!

31 Aug. 72 - Thursday

Individual sitting with Kasturi. In the beginning I felt as if there was a road-roller in front of my fast car, blocking my path and impeding advance. The road-roller suddenly disappeared. Flight or diving started — felt myself falling forward. Suddenly, about half way through the 40 minute sitting, I found myself sitting in front of a fair, huge, handsome, seated figure. It was not Master, but was probably Lalaji — and I fell forward **into** him. Then I felt myself going deeper and deeper. In one minute part of the mind some evil thought occasionally interrupted — but I went in deeper and deeper.

When the sitting ended Kasturi confirmed the initial block, but said she had seen a hand-cart blocking me!

About the huge person into whom I fell, she confirmed that it was Lalaji, and said, "I am observing that as the merger in Babuji Maharaj is proceeding, simultaneously there is also merger in Him (Lalaji). So what it means is that when connection is established with Babuji Maharaj then it is also established with "Him".

Then she continued, "This is the extent of my experience in reading the condition, but nevertheless I have made a lot of efforts, but brother, no coverings were visible to me — and they are not now visible to me. And when you are becoming merged with Babuji Maharaj, how can anything come to you from your father, I mean such tendencies? Especially when you have no connection with him? I have seen that sometimes when something strikes the mind of our Master, it does not easily leave Him, and He keeps saying the same thing even after years."

She referred to Master's recent comment about me that as he removed one layer or covering, another seems to come up, and attributed this to certain tendencies which keep coming into me from Appa. I too cannot understand this. Heredity is alright, but up to the time of birth only — how can tendencies be inherited afterwards too?

6 Sep. 72 - Wednesday

Sitting with Kasturi. I felt as if I was floating on water on my back. Somebody says, "Aré! Just plunge in and see for yourself how deep it is.", and someone answers, "What is the need to plunge in now? He has already drowned in it, and he knows its depth."

Then there was brilliant light, and a very very light feeling in the Mind Region. Towards the end I felt as if Kasturi was moving farther and farther from me, until, at the end, she vanished altogether, and I felt I was the only person in the whole Universe — all alone!

Kasturi said she saw me floating like Krishna on the leaf, and felt my expansion. She said she tried to remove some samskaras which have been giving me official worries, but she found that the sitting took its own course and she could not guide it in the way she wanted to.

22 Sep. 72 - Friday

Sitting with Kasturi. As soon as I closed my eyes I felt I was very big, bigger than anything, and Kasturi was not someone outside me but was within me, and transmitting to me from within myself! I got lighter and lighter.

Kasturi said, "As soon as I closed my eyes, I felt that I went inside you and then I forgot myself, and then I understood that the training is proceeding by itself."

I told Kasturi I had a dream last night. I felt in the dream that I had gone somewhere and brought my father back with me. Kasturi felt this to be a very good sign.

5 Oct. 72 - Thursday

Sitting with Kasturi. After some time I felt myself to be very big, like an enormous balloon, as large as the earth. I knew this to be my Soul. I saw a tiny solid object suspended from this, and this I knew to be my body! I knew that even though the body was heavy, the atma had so much lightness and buoyancy that it was carrying the body along without difficulty.

6 Oct. 72 - Friday

Sitting with Kasturi. Lot of impressions at first. Then I felt I was swimming on the surface of a vast ocean, but I had the strange feeling that the whole ocean on which I was swimming was inside my head, while simultaneously I am outside it! A little later I saw the ocean inundating the whole surface of the earth, but there was no destruction.

7 Oct. 72 - Saturday

The whole afternoon I felt intoxicated. There was also the feeling that I am going far far away from this world — almost like extra-galactic travel, when the world becomes less than a pin-point. From 2:00 P.M., I had the feeling that I had left spirituality behind me — that it had dropped off! The thought came into my mind that I am at the stage where "spirituality ends and Reality begins".

In the evening at 8:00 P.M. I discussed this with Kasturi. She told me that at 4:00 A.M. this morning she felt Master transmitting to me, and since then some deep change had been taking place.

8 Oct. 72 - Sunday

No "intoxication" today but the same feeling as yesterday still persists.

Kasturi told me at 9:00 P.M. that she sees something surrounding, or rather enveloping, me like gas or vapour, but it has no colour or other characteristics. She can't make out what it is, but thinks it is something Master has put around me so that it can gradually flow into my heart — as I probably can't take it all in in one go!

9 Oct. 72 - Monday

Had a good sitting with Kasturi. She says the thing enveloping me is "Reality".

13 Oct. 72 - Friday

Master arrived from Delhi by IC-439 at 14:35 hours. We met him at the airport and took him to Umesh's house at Besant Nagar. On the way he said to me, "I shall take up your case this evening. Lalaji says, 'Hurry up! Hurry up!' He is in a very great hurry! Look here, the post is lying vacant and of course I have also taken upon myself some work already, but how far I should take you up — now it will be completed."

Master was tired. One eye, the left, was sunk in. His face was lined with pain. He appeared far away. But in an hour he became cheerful.

Master: How was grossness created in us? As soon as the sankalpa was made for the creation, this grossness came with that sankalpa. Sankalpa is a heavier thing than Reality. And therefore it is that sankalpa itself which comes into us in the form of grossness. In the stomach of spirituality there was sankalpa!

Master: You will find a lot of worshipers of God; but you may not find any seekers of God.

Master: Why do thoughts arise? Sometimes I have thought over this. If thoughts do not rise in us we would come to a totally balanced condition as was present in the beginning, and the body will be shattered. Now why do thoughts arise? Our mind has descended from the original mind, the divine mind, and it has come out of it. Because of this there is the original divinity certainly present in it. Because it is associated with the divine mind, it will not permit any dirt or uncleanliness to be taken into itself, and keeps throwing them off. That which is thus thrown out comes to our experience as thoughts arising in us.

We left Master with Appa and Kasturi at Besant Nagar and came home. I went again at 5:00 P.M. and we all came back at 8:00 P.M.

Master gave me a two minute sitting — I felt opening of the Chit Lake or Brahmanda Mandal, like a camera shutter opening, and the inside being filled with light.

14 Oct. 72 - Saturday

Went to Besant Nagar at 8:30 A.M. and brought Master home to Gayathri. He took me up to the library for the special sitting for "Dhruvathipathi".

He gave me a transmission for five minutes and asked me to rest for five minutes. This was followed by a second period of five minutes of transmission, and five minutes rest. Then a final five minutes of transmission. At 9:20 A.M. Master said, "Now you have been given the position of Druvathipathi. Now you may do the work according to this post."

After this we meditated for about two minutes and then it was over.

Master explained that at any one time there are only 2 or 3 persons at this stage. My appointment is consequent on a vacancy at this level created by the demise of a person recently (Shri Karuna Shankarji of Pilibhit). Shri R. Viraraghavan was given this position some years ago but has not worked to Master's satisfaction. All along, on our recent overseas tour, Master was remarking again and again about his disappointment with Shri Viraraghavan — and at one stage started saying that he would have to be punished for non-utilisation of powers conferred on him. Master has been very upset even after our return to India.

Master went back to Besant Nagar at 11:30 — I dropped him there. Then I went to Besant Nagar again at 6:00 P.M. and stayed till 8:00 P.M.

15 Oct. 72 - Sunday

To Besant Nagar to bring Master to Gayathri at 8:30 A.M. after usual group satsangh. Satsangh from 7:30 A.M. to 8:40 A.M. taken by Shri R. Viraraghavan. Nearly 40 abhyasis were present. Master came to Gayathri after the satsangh at 10:30 and stayed the whole day with us, taking special evening group satsangh at 6:30 for 20 minutes. More than 70 were present. Master spoke to them for over half an hour. M.D. Jahagirdar is here since yesterday. Master left for Besant Nagar at 9:00 P.M. after dinner with us.

22 Oct. 72 - Sunday

Master called for a special meeting at Besant Nagar to consider organisation matters. The meeting began at 9:30 A.M. and lasted one hour. It was presided over by Master. It was attended by:

1) Shri Raghavendra Rao
2) Kum. Kasturi Chaturvedi
3) Shri M.D. Jahagirdar
4) Shri Vittal Rao
5) Dr. V. Parthasarathi
6) Shri R. Ramachandra Reddy, and
7) Myself.

I proposed to Master that state-wise organisation must be changed as it led to regional loyalties developing and, to some extent, regional thinking too. Master agreed. The old scheme of organisers was therefore dropped, and a new one ordered as under.

There would be 4 zones in South India with 4 organisers, one in charge of each zone.

1) Shri Raghavendra Rao would control North Mysore State and parts of Andhra, namely the centres of Raichur, Gulbarga, Sedam, Bidar, Narayanapura, Dharwar, Sholapur, Anantapur, Mahbubnagar and Hyderabad. He will be assisted by Shri S.A. Sarnad.

2) Mr. M.D. Jahagirdar will control South Mysore State and parts of Andhra, namely the centres of Bangalore, Channapatna, Hassan, Mysore, Kollegal, Tirupathi, Chittoor and Madanapalle. He will be assisted by Shri Janardhan of Hassan, who will be trained for the work.

3) Dr. V. Parthasarathi will be responsible for coastal Andhra North of Guntur — centres at Vijayawada and Rajahmundry. His assistant will be nominated later.

4) Shri C.A. Rajagopalachari for Kerala, Tamil Nadu and coastal Andhra, South of Guntur.

Simultaneously North India was also taken up for reorganisation and organisers appointed as under:

1) Shri Nasib Chand for Lucknow, Kanpur and suburbs.

2) Shri Lakshmi Shankar for Allahabad, Rae Bareilly, Banaras and Pratap Garh.

3) Shri Uma Shankar Arya for Sitapur, Hardoi, Lakhimpur-Kheri and Bahraich.

4) Mr. D.B. Patel for Assam.

5) Shri Raghavan for metropolitan city of Bombay.

It was decided that Master himself would look after Delhi, Moradabad, Kanth, Roorkee etc. centres for the time being.

26 Oct. 72 - Thursday

Master took evening satsangh at Gayathri between 6:30 and 7:05 P.M. He stayed on for dinner and left for Besant Nagar at nearly 10:00 P.M.

"A disciple is one who is well disciplined." (Master)

27 Oct. 72 - Friday

Master, accompanied by Kasturi, left for Delhi by IC 440 which took off 20 minutes late at 19:30. Shri V. Krishnamurthi of M/s. T.T.K. Delhi office travels on the same flight and has promised to look after them.

30 Nov. 72 - Thursday

Mrs. Geraldine Nash of Cleveland, Ohio, arrived from Delhi by IC 439 A at 15:30. She has been with Master for a week. She was to have gone to Hyderabad and Warangal (to see K.C. Narayana) but cancelled these visits due to Mullki agitation going on for the last 10 or 12 days, causing havoc in Andhra.

3 Dec. 72 - Sunday

Gerry Nash left for Tirupathi by 9:00 A.M. bus after satsangh.

4 Dec. 72 - Monday

Gerry Nash came back from Tirupathi at 1:00 P.M.

5 Dec. 72 - Tuesday

Gerry Nash was due to leave for Bangalore today but we had to return from the airport as the flight was cancelled due to a severe cyclonic storm.

1972

6 Dec. 72 - Wednesday

Gerry left at 14:30 hours by IC 503 for Bangalore. She will stay with Annaiyappa, leave for Bombay on 8/12, and leave for New York on 12/12.

20 Dec. 72 - Wednesday

Luciana Dalla Torre of Rome arrived from Calcutta without prior notice and rang up at 3:00 P.M. from Woodland's hotel. I went and picked her up and took her home. I could spend just a few hours with her as I have to leave for Coimbatore at 6:30 P.M.

23 Dec. 72 - Saturday

Returned from Coimbatore. At 1:00 P.M. when I got home from the office, I found Lucy at the house, along with Ole and Leif Larson of Denmark, and Mrs. Tigger Outlaw of U.S.A., the last named of whom I met for the first time. She has been introduced to the Mission by Fred Weinstock and has been in Shahjahanpur for nearly a month during which time she has been made a preceptor too. She stays about 60 miles west of Boston in the state of Massachusetts. Ole and Leif have also been in Shahjahanpur for nearly a month, and after visiting Puri they have come here for the Music season. Lucy has been in Shahjahanpur for 6 weeks, and after leaving there she has been to Agra, Jaipur, Banaras and Calcutta. At Banaras airport she met Rakotondrainibe of Tananarive, who had spent a couple of days with Master at Shahjahanpur and was on his way to Kathmandu. Rako has been very fortunate. He gave a talk at the Aurobindo Mission at Tananarive. This seems to have attracted attention, and the Government of India invited him to attend the Aurobindo Centenary Celebrations at Delhi in December at Government expense! So he has got a free trip to see Master!

Vibe, Thomas, Rikke etc. have also arrived from Shahjahanpur on 12/12 — the influx has started.

"India in the West" is in press — page proof for the first four forms received today as also galleys 17 - 32. I think it will come out well. It has 67 pictures in it, 22 of our overseas preceptors and others in general.

24 Dec. 72 — Sunday

Lucy came at 1:00 P.M. Took her to Mahabalipuram along with Sulochana, Krishna and T.T. Sridhar.

25 Dec. 72 - Monday

Took Lucy, Tigger, Leif, Ole, Sulochana, Krishna and Narayanaswamy to attend T.R. Mali's flute performance at Vani Mahal — but the programme was postponed (at 6:45 P.M.) due to the passing away of the great leader C. Rajagopalachari at 5:44 P.M. in the Government General Hospital. He had only just recently completed 94 years of age on 8/12.

26 Dec. 72 - Tuesday

Rakotondrainibe put in an unannounced appearance at 10:30 A.M. He, it seems, arrived in Madras on the 24th evening from Calcutta, and went off straight to Pondy and has come in to Madras only this morning. He had lunch with us at Gayathri and left for Bombay by the 14:10 flight. Appa took him to the airport and saw him off.

27 Dec. 72 - Wednesday

Luciana Dalla Torre left for Madurai at 20:30 by Trivandrum Mail. In her stay of one week here she has become very affectionate, and it is a pity she could not stay with us at Gayathri. Seena and his family are here since the

19th but have been at Ambattur since last Saturday, and if we had known that they would be there for a whole week, Lucy could have stayed comfortably with us. Rangappa will meet her at Madurai and take care of her till she leaves for Trivandrum in the evening. Leif, Ole and Tigger are continuing in Madras. It seems that Ole has gone on to drugs again — LSD!

C.A. Rajagopalachari (Appa) with Babuji Maharaj

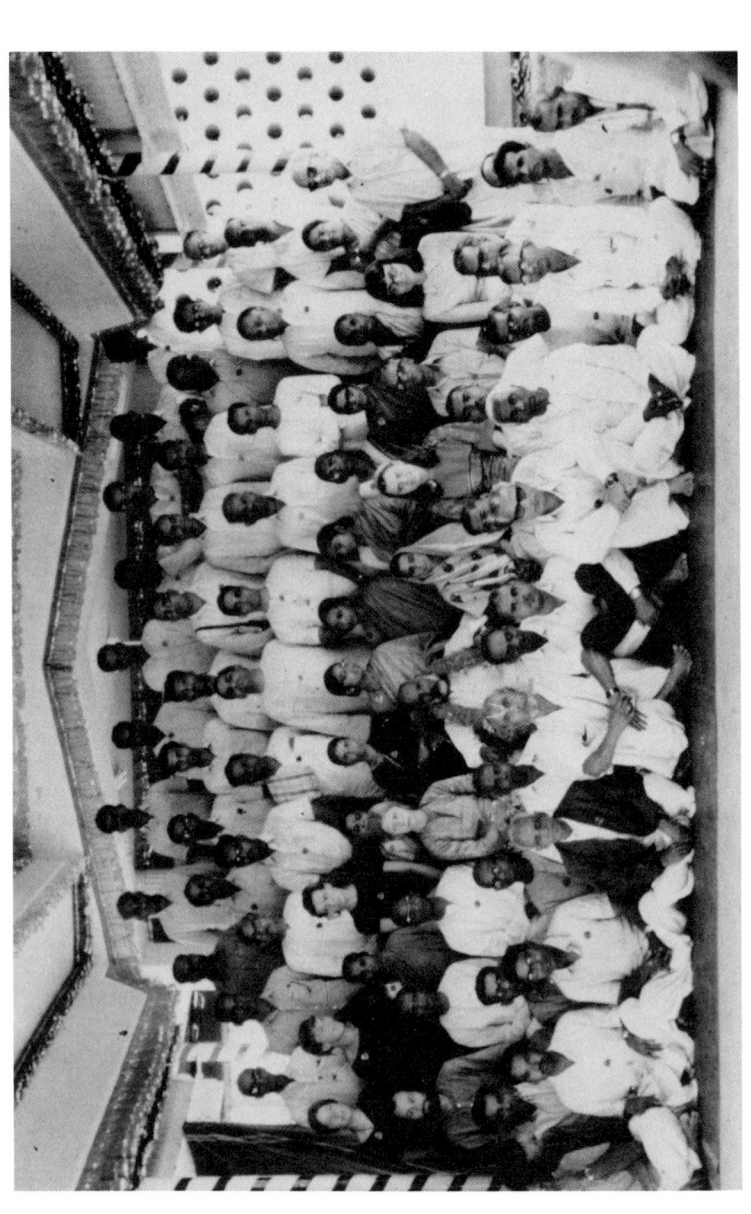

Preceptors present at the Birth Centenary of Lalaji Maharaj

1973

1 Jan. 73 - Monday

The New Year has come around again, inexorably, but in welcome fashion, as denoting one more year of sadhana concluded — and doubtless that much nearer the goal! For me, materially speaking, the year just concluded has been one of dissatisfaction, much aimless effort; confusion as to my own parameters of work; more confusion arising out of so-called reorganisation in the office. The entry of T.T. Jagannathan — TTN's second son — into the business as 'consultant' has led to much major change and, in many ways, I feel as bewildered as a new entrant into the firm.

Spiritually, it has been a most satisfying year. My close proximity to the Master during three months of overseas travel has had much to do with it. I have completed a 3-year term as General Secretary of the Mission. I tried, very very tactfully, to get out of this while we were abroad, pointing out that my appointment had brought into play divisive forces within the organisation arising out of personal jealousy. I told Master I was afraid he may face the possibility of losing many of his *chelas*. He then replied, "If they go, let them go. I am not worried about it. I am happy that I have got you." So it appears I am stuck to this post for at least another term.

India in the West is half through the press — my first and perhaps the only literary effort of any size! It was slated for release today but the book has turned out to be much longer than originally assessed by the printers from the typescript. They estimated 10 forms of 16 pages each, but it is likely to be finally no less than 22 forms of which 17 have already been composed and proofed!

Tigger Outlaw, Ole and Leif Larson left for Nagercoil by the night bus. They go on to Coimbatore, Bangalore, Bombay and reach Shahjahanpur around the 20th of January.

9 Jan. 73 - Tuesday

At Madurai — Appa telephoned from Madras to say he has received a long telegram from Vibe at Shahjahanpur to say that Master is very unwell. I asked Appa to send her a telegram asking for details, and I also sent one off from Madurai.

11 Jan. 73 - Thursday

Just before I left Madurai for Madras, B. Ramachandran telephoned from Virudhunagar to say that two telegrams had been received, one from Master saying that his stomach ache is subsiding, and the other from Vibe confirming some improvement.

14 Jan. 73 - Sunday

Another telegram from Vibe saying that Master is fine again.

I have been getting headaches more frequently the last few months. They are also more severe and last longer. But I notice one change. After the headache subsides, I feel better in a peculiar, inexplicable way. I have written to Master about this. Master has always held that illness, if taken rightly, confers spiritual benefit. Perhaps this condition is being created in me by Master's grace!

The Mission emblems in metal have been delivered — the first lot of 1000 — and distribution commenced today. The emblem has come out well.

Lalaji's work *Truth Eternal* has been finally revised and typed and is ready for the press.

18 Jan. 73 - Thursday

Telegram from Master at 10:30 P.M. to say he is well again. *Truth Eternal* has been given to G.S. Press for printing. It was G.S. Press which printed Dr. Varadachari's *New Darsana*, the first book entrusted to us for printing. It had to be given to G.S. Press because Kabeer Press is still busy with *India in the West* — 16 forms printed so far, and possibly another 6 to 8 forms to be composed and printed! It has come out very long, and threatens to be about 360 pages at least.

Raichur Shri Raghavendra Rao sent in a report on his visit to centres celebrating Lalaji's Centenary — it indicates a recrudescence of jealous criticism against Appa and me again — indications are that Bro. X has been there recently and this has sparked it off!!

24 Jan. 73 - Wednesday

Final 5 forms of *India in the West* page-proofed and handed over to the press for 'strike' — the total is exactly 21 forms or 336 pages! Printing will be over by tomorrow evening and then since there are three days holidays, stitching and binding will commence on Monday 29th January. Shankaran of Kabeer Press has promised delivery of 25 copies on Wednesday the 31st if wrapper (designed by me and given to Ogilvy, Mather & Benson for execution) is ready. Wrapper block should be ready by tomorrow.

Simultaneously G.S. have given 'proof' for 56 pages of *Truth Eternal*, and striking will commence on Saturday. This book will be ready, I think, by the 10th of February, complete in all respects.

Also, work for the Hindi section of the Lalaji Birth Centenary Souvenir with the Hindi Prachar Sabha, and English section with India Printing Works, are all in full swing — much load on Appa, the Hindi galleys needing much work! I am in charge of *India in the West* and *Truth Eternal*, and the former having been completed, I am at rest. But Appa is under great pressure of work for the Souvenir and general arrangements for the Centenary.

31 Jan. 73 - Wednesday

Received the first completed copy — bound and wrappered — of *India in the West* from Kabeer Printing Works. It is good in get up, printing etc. though I am quite disappointed that some of the full-page blocks of exterior scenes have not reproduced well. Anyway, on the whole it is good — one job off our hands! This first copy will go to Master at Shahjahanpur.

7 Feb. 73 - Wednesday

Basant Panchami Celebrations commenced with a one hour sitting in the evening at 6:30 P.M. at 'Gayathri'. A new, coloured photo of Lalaji has been prepared for this — and for our 'gallery' of Sahaj Marg. It has been placed today in the *Guru Sthan* during the satsangh. About 45 persons were present. The second half was very good.

8 Feb. 73 - Thursday

Basant Panchami day — two sittings, at 6:30 A.M. and 6:30 P.M. respectively — of one hour each. The evening session was superb! M/s. C.S. Ramakrishnan and S.

Narayanaswamy spoke in English after the evening satsangh, followed by Miss N. Sundari, the latter's daughter, in Tamil.

Printing of *Truth Eternal* is completed. Now only title page and contents page are to be printed, and cover and jacket designed and printed.

9 Feb. 73 - Friday

Closing session of Basant Panchami celebration at 6:30 A.M. Only about 35 abhyasis were in attendance. Mr. Viraraghavan was otherwise engaged and so Appa took the sitting.

My headache has been troubling me — and now I find polyps growing inside the nostrils again! One appeared externally on the septum but has no pedicle, and is flush with the skin. It made its appearance about a year ago, but the ones inside the nose are new ones. My breathing is obstructed particularly when I am supine on my back. Some small ones, polyps no doubt but looking like pimples, have also appeared above the upper lip below the nose.

16 Feb. 73 - Friday

I had a dream last night. There is a large courtyard with a raised room at one end. It is twilight or like that. A lot of people are asleep in the courtyard. I am going round, almost like a night-watchman. I have gone around two or three times, and on the next circuit I find Master sitting on the platform. I salute him. He looks up, smiles and says, "I see. You are still going round and round in this place?"

My big question to myself in the morning was: Is this a mere comment on my perambulation around the courtyard, or is it an inner feeling of spiritual stagnation and an urge to onward movement?

The Andhra agitation for creation of a separate Andhra is now a month old, and rail services in all directions are paralysed as all major lines run through that state. How our abhyasis from the North will get into Madras for the Lalaji Birth Centenary is the big question. The Bombay line which was initially unaffected is also in difficulty now.

In the evening P.T. Seshadri came. He had a sitting from Appa yesterday evening. In the night he dreamt that Master appeared to him and told him that even though Krishna and Arjuna were very close and inseparable, and had been together for very many years, yet Arjuna did not know the real Nature of Krishna, and Krishna had to reveal Himself to Arjuna on a special occasion. Similarly Master, under the orders of Lalaji, would reveal his true nature and identity to all who are present on the 25th February. Master therefore asked him not to miss this opportunity.

Truth Eternal printing is over and binding is going on. Cover (wrapper) design is final and block made. Wrapper proofs have come in for approval.

Centenary preparations now in hectic swing with regular meetings etc.

17 Feb. 73 - Saturday

Mr. G.S. Mani of Madurai, who had gone to Shahjahanpur to attend Basant Panchami, returned by air from Delhi. He called on us and confirmed that Master will arrive by air from Delhi tomorrow.

Learnt late at night that 21 Europeans have arrived from Shahjahanpur at noon. They came to Hyderabad by rail, and then 18 of them came by a mini-bus while 3 flew in. Party includes Vibe, Thomas, Rikke, Jan Gravesen,

Ole, Leif, Tigger Outlaw of USA, Jean of Denmark, Fred Weinstock, John and Ose, Richard and his Danish wife Karin etc. It is a good thing that they have come in without any trouble on the way. Hans Hvid and his wife are also here.

18 Feb. 73 - Sunday

Morning satsangh as usual. Tigger Outlaw, Leif and Ole attended. The satsangh was followed by a long 'Volunteers' meeting. S.P. Mani has been nominated 'Volunteer Captain' and will be in charge of the volunteer force of nearly 70 abhyasis. The meeting ended at 10:00 A.M. Vibe and Thomas arrived at 10:30 A.M. Vibe is not well, and has an infected throat and a bad cough, same as she developed last year when she came to Shahjahanpur.

We left for the airport at 1:30 P.M. Master, accompanied by Mrs. Birthe Haugaard and her son Hendrik arrived at 2:25 P.M. Over 30 persons assembled at the airport to welcome Master, including Tigger Outlaw, Fred Weinstock, an old Danish lady Marianne, who speaks no English, and others of Madras centre. Drove Master to Besant Nagar and stayed with him till 4:00 P.M. and got back. At 5:00 P.M. I picked up Vibe and Thomas at Woodlands, then picked up Mr. K.D. Menon at his residence, and went back to Besant Nagar. Mr. K.D. Menon belongs to T.T. Consultants and has been with the Shell Group as a top finance/audit executive for over 30 years, mainly in Sumatra, Borneo and Iran. He has been a member of the Yogoda Satsangh Society for 20 years, having received initiation from Daya Mata in Los Angeles in 1953. He spoke to Master and had a long sitting of 30 minutes with Master. Sulochana and Krishna came at 7:30. We all left at 8:30 P.M., dropped Vibe and Thomas at Woodlands, and got back home at 9:30 P.M.

19 Feb. 73 - Monday

To Besant Nagar at 8:30 A.M. to pick up Master. We brought him home to 'Gayathri' at 10:00 A.M. Thomas had arrived just before I left. Master gave him provisional permission at 11:00 A.M. This is the 8th preceptor in Denmark. Thomas has been told that he will be held responsible for Mission development in Sweden and Holland.

Overseas abhyasis came in. Birthe, Jan, and Jean left for the airport at 12:30 to meet the last batch of Danes coming in from Bombay.

At 12:50 Master suddenly called me in. "Look here, Lalaji is urgently calling you. Please sit in meditation." I sat in meditation facing Lalaji while Master sat on a chair. The sitting lasted about 8 minutes. Master said, "You have worked a great deal, and because of this some heaviness had been created in you — now you have been made fresh — now you will be able to do a great deal of work."

Suddenly he said, "Sit again," — and I had a second session, minutes after the first, for about 15 minutes. I felt drowsy. During the sitting I felt as if my head was cleaned inside by a hand going in and scrubbing — very much like a vessel being cleaned. Then wave upon wave of in-filling light — there was bliss. The sitting ended and I was sitting quietly. Suddenly Master, after just a few minutes, again said, "Sit again," and I had a third session of about 10 minutes! I felt a little intoxicated at the end of it.

The overseas party had dispersed as we have a press conference this evening at 5:00 P.M. — 10 editors of local newspapers have been invited to send their reporters for a briefing.

Mr. S.K. Rajagopalan arrived at 3:00 P.M.

5:30 P.M. press conference with just two press reporters, one from the Kalki and the other from Dinamani/Indian Express. It lasted till 6:30. By then the full overseas group of 30 or so had assembled, including Birthe, Elsebeth, Vibe, Thomas, Jan and Jytte, John and Ose, Mikala and Palle, Richard and his wife Karin, Irene Imperiali of Naples, Tigger Outlaw, Fred Weinstock, Hans Hvid and his wife. Anne and Leif Larson are missing this evening.

7:00 P.M. — Master called a meeting of Danish preceptors to discuss matters in general, and the particular problem of Bent Ruus. The meeting ended at 8:00 P.M. Present — Birthe, Elsebeth, Vibe, Thomas, Hans Hvid and Jytte.

After the meeting Master gave a separate sitting to Fred Weinstock, Irene Imperiali and Hans Hvid. All the others had group satsangh with Appa. Then Master sat with the group in the hall till 9:00 P.M. Then I drove him to Besant Nagar. A full day!

When I returned at 9:30 I found V.C. Sriram of India Printing Works had brought two copies of the *Lalaji Centenary Souvenir* — well done indeed. The cover picture of Lalaji, in three colours with a gold frame and completely varnished over, has come out like a Grand Master's oil painting — indeed with a mystic effect not seen in any of Lalaji's pictures so far.

I asked Master about P.T. Seshadri's dream. At first, in Hindi he said, "Yes, he is correct," but later when talking to P.T. Seshadri he changed his answer and said, "Well, he has said it, and let us see what he does."

20 Feb. 73 - Tuesday

To Besant Nagar at 9:00 A.M. Master better than yesterday but weakness persists — it can be seen in his eyes. We brought him to Gayathri at 10:00 A.M. A large crowd gathered. I had to give several sittings in the morning. Two dozen overseas associates present. Irene Imperiali did not come till 1:30 P.M. Master rested from 1:30 to 4:00 P.M. Evening group meditation at 6:30 P.M. taken by Thomas Mogensen. Then dinner for about 50 at Gayathri. Shri S.K. Rajagopalan came yesterday from Mettur and is with us. I dropped Master at Besant Nagar at 10:45 P.M. It was midnight when we went to bed.

Sivakami Kalyana Mantapam will be released to us at 3:00 P.M. tomorrow.

21 Feb. 73 - Wednesday

The Lalaji Birth Centenary Celebrations will be the big affair planned as today's newspapers report resumption of the Grand Trunk Express which has not run for nearly a month now. This means that Northern centres will be represented better than we hoped.

I went to Besant Nagar and brought Master to Gayathri at 11:30. He stayed till 1:15 P.M. and then went back home. M.D. Jahagirdar has arrived.

Arranged for V.S. Raghunathan to take Richard, Karin, Ose and John to the C.L.R.I. and Handymen Ind. All the crowd evaporated by 2:30 P.M.

Mikala Erstad came at 6:00 P.M., ostensibly to have a sitting with Sulochana. After the sitting she presented me a gold 'Omega' Seamaster watch with a gold band-type strap, engraved inside with my name — "Chari" — the present being hers and Vibe's jointly. I was unwilling to accept such an expensive gift and she was weeping for some time. Later I **had** to take it as she was so distressed. I then took her and Sulochana to see Master at 8:30 P.M. after she had dinner with us — we stayed one hour with Master, dropped Mikala at Woodlands after showing her the beach, and got back home at 10:30 P.M. S.K. Rajagopalan accompanied us. He is staying with us.

Sivakami Kalyana Mantapam was given to us at 3:00 P.M. Appa busy with S.P. Mani, Mutthiah, Swaminathan etc. going over the final arrangements. On our way back from Besant Nagar at 10:00 P.M., we stopped to inspect the arrangements. All appears in order. Security men have been posted by Krishnan & Krishnan. Some abhyasis have already arrived.

22 Feb. 73 - Thursday

To Sivakami Kalyana Mantapam at 6:30 A.M. All in order. Various desks in functional order too. Registration of incoming members started. Throughout the day about 150 came in. Biggest group is from Hyderabad who have come by bus. M/s. Kumaraswamy, Joga Rao, Satyapal from Amritsar, Dr. Jajodia and his wife from Bombay, Devram Chavda of Navsari, D.B. Patel of Tinsukia have arrived so far.

Morning satsangh was taken by S.K. Rajagopalan for over 100 persons — all Danes, etc., in attendance except for Hans Jorgen Hvid and his wife. The dining room arrangements with meal coupons printed in sets of four for each day, is working perfectly. The 'hard core' of volunteers with my official group forming the 'hard core' is perfectly disciplined and efficient. Cooking is near-perfect, with chillies completely toned down for the benefit of our overseas abhyasis.

Brought Master to Sivakami Kalyana Mantapam at 4:30 P.M. Nearly 200 abhyasis were present. Master conducted the evening satsangh at 6:30 for 45 minutes. It was superb.

Breakfast served was about 90 coupons, but by dinner it had risen to 220 when we left at 10:00 P.M. A grand day. Mission badges in metal were introduced for the first time. 140 badges were sold for Rs. 700/- while donations and book sales brought in a further Rs. 900.

We left Sivakami Kalyana Mantapam at 10:30 P.M.

23 Feb. 73 - Friday

To Sivakami Kalyana Mantapam at 6:30 A.M. Group meditation at 7:00 A.M. conducted personally by Master. A superb 55 minutes! I think the transmission here is different from that during Basant Panchami at Shahjahanpur. It seems to be deeper and subtler.

Group discussions from 10:00 A.M. All systems working smoothly. At 11:00 A.M. we were allowed to occupy the Rajeswari Kalyana Mantapam. Delegates are arriving in large numbers. About 375 delegates were registered this morning by 10:30 A.M. The number rose to 625 by 8:00 P.M.

At 3:30 P.M. we had a preceptors meeting at the Sivakami Kalyana Mantapam, presided over by Master himself, with Sister Kasturi in attendance, and with me conducting the session. The session lasted about an hour and a half, and was attended by all preceptors, Indian and overseas, present today. The overseas preceptors were the most active, asking a lot of questions, mostly routine in nature. The meeting served the good purpose of bringing the overseas preceptors on common ground with their Indian brothers and sisters of the Mission.

Master conducted group meditation at 6:00 P.M. Guests continue to arrive in large numbers. By dinner time we had a large gathering. However the full complement of 1500 Indian abhyasis is unlikely to turn up due to Andhra Pradesh disturbances (for separate Andhra state) consequent on which trains are not running.

We have a large volunteer force and work has been assigned as under:

Reception and Transport: Shri K.V. Rao, Shri N.S. Rao, Shri Sambasivan, Shri Acharya, and abhyasi drivers M. Palani and Rajan.

Registration of Arrivals/Delegates: Bro. B.P. Anand and Master P.R. Krishna.

Accommodation Allotment: Shri S. Sadasivam and Shri K. Mahalingan.

Badges, Tokens: Shri N. Srinivasa Rao, Shri T.T. Santhanam, Shri Jambulingam and Vasan.

Book Sales: M/s. Shri P.T. Seshadri, B. Ramachandran of Virudhunagar, B.B. Motiwalla, S. Parthasarathi, R. Krishnamachari, P. Rangarajan, P.V. Raman.

Stores: S. Muthiah (in charge), S. Raghavendra Rao, R. Thiagarajan, Balakrishnan, Janakiraman, V.N. Kalyanarama Dass and Manickam.

First Aid: Shri V. Kalyanaraman

Sanitation: Shri V. Kalyanaraman

Dining Hall and General Administration:

Gents:	Ladies:
Shri T. Padmanabhan	Mrs. Sulochana Parthasarathi
Shri P.S. Doraivelu	Mrs. Motiwalla
Shri V.S. Raghunathan	Mrs. Lalitha Rao
Shri R. Ramanan (Bhavanisagar)	Mrs. Indra Raghavan
	Mrs. Sundaravalli Padmanabhan

Shri B. Rajagopal (Virudhunagar)	Mrs. Vatsala
	Miss. V. Jayashree
Shri R. Rangappa (Virudhunagar)	Miss. N. Sundari
	Miss. N. Sarada
Shri K. Babu	Lakshmi
Shri S. Ranganathan	Mrs. Sahkubai (Tiruttani)
Shri S.V. Raman (Bangalore)	
Shri P.S. Vasu	
Shri T.T. Jagannathan	
Shri T.T. Sridhar	
Shri Subramanian	
Shri Balasubramanian (Virudhunagar)	
Shri P.V. Srinivasan	

Reserves: M/s. Satya Pal, Joga Rao, Venkatasubba Reddy, Devaraj, Lakshminarasimhan, Periakaruppan, Ram Raj.

The volunteer force was under the overall command of Shri S.P. Mani as Volunteer Captain with Shri R. Swaminathan as his ADC and General Adviser. The meal times are kept up (Breakfast: 7:45 A.M.; Lunch: Noon; Tea: 4:00 P.M.; and Dinner: 7:30 P.M.).

24 Feb. 73 - Saturday

It was the first day of the formal Centenary Celebration. The day opened with group meditation at 7:00 A.M. Nearly a thousand persons were present for this sitting. Master transmitted for an hour and a little more.

At 10:35 A.M. the formal session commenced — the public session — with an invocation. A prayer song was rendered by a group led by Mrs. Sulochana Parthasarathi, the other participants being Miss. V. Jayashree, Mrs. Indra Raghavan and Mrs. Sundaravalli Padmanabhan. Justice P. Ramakrishnan presided over this session. I garlanded Master with an enormous jasmine and rose garland specially brought from Madurai for this occasion. B. Rajagopal of Virudhunagar garlanded Justice P. Ramakrishnan. Then Shri C.A. Rajagopalachari gave a welcome speech. This was followed by the judge's presidential lecture, following which he formally released *Truth Eternal*, Lalaji's only extant work. This publication was undertaken at Madras and 500 copies got ready just the day-before-yesterday. As a matter of interest it is recorded that all 500 were sold out, at a price of Rs. 10/- per copy, immediately after release!

This was followed by Master delivering his special "Message" printed in the *Special Centenary Souvenir.* He read from his prepared script for about 20 minutes — and twice choked with emotion on references to Lalaji. Tears streamed down once, and he had to stop to wipe them off before he could continue to read! What love and devotion he has for his Master! Can we ever duplicate it for our own Master? The souvenir was released by Master.

This was followed by a short speech of dedication by Shri S. Narayanaswamy. After this the Joint Secretary Shri J.R.K. Raizada gave a good speech "Ourselves" — all about the Mission, its founding, its activities, aims, etc. It was a very good speech indeed. Mr. Palle Kousgaard of Denmark spoke next, and formally released my work *India in the West.* The morning session ended with a thanks giving talk by Shri C.A. Rajagopalachari.

Group discussions were held from 2 to 4 P.M. Several groups formed themselves around Sister Kasturi, Br. Raghavendra Rao of Raichur, and other senior preceptors present — with of course an ever-present group surrounding Master in his room. The group around Master was permanent, only changing members. After this Shri G. Vijayarangachari of Hyderabad, Mr. Srinivasa Rao Kashampurkar of Bidar, Shri D. Srinivasa Murthi of Kavali, Shri Sriman Narayanamurthi of Bhimavaram all gave short lectures. The lecture session was presided over by Dr. V. Parthasarathi of Vijayawada.

Master took evening meditation at 6:30 P.M. Nearly 800 present at satsangh.

From 7:15 P.M. a lecture session was held — speakers were Mrs. Birthe Haugaard and Mrs. Jytte Gravesen of Denmark, followed by Mr. V. Venkatapathi of Tiruttani. Birthe gave a nice talk, totally sincere and from her heart.

At 9:00 P.M. Shri Srinivasa Rao, well known *bhajan* musician brought his group to sing *bhajans* for one and a half hours. It was a lovely programme and the groups rendering of Tulsidas' "Shri Ramachandra Kripalu Bhajamana" was extremely moving and brought tears to my eyes.

There followed an impromptu session with Master and then we 'closed' formally for the day at 11:15 P.M. A wonderful day indeed.

While with Master I had a strong feeling that I shall be his representative. I hid this thought in my mind lest "He" should read it.

25 Feb. 73 - Sunday

The second day opened with group meditation conducted by Master from 7:00 A.M. to nearly 8:00 A.M. A superb atmosphere prevailed. I felt it was finer and subtler than the Basant Panchami atmosphere that prevails at Shahjahanpur. The hall was packed full, and surely 1200 must have been present for this satsangh. After the sitting 'prasad' was offered by Master to Revered Lalaji Saheb.

At 10:00 A.M. the morning lecture session commenced. Shri Raghavendra Rao of Raichur, Shri S. Raju of Trichy and Shri Kumaraswami of Hyderabad were the prominent speakers.

There was a group discussion at 2:00 P.M.

Master took evening satsangh at 6:00 P.M. — again a packed hall, and again a superb atmosphere of pure spirituality!

Evening lecture session commenced at 7:00 P.M. Speakers were Irene Imperiali of Rome, Thomas Mogensen of Denmark, Dr. Chandrika Prasad of Roorkee, Prof. Suresh Chandra, and Jaggan Raizada, the Joint Secretary of the Mission. Jaggan spoke very well.

After dinner there was a devotional music session, the participants including Sister Kasturi, Sulochana, Shri G.S. Mani of Madurai and Shri V.V. Balakrishnan of Virudhunagar. Master was present throughout. After this, in an electric mood, a large group formed in the main hall around Master and Master kept them spellbound for over an hour.

We have succeeded in getting Rajeswari Kalyana Mantapam for an extra day at NO EXTRA COST! God Bless the trustees. This was necessary as a large number of abhyasis could not leave due to rail disruptions and was therefore a boon.

26 Feb. 73 - Monday

Group meditation at 7 A.M. The attendance was a little reduced as a number of abhyasis left yesterday — mainly those from Tamil Nadu Centres.

11:30 A.M. — a short question and answer session with Master doing the answering.

3:30 P.M. lecture session. Talks by Shri S.K. Rajagopalan of Trichy, Shri B. Rajagopal of Virudhunagar and Shri C.A. Rajagopalachari.

6:00 P.M. group satsangh — with a further reduced gathering. A fairly large number have left during the day.

7:00 P.M. music by Sister Kasturi and Sulochana Parthasarathi.

I gave the concluding talk, bringing the Centenary Celebrations formally to a close. At the end I prayed to our beloved Master to grant us the magnanimity of being physically present to preside over his own Centenary Celebrations at the turn of this century.

A mood of sadness prevails at this moment. Tomorrow morning we have to vacate the hall by 8:00 A.M. Master left for Besant Nagar at 11:00 P.M. He has been staying here since the 22nd afternoon!

Meal Statistics

Date	B'fast	Lunch	Tea	Dinner	Total
22/2/73	154	159	168	261	742
23/2/73	321	363	452	881	2017
24/2/73	986	1018	984	1020	4008
25/2/73	1052	1048	814	1070	3984
26/2/73	581	447	350	212	1590

27 Feb. 73 - Tuesday

To Rajeswari Kalyana Mantapam at 8:00 A.M. The place was deserted and cleaning was in progress. With the assistance of abhyasis who were allotted work I settled the bill. Later at 9:30 A.M. I gave a final sitting to some overseas abhyasis Vibe, Mikala, Irene, Birthe, Elsebeth,

Thomas, Jens, Anne, Jytte, etc. How forlorn they looked, after the exuberance of the past four days! And how lonely and deserted the Mantapam looked!

Sister Kasturi told me in the evening at Gayathri, "Babuji Maharaj is very happy. Poor Babuji! The night before yesterday, approximately at 1:00 A.M. we were speaking together there were tears in his eyes. He was saying, 'Daughter, do you remember that when I began this Mission we were only three or four persons — you, Ishwar Sahai, Harihar Sahai and that's all — and in those days I could not even dream that a day would come when I would be able to celebrate my Master's Centenary in front of 1,500 persons or more. The people of this place have done a lot of work.'"

Master came to Gayathri in the evening and when we were alone, embraced me and said, "I am very pleased with you; you have performed a very big work."

Master spent the whole evening with us. Most of the overseas abhyasis who are still in Madras were present — Birthe, Elsebeth, Vibe, Thomas, Mikala. We had some music. Later Master sang, "Deenana Dukh Harana Nath...." which I recorded on cassette. A memorable day.

The Centenary has been financially a great success. The following facts would bear recording:

Donations received 47,002.15

Souvenir Advertisements. 69,658.55

Badge sale ...... Taken to Gen. a/c

Souvenir sales .... 7,470.00 (loss of Rs. 2100)

1,24,130.70

Total expenses 36,075.73
          (Festival 25,379.58; Souvenir 9,505.91)
Profit to Mission 88,054.97

Master has instructed that the profit should be earmarked as the nucleus of a separate fund for the construction of a Mission Ashram at Madras!!

4 Mar. 73 - Sunday

Master left for Calcutta by evening IAC flight. The flight was delayed. He will spend a couple of days with Mr. Mimani and then go on to Shahjahanpur.

12 Oct. 73 (Calcutta)

Spent three days with Master at Calcutta. I arrived here on Friday the 9th night. The plane was one hour late and arrived near midnight. I was surprised to see Shri Raman Lal Mimani with his brother-in-law Shri Raman Lal Bhattar and two other Bhattar brothers all at the airport to receive me. So very nice of them. Sankar of TTK, Calcutta also at the Dum Dum airport. Since Sankar had a car, Swaminathan and I drove off with him to the Grand Hotel where we are staying.

13 Oct. 73 - Sunday

Master and Sister Kasturi accompanied by Shri Kashiram Agarwal arrived by air from Lucknow. Master looked very tired and drawn. About 35 persons of the Calcutta centre met them on arrival. They are put up in a *dharamsala* next to Mimaniji's house. I spent the whole day there with Master. Shri Saudagar Singh is here now — a Major in the army — a very nice man indeed, very devoted and sincere — his wife too — as also his son and daughter. Kasturi looked ill. She told me that ever since she left

Modinagar a week ago she has been ill, and particularly the last two days at Lucknow she has been very ill. It would have been good if she had stayed back.

14 Oct. 73 - Monday

Whole day with Master — a bonus day, since it happens that today is Vishwakarma Puja day and everything is closed here in Calcutta.

I had to have medical attention. Since 10 days I have been having some abdominal pain — it was quite bad at Meenambakkam airport when I left Madras — today it turned severe. The doctor was not very happy and gave me intravenous Baralgam 5 cc. He wants blood and urine tests. Took blood, but urine was a problem as it has become very very painful and difficult to excrete even a few drops. The doctor suspects some urinary infection. After seeing him I went back to the *dharamsala* and rested the whole day.

15/16 Oct. 73 - Tuesday and Wednesday

Spent as much time as possible with Master while attending to the work (official) which has enabled Swaminathan and me to come here. Recommended Swaminathan to Master for provisional permission, but for the first time ever, Master turned it down saying Swami is "vicious" and undeserving.

11 Nov. 73 - Monday (Madras)

Started work on Master's autobiography to get it ready for printing. Manuscript revised twice, and final script handed over to Kabeer Printing Works so that proofs can be ready when I get back from Shahjahanpur.

18 Nov. 73 - Monday (Shahjahanpur)

Arrived Shahjahanpur with Sulochana and Krishna. Also accompanying us are Swaminathan, B. Rajagopal and Seshan. Master gave us a superb sitting at 9:00 A.M. In residence here are Jean-Michel Piquemal and Jean-Marie Bertrand of Nice with another French couple, and Fred Weinstock of USA. Muthiah of Madras centre has also been here for some days.

19 Nov. 73 - Tuesday

Shahjahanpur — a quiet day with a single group sitting taken by Master. Went to new Ashram site. Master also took me to his Hakim for medicine.

20 Nov. 73 - Wednesday

Spoke to Master about Krishna starting meditation. Master kindly agreed and gave Krishna his first sitting personally. Master told Sulochana that Krishna should go slow on this, meditate only for 10 minutes or so, and sit only with junior preceptors having provisional permission.

The French group left for Delhi en route their homeland.

We went to Ashram site again. Recommended B. Rajagopal for initiation. Master kindly agreed to it.

21 Nov. 73 - Thursday

Shahjahanpur — Seshan left for Lucknow by morning train and will come back by midnight Lucknow Mail by which all of us are to depart. B. Rajagopal initiated.

I have had one long session with Master clarifying various matters in his autobiography.

We left at 12:15 (past midnight) by Lucknow Mail. Master said he has put Sulochana in the 4th point. She is

not happy with this and has told Master so. It is almost eight years since she commenced, and has just come to the 4th point. Master is taking her extraordinarily slowly — only he knows why, though he seems to be praising her for her devotion all the time.

23 Nov. 73 - Saturday (Delhi)

Public meeting at Moti Bagh South addressed by Shri C.A. Rajagopalachari.

24 Nov. 73 - Sunday

Attended general satsangh at Delhi centre in Mr. Sundara's house. Left for Madras by the G.T. Express at 17:10 P.M. Appa leaves for Shahjahanpur tonight.

31 Dec. 73 - Monday (Madras)

Two forms of *Autobiography of Ram Chandra* final proofed and strike order given. I hope the book will be ready by 12th or so of January so that some copies can go to Shahjahanpur with abhyasis going for Basant Panchami for sale.

Beloved Babuji Maharaj recovering after illness with nurse, Donald Sabourin, March, 1974

1974

1 Jan. 74 - Tuesday

One more year has gone by. According to Master good progress has been made spiritually. I feel the effect within me. There is more calm in the depths of my being, more peace; more fearlessness; more rest. My physical well-being has also been enhanced. The hakim's treatment seems to be doing quite a bit of good. In the last six weeks I have had no severe headache at all, and I have been **free** of an attack for more than two weeks at a stretch!! Master be praised. A major source of happiness, and a milestone, is Krishna commencing meditation, and that too being privileged to get his first sitting from Master himself. A great disappointment is Sulochana's snail-like pace of progress. Master promises to take her up fast but is really disinclined to do so. She, on her part, is far too hard and rigid in many of her ways, and will not bend. She certainly has love for Master, but coupled with an unbending stance, too proud, too haughty to ask Master, but willing only to receive **if** given; yet interiorly unhappy, with a keen sense of being discriminated against, and a keen and bitter disappointment that Master moved her up just one point (to the 4th) when she went to Shahjahanpur!

The past year was one of major activity, seeing, as it did, the birth centenary celebration of Pujya Lalaji Saheb. That was a great event, a great effort, and a great success, culminating in a most enchanting celebration which pleased Master greatly.

I have not been writing my diary regularly — and when writing in retrospect much is forgotten. Several dreams had been referred to Master for clarification and fortunately he has replied to them — or at least to those that he thought needed interpretation.

In Shahjahanpur he casually asked me whether I was doing some work which he had assigned to me as *Dhruvadhipathi*. I said I was doing it off and on, and I referred to him one regular experience in this work. I generally do the transmission between 1:30 P.M. and 2:00 P.M. lying on my bed. Almost as soon as I start transmitting, I seem to go into deep unconsciousness, from which I seem to 'wake up' after 30 minutes or so. The state resembles deep sleep, very deep sleep. Master said this was very good indeed and said this is what happens to him when he works!

Master has decided to go to Europe and UK in late spring or early summer of this year, and I am to accompany him. I have completed four years as General Secretary of the Mission.

2 Jan. 74 - Wednesday

I sat in meditation for half an hour, and seemed to go into some sort of unconsciousness. Felt as if black waves were coming into me sometimes from outside, and sometimes from within me, and each wave sent me deeper into unconsciousness. After this I transmitted to B. Rajagopal who should have reached Hong Kong today on his first Far East tour. He has been away for a week now and will go up to Japan. Master has asked him to do some work wherever possible.

4 Jan. 74 - Friday

Very busy time with Master's Autobiography. Six forms printed today. By this evening 10 forms are over.

Book advance sales encouraging. About 400 copies of both editions have been paid for. For the first time the book is in two editions, a calico-bound edition priced @ Rs. 10/- and a paper edition @ Rs. 7/-. Surprisingly, or not so surprisingly at that, when offered a choice people seem to invariably go for the expensive one. Orders so far are for 300 calico as against just 100 of the paper edition.

Proof sheets of the last two forms have come in this evening and printing will be over on Monday. I hope to have at least 400 copies ready by the 14th or so, to be sent to Shahjahanpur for Basant Panchami sales.

The Honolulu lady, Kantha Devi, has been coming to Appa for sittings regularly since she was introduced by T. Srinivasan, IAS, a week ago. She is getting very devoted.

5 Jan. 74 - Saturday

Dream early in the morning. I am sitting in a room with Sulochana and Krishna. Someone brings in a really handsome male child aged about two years old. The child is very handsome and charming. Someone present there says it is my child. I wonder how this can be. Children rarely come near me, but this one comes to me, smiles bewitchingly, climbs onto my lap and rubs its cheek against mine — and goes on doing it. Then it traces the outline of my lips with its forefinger, looking admiringly. Laughingly it asks whether I have brought anything for it. I say, "No." Then from behind its back it brings a sweet, breaks off a piece and puts it into my mouth. The dream fades off.

Then I am in a railway station at 11:00 A.M. to receive someone. Some friend is with me. We wait and wait, but till 4:30 P.M. the train does not come.

7 Jan. 74 - Monday

Final page proof of form 12 of *Autobiography* corrected and given to press this morning. Expect printing to be completed by Wednesday evening — have requested 400 calico and 100 paper bound copies by Saturday the 12th.

12 Jan. 74 - Saturday

Kabeer Printing Press delivered 400 copies calico bound and 200 copies paper bound of *Autobiography of Ram Chandra*. Mr. D. Rangarajan of ITPT goes to Delhi today, and I have sent 200 calico copies through him to be delivered at Shahjahanpur. The book has come out well.

I am getting more than usually irritated the last week or so. I have written to Master requesting him to release *Autobiography* formally on Basant Panchami Day (28th) and then put up copies for sale. I have also said that I do not see any possibility of my going to Shahjahanpur for the Utsav.

13 Jan. 74 - Sunday

Missed satsangh due to demise, this morning at 1:15 A.M., of my uncle (Athimber) Shri S. Aravamuda Ayengar, at H.M. Hospital.

13 Jan. 74 - Sunday

Mr. G.S. Mani of Madurai came home. He goes to Delhi tomorrow by the Link Express, and carries 100 paperbound copies of Master's *Autobiography* with him to Shahjahanpur.

19 Jan. 74 - Saturday

Letter from Master, in his own handwriting, to say, "Basant Utsav is fast approaching and awaiting your arrival." Hitherto, I had decided not to go for Basant to Shahjahanpur this year. There is a strange reluctance in me — I have written about this reluctance to Master a few days ago. But today's letter reverses my decision.

Shri Thasma Swami, our preceptor-in-charge of Madurai, has been here for the past few days.

Don Sabourin and his wife Jackie, of Canada, have arrived at Shahjahanpur. He brings a special stained-glass window of the Mission emblem for our Headquarters Ashram. They came from Burnaby in the district of British Columbia of Canada. David Bolevice, of Troy, N.Y., USA, has already been in Shahjahanpur for some time. He was to come to Madras, but by a letter I received from him today, he has confirmed he will not come. When he arrived he was quite unsure of himself, and came avowedly to "look around". He was quite frank about this to our S.S. Ramakrishnan even before he left Troy. He had made it quite clear that though he had started our meditation, he had neither accepted the Master nor the method finally. Today's letter says all this, and adds that he has become a preceptor, and has decided "there is nothing more to be found outside the four walls of the Mission, and so I will go back to the States from here on 30th January. What money I would have spent on travel in India, I am donating to the Mission." So Master has again made his conquest!

22 Jan. 74 - Tuesday

Conducted group satsangh at Valamjee Mansion in Madurai. Swaminathan is at Madras, busy with our travel plans to go to Delhi on Wednesday 23rd, en route Shahjahanpur. Tickets are proving difficult but he phoned that we will certainly go!

23 Jan. 74 - Wednesday

Returned from Madurai in the morning. A postcard was waiting from Master saying,"Basant Utsav will be celebrated from 27th to 29th and you will naturally be the guest and the host too. So this is for the information only." Also a letter from Don Sabourin, stating that he may possibly not come to Madras. Also received a long letter from Shashi Dhawan.

Our tickets are unconfirmed, but Swaminathan has been at it the whole day. Went to airport but finally returned at 6:00 P.M. without success. Vijayaraghavan travels to Delhi and will go to Shahjahanpur for Basant and has been requested to convey this to Master. Superficially I am unaffected but in depth I am deeply disappointed.

24 Jan. 74 - Thursday

Woke up with tears in my eyes. The deep disappointment has been working on my mind all through the night. There is no possibility of going due to severe curtailment of flights as a result of Indian Airlines lock-out for over two months now, combined with Rail strikes. Is my inability to go a result of my earlier reluctance? I do not know. I believe the reluctance was only in the superficial layers of the mind, whereas I see that the disappointment at not going is very much deeper.

S. Narayanaswamy and Dasarathan (of Trichy) left by the G.T.Express on 22nd. Yesterday morning N.S. Rao, his wife and mother accompanied by S. Raghavendran left by the Link Express. V.J. Chandrasakar should have left by G.T. of 23rd. No information of any others from this side.

Can it be that Master, from the merely human level, wished me to go, but in a different way wanted it otherwise? This duality between what he expresses as his desire and what actually happens, has come to my notice on several occasions. I must put it up to him for clarification.

26 Jan. 74 - Saturday

D. Rengarajan of ITPT returned from Shahjahanpur, deeply bitten!

27 Jan. 74 - Sunday

Morning satsangh as usual.

Basant Panchami celebrations commenced with special sitting in the evening from 6:30 to 7:30 P.M. About 80 abhyasis present. B. Rajagopal arrived this morning from Colombo after completing his one month tour of the Far East. Evening sitting was very good and deep, especially the second half hour.

Krishna, sick since Thursday, missed joining in as he continues to have fever.

28 Jan. 74 - Monday

Basant Panchami day. Morning sitting 6:30 to 7:30. Nearly 100 abhyasis present. Sitting very good throughout.

Evening sitting 6:30 to 7:30 P.M. Also very good. This was followed by a music interlude, Sulochana and Jayashree singing 'Dinana Dukh Harana Dev', 'Shri Ramachandra Kripalu Bhaja Mana', and a final Purandara Dasa song. After this Appa formally released *The Autobiography of Ram Chandra* with a short talk, handing over the first copy to Shri R. Viraraghavan. Shri Viraraghavan gave a short talk, followed by Dr. S.V. Raghavan of Bombay, B. Rajagopal (who spoke well), R. Swaminathan, C.S. Ramakrishnan, and V. Seshan. Copies of the book were distributed to advance buyers. The evening session concluded with a 20 minute exhibition of coloured slides about Master. The meeting broke up at around 9:10 P.M. It was a delightful evening.

29 Jan. 74 - Tuesday

Final session of Basant Panchami with special one hour meditation from 6:30 to 7:30 A.M. Poor attendance — around 40! I felt disturbed, waiting for the session, which seemed unending, to end.

1 Feb. 74 - Friday

S. Dasarathan of Trichy centre called, on his way back from Shahjahanpur, in the morning. V.J. Chandrasekar of Madurai centre called late in the evening, also back from Shahjahanpur after attending Basant Panchami celebration there.

3 Feb. 74 - Sunday

S. Narayanaswamy returned from Shahjahanpur. He came to 'Gayathri' at 5:00 P.M. with *prasad* and the fifth Volume of 1973 Patrika for distribution to life subscribers. Reports about Master's health are disquieting. He is reported to be suffering from severe back pain, abdominal acidity and ulcer pains, and almost constant headache. A letter from R. Vijayaraghavan to me says Master is considering undergoing a thorough check-up at Madras shortly.

Ashram roof slab at Shahjahanpur was laid by our members, present for Basant Panchami, offering *shramdan*! About 700 members are reported to have attended the Utsav this year.

Abhyasis participating in ashram construction
Basant Celebrations, January, 1974

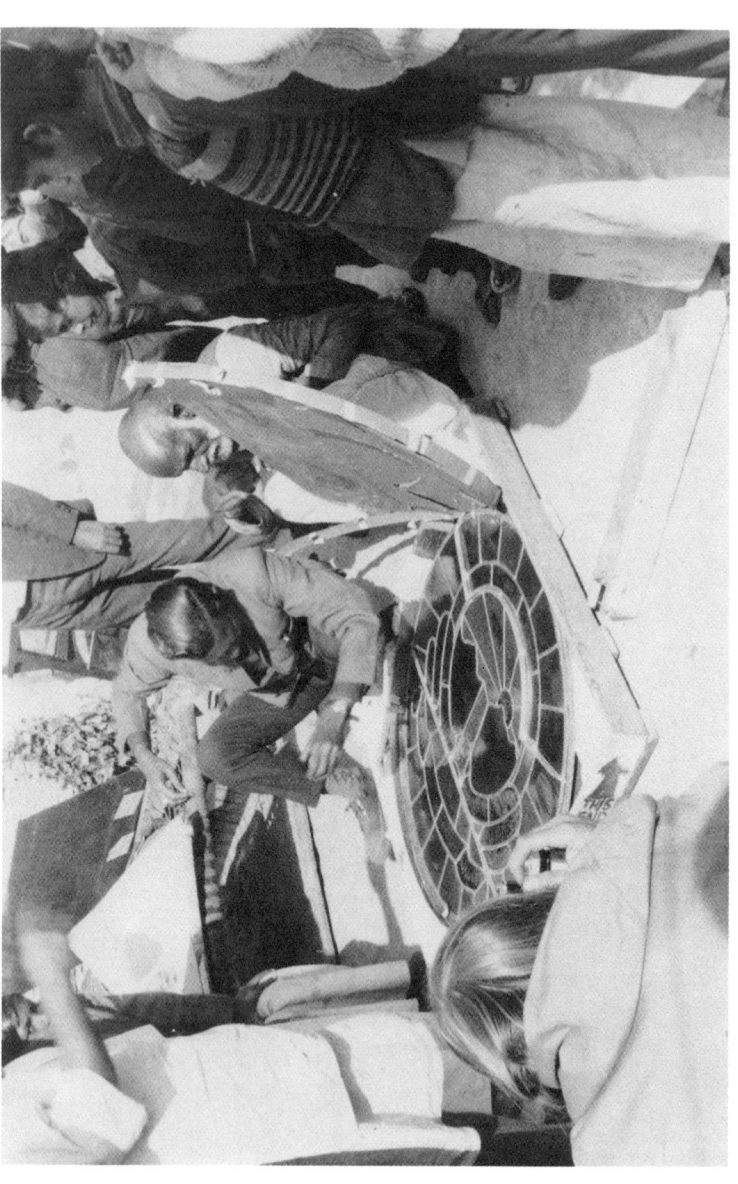

Reverend Babuji inspecting stained glass window for the Shahjahanpur ashram, January, 1974

Appa took general satsangh this morning — it was very good.

4 Feb. 74 - Monday

Don Sabourin, preceptor, from Canada, accompanied by his wife Jackie, arrived at Madras by G.T. Express and telephoned from Woodlands Hotel to say they have arrived. I picked them up at 5:00 P.M. and took them home for a couple of hours, primarily to discuss the Mission constitution for the British Columbia (Canada) branch of the Mission.

5 Feb. 74 - Tuesday

Mr. G.S. Mani passed through, on his way back from Shahjahanpur to Madurai. All returning brothers are bringing information of Master's arrival here shortly, but we have no direct information from Master himself yet. Don told me yesterday, "Master said that there was a strong pull from Madras, from Parthasarathi, and he feels he must come here. He will surely come soon."

6 Feb. 74 - Wednesday

Don and Jackie Sabourin came at 5:00 P.M., joined in the evening meditation, had some rice and koottu with us, and left around 9:15 P.M. Don bought 797.50 Rupees worth of books from our stock, which he will donate to the Canadian Mission, which will sell the books locally and so build up some funds to start with. A very generous gesture, giving money to the Mission at both ends! May Master bless them.

7 Feb. 74 - Thursday

At about 4:00 P.M. an abhyasi from Denmark, Niels Erik Harup-Hanson, accompanied by a non-abhyasi girl friend Elsa, landed up at Gayathri, having come from Ceylon by train. They had some tea — and then I managed to put them into the Woodlands Hotel. I sent a telegram to Master, asking for date of his arrival.

7 Feb. 74 - Friday

Jackie, Don and Niels came for satsangh in the evening.

8 Feb. 74 - Saturday

Letter from Grace Kimball from Shahjahanpur saying Master is quite ill and any travel is now out of the question. No reply to my telegram yet.

11 Feb. 74 - Monday

At Coimbatore Sulochana phoned to say that a telegram has been received from Shahjahanpur, "Master indisposed. Await revised programme."

Conducted satsangh at Shri Sukaswami's residence in the evening at 7:00 P.M. About 11 persons present.

12 Feb. 74 - Tuesday

Evening satsangh at Alankar Hotel at 8:00 P.M. K.R. Subramanian, Swaminathan, Rangarajan and Varadhan were present. Grace Kimball arrived in Madras.

13 Feb. 74 - Wednesday

Madurai — Evening satsangh at Valamjee Mansion taken with about nine abhyasis present.

14 Feb. 74 - Thursday

Sulochana telephoned me at 10:30 A.M. at Madurai to say reports of Master's health are alarming. Grace Kimball, who arrived at Madras on 12th and telephoned me at 7:00 P.M., and who is staying at our house, seems to have given an alarming report to Sulochana. Sulochana seems to be frightened. I spoke to Umesh at Madras, who said Ramanlal Mimani had telephoned from Calcutta at the request of Kashi Ram Agarwal, asking me to proceed to Shahjahanpur. I asked T.S. Rajagopal to send a telegram asking for current information.

Held two group satsanghs at 6:30 A.M. and 7:00 A.M. followed by one individual sitting, and one individual sitting again at 4:30 P.M. followed by group satsangh for about 15 at 6:30 P.M.

15 Feb. 74 - Friday

Telegram from Prakash Chandra Saxena from Shahjahanpur saying, "Father's illness persists. Consultation necessary. Come." I sent a telegram to Mr. Mimani at Shahjahanpur — presuming his arrival there — asking for factual information and asking him to consult Master and wire me.

16 Feb. 74 - Saturday

Back in Madras. Letters received by Appa and Shri S. Narayanaswamy from Mr. N.S. Rao (who is still at Shahjahanpur) indicate that Master is better.

17 Feb. 74 - Sunday

Conflicting reports from Shahjahanpur about Master's health. Kashi Ram Agarwal has sent a telegram to Umesh which is quite contradictory to other reports.

Received a telegram signed by Prakash, dispatched from Shahjahanpur yesterday 16th at 8:30 A.M. reading, "Master delirious. Inform Umesh and Sarvesh. Come."

This was received at about 8:00 P.M. today. Umesh has however received a telegram dated this morning which says Master is better and asking him to inform Sarvesh accordingly. This is also signed by Prakash. Umesh has decided to leave with Sarvesh, for Shahjahanpur on Tuesday.

This morning general satsangh was taken by Don Sabourin of Canada. I understand he took satsangh last Sunday also — and it was exceptionally good.

18 Feb. 74 - Monday

Umesh left for Shahjahanpur (via Jhansi and Lucknow) by G.T. Express in the evening. Sarvesh stays back at Virudhunagar. I have decided to leave tomorrow with my brother-in-law Jagan by G.T.

19 Feb. 74 - Tuesday

Telegram from Prakash to say that Master was admitted in the Vivekananda Hospital at Lucknow yesterday. Again a period of indecision — and finally my departure for Delhi this evening cancelled. I shall await news before deciding.

My heart feels light. I have no worry in depth, though since this morning there is superficial heaviness in the heart. Last Thursday, at Madurai, when Sulochana telephoned me about Master's illness, there was overwhelming heaviness in the heart, almost unbearable. From 12 noon on that day I prayed till 2:00 P.M. to Lalaji Maharaj, lying on my bed. From 3:00 P.M. my heart became much lighter, and by evening I was more than normally cheerful and light-hearted. It has continued till this morning — only today there is arising a superficial heaviness of the heart. Wrote to Nasib Chandji at Lucknow for details.

20 Feb. 74 - Wednesday

Seshan has been trying to contact Shri Kalyanakrishnan, IAS, Private Secretary to the Chief Minister of UP at Lucknow for help and assistance in looking after Master there — but as luck would have it the Delhi-Kanpur lines are out of order, and telephone connection was unavailable the whole day. From 4:00 P.M. I felt heaviness, and by 6:00 P.M. on the verge of tears. Better after that. A telegram has been sent to Shri Kalyanakrishnan, IAS, Lucknow.

21 Feb. 74 - Thursday

A dream early in the morning. I find myself emerging out of a factory after inspection, and am about to cross a track which looks something like a rail track. It is like dawn or dusk. Suddenly I became aware of some object moving towards me from my right, along the track, and I jump back. I escape being killed. The object is like a small wagon, or a block of steel. The workers concerned are reprimanded by B. Ramachandran whom I find behind me. Then I leave and go along a path that seems to go down, like a hill-path. I am alone. I go down some distance and at a sharp descent I have to go into a cleft through which the path seems to go on. I enter it and keep going. The road has become like an enclosed tunnel, but illuminated. The road continues to go down and down, and at places steps seem to have been cut into the floor to facilitate foothold. At places there are openings on the roof which appear to be in-flow channels for streams. Increasingly I feel I am not on the road by which I went originally to the factory, and the road I am on seems to be a subterranean river bed. But I have come down in level so much I am hesitant to turn back and climb the distance all over again. So I keep going. The tunnel begins to narrow and close in, twisting and winding, and all the time going down, down, so that I can't see the way more than a few feet ahead. I realise it is getting darker, and I become anxious as to how I will ever go back the way I have come, and if I keep on where it is going to lead. At this stage I become aware that there is someone ahead of me, though I can't see him for the twists and turns. I shout out to him, but there is no reply. At this stage I woke up. Soon the clock strikes 5:00 A.M.

In the morning received a telegram from Shahjahanpur sent by Om Prakash, given at 19:20 on 19 February reading, "Master admitted Vivekananda Hospital Niralanagar Lucknow delirious condition." It is an Express telegram and has taken 36 hours!

At 3:30 P.M. Seshan's wife received a reply telegram from Shri Kalyanakrishnan, IAS, "Swamiji well looked after. Abdominal pain, X-ray done. Radiological tests in progress. Diagnosis in day or two." The message was dispatched from Lucknow at 11:15 A.M. on 20 February.

A reply was sent reading, "Your telegram thanks. Awaiting details of diagnosis. Hope no cause for anxiety." It was sent at 17:45 hours.

22 Feb. 74 - Friday

At about noon a telegram was received from Umesh sent from Lucknow at 19:00 yesterday evening. It says Master is progressing. Umesh has called Sarvesh from Virudhunagar to go over, and wants old medical reports collected from us here — I don't know if we have any.

23 Feb. 74 - Saturday

Sarvesh arrived from Virudhunagar en route Lucknow. Appa has received a letter dated 21 February from Kasturi from Lucknow which says from 16th to 19th Master was in a very serious condition — bad headache, lolling of head from side to side almost ceaselessly, high fever, lung congestion, unconsciousness, delirium, and inability to recognise anyone. They suspected cerebral meningitis at Shahjahanpur, and after Shri Mimani reached there, they decided to shift Master to Lucknow. Lucknow doctors examined Master and ruled out the cerebral meningitis, saying that the lung congestion had, to some extent, interfered with blood circulation to the brain. On 21st Master has been pronounced to be out of danger. He has become conscious, talks coherently and recognises persons. No fever now, lung congestion removed.

I telephoned Ramanlal Mimani at Calcutta who told me much the same thing.

24 Feb. 74 - Sunday

Sarvesh left for Lucknow. My nephew Srivatsa's *upanayanam* was performed.

25 Feb. 74 - Monday

I left for Lucknow by Delhi Link Express at 8:10 A.M. with T.T. Jagannathan, my brother-in-law, accompanying me.

27 Feb. 74 - Wednesday

Arrived at Lucknow at 13:35 hours after a long and tedious journey of just over 53 hours. Chi. Sarvesh met us at the station and took us by cycle rickshaw to Niralanagar. He himself reached Lucknow only last night at 10:30 P.M. — many hours late. We eat at Mr. R.N. Saxena's house, but stay 50 feet away at Mr. S.N. Saxena's place. After a bath at the latter's place, we went to Mr. R.N. Saxena's place (father-in-law of Umesh) where we had lunch and then left for the Vivekananda Polyclinic, about three quarters of a mile away, on foot. We arrived there at 3:00 P.M. and found Kasturi, Nasib Chand, Narayan Sahai, Bishnu Sahai and some others around Master. Master was awake, fully conscious and recognised me immediately on arrival. I was told that he had been delirious for nearly 5 days from the 19th, and also had lost his memory for quite some time, during which time, according to Kasturi, he recognised no one except her. It was only on 25th evening that the delirious state left and he regained his memory. According to Kasturi Master had forgotten even Lalaji, and also the fact that he himself was the President of the Mission. "Which Lalaji? About whom are you speaking? I don't know him." He is reported to have said. What terrified Kasturi at one stage was the fact that Master's intercommunication with Lalaji seemed to have been interrupted for a long time at that period. Kasturi said that at one stage the doctors had been baffled and could do nothing — except to negate a diagnosis of cerebral meningitis made at Shahjahanpur. She then 'read' his condition and found the life cell dull, with surrounding nerves inflamed. She said she had got medical confirmation of this from another doctor who, however, was not in attendance. She claimed that over two nights she 'worked' and cleared this, and only thereafter Master regained memory. Kasturi said she had not slept for 14 days and 14 nights continuously — and looked ill herself and in much need of rest. She was anxious that I should take Master away at once to Madras — for which purpose I have come. But Master, who has already cajoled doctors into discharging him tomorrow morning, is adamant on going back to Shahjahanpur. His discharge papers are ready and Kashiram Agarwal comes early tomorrow morning with a car to take him back.

Everyone feels that Master will be neglected at Shahjahanpur and are afraid of a relapse setting in.

Kasturi told me how Mr. X had tried his very best to prevent Master being removed to hospital. He kept on saying that Master was progressing. It was only when Raman Lal Mimani came to Shahjahanpur from Calcutta that he and Kashiram Agarwal could force a decision — and even that after a violent outburst from Mr. X, "Babuji is progressing. Why do you wish to take him away from here? I have full authority over him. What do you think, that you can buy him by giving Rs. 50,000?" and so on...! Finally Raman Lal Mimani is said to have threatened him with mobilisation of the opinion of all the members of the Mission, after which he conceded the point and agreed to Master's hospitalisation at Lucknow.

However Master is unwilling to go to Madras now. He said, "I know that you have come only to take me away with you. And of course I shall come to Madras. This I promise, but only after my health is restored somewhat. And this can happen only in my own house. As soon as my health is restored I shall definitely come to Madras. There is also some very necessary work which I have to do, which I can only do from here. Without completing this work I cannot find rest anywhere. But I make this promise to you that after two or three weeks I shall surely come to Madras."

So I stopped persuading him and agreed to his going back to Shahjahanpur.

Outside, on the fourth floor roof-top lawn of the hospital I asked Kasturi whether she knew what this urgent work was, and whether Master could not complete it from Madras. She answered that one matter over which Master is worried is the marriage of Sarvesh which he desires to finalise, now that Sarvesh himself is here. The other matter she explained at great length. "When our Babuji Maharaj came out of the condition of delirium, he told me that he had to carry out some very essential work now — and this was about his representation. He asked me, 'Kasturi, whoever I may appoint as my representative, will you co-operate with that person, and help him to carry on the work of the Mission? And will you help him to conduct the affairs of the Mission with your full co-operation?' Brother all that I said was, 'Whomsoever you may appoint as your representative I shall think him to be my brother and give him every possible co-operation for the growth and spread of the Mission.' Then Babuji said, 'To represent me, I have already selected Parthasarathi, and it is only he that I am going to appoint as my Representative.' But dear brother, please never tell him that you have heard this matter from me because he does not want this matter to become common knowledge yet. Perhaps it is of this work that he was speaking."

My own fears of the past nearly five years seem to be coming true. Ever since the middle of 1971 I have had the feeling, amounting at times to total conviction, that I am going to be appointed Master's Representative and given the job of running the Mission — today sees the public utterance of this idea for the first time. Naturally I am elated that Master's choice should fall on me, but I am also deeply worried by the tremendous responsibility I shall have to shoulder.

Kasturi told me she will not go to Shahjahanpur with Master tomorrow. She feels, and looks, quite ill and exhausted. She, therefore, proposes to leave on the 1st of March for Delhi and go on to Modinagar.

We were with Master till 8:00 P.M. Kasturi left for her brother G.D. Chaturvedi's residence. Jagan and I went back to Shri R.N. Saxena's place, had dinner, and came back to the hospital to stay with Master till 11:00 P.M. Narayan Sahai left for Kanpur.

28 Feb. 74 - Thursday (Lucknow)

To the hospital at 9:00 A.M., after calling on Mr. Satagopan, manager of Rallis, and father-in-law of P.S. Vasu, to telephone Delhi for my own onward travel reservations. Master cheerful — was having a beard trim and haircut done. Master left at 11:00 A.M. in an Ambassador car with Kashiram Agarwal, daughter Chhaya, Bhitto, and Sarvesh. Kasturi went with her brother. Jagan and I returned to Umesh's place. Umesh will go back to Madras from here without visiting Shahjahanpur.

Jagan, my brother-in-law, and I left Lucknow by the Punjab Mail at 4:00 P.M. and arrived Shahjahanpur at 8:00, approximately one and a half hours late. We reached Master's place at 8:30 P.M., and I was assigned my usual bed in Master's bedroom. Chhaya will stay for a few days to nurse Master.

1 Mar. 74 - Friday (Shahjahanpur)

At Lucknow itself Master agreed to cancel the proposed overseas tour 1974. Since no typist was available, I drafted two circulars, one for Indian centres and the other for overseas ones, typed them myself and gave them to our Press for printing. Spent nearly three hours typing addresses on 102 envelopes for dispatch of the circulars. My part of the work was over by 3:00 P.M. Master agreed to my suggestion to call Don and Jackie Sabourin from Madras to nurse him. They are both trained and registered nurses, and will be able to nurse him with professional competence. I sent an express telegram to Appa reading,

"Request Don and Jackie proceed Shahjahanpur immediately to nurse Master. Master better. No anxiety."

Master then asked me to send a telegram to Shri Bhairon Prasad at Lakhimpur, "Sarvesh here. Send Bartariya Sunday." Shri Bartariya is the father of the girl proposed to wed Sarvesh.

In the morning Master told me that power had begun to descend into me. Now, at 3:30 P.M. I felt tired, and went to sleep. I slept like a drunkard till 6:00 P.M. — a very very deep sleep, which could not be differentiated from unconsciousness. When I went in to see Master he asked me how I had slept and I described my deep sleep to him. Master said, "Sabash! I am very happy. Now I am telling you one thing, when my condition started opening up, I slept for 14 days! Look here, this does not mean that this should happen with everybody, but I am extremely happy because this has happened to you. Do you remember that I had told you that I have some very important work to do? I now wish that you should take up the work of the Mission upon yourself. Of course I am there, but I have to do some other work. I have prepared three persons for this work, and you are one, Shri Raghavendra Rao is another, and Dr. S.P. Srivastava is the third person. I wish that in the beginning you should form a committee, or a Cabinet, for yourself in which you may include both these persons. You may organise the work of the Mission in consultation with them. Both are very capable, but your orders shall be final. And whenever you feel that the existence of the Cabinet is no longer necessary you may then dissolve it. The Cabinet should be there to help you, and when you feel that there is no further need for it, then its existence becomes useless. Shall I tell you one thing? For the past four or five years whenever I thought about the Representative of the Master, I have always found him as coming from the South. Dear

Brother, this is the work of Lalaji that in such a short time people can be prepared, and also can be applied to the work. I am now thinking about this. By Lalaji's grace, everything will of course go on well. I wish that the Mission should spread everywhere, and of course it is already spreading and shall continue to spread too. This is Lalaji's blessing. If the weakness of the brain can be removed then I will continue to think over this and other matters. Of course I am not worried about the body, but if the weakness of the brain leaves me, then I shall think a great deal and achieve a great deal too. Now you tell me one thing — what word should I use in making the Representative — the word 'appoint' or something else?"

I suggested the word 'nominate'. Master said, "Yes, it is appropriate. It also sounds nice. I have also spoken about this to Babu Raghunandan Prasad, Maya's father-in-law who is a very capable person. Now do you understand what I am saying? At the appropriate time, I shall send to you signed papers but now I have to consider whether I should reveal this publicly or not. It is quite possible that X and Y may join together and try to create some division, but by Lalaji's grace this work shall be successful, and it must be so. In one way X is not against me. Very recently I had a letter from him that he accepts me as a Master but he is not prepared to accept the Mission. He is only prepared to accept me personally. Look here. I have also been thinking about whether I should call him to Madras, or here, and have some talk with him. I wish to say one more thing to you. I am not worried whether anybody remains in this Mission or not. The Mission will surely grow and spread, and about this there is no doubt. But I do not wish that we ourselves should send anybody out of the Mission. I shall think about this. Maybe I shall call him to Madras and speak to him. All these things have to be thought about. The people of Tirupathi have told me that there is no one there who is annoyed with you or against you. They all have much regard for you; but they are all somewhat annoyed with your father."

Later on, in the evening, Master asked me how I was feeling. I told him I was feeling very very light. Master said, "This is the real thing. Now what is there for me to do! It is all Lalaji's work that within such a short time a person has been prepared, and he has also been entrusted with the work. Except for Him nobody else could have done this."

"I cannot say anything about the past. But I can say one thing, that such a system neither exists today, nor will it exist in the future. Shall I tell you now what is going on inside you (with a mischievous twinkle in his eyes)? In the left-side of your head the state of super-consciousness in the mind has begun to open up. The walls surrounding it are being removed. I have written about this in *Efficacy of Raja Yoga*. I shall tell you one more thing. There are also some signs in you indicating the beginning of intercommunication. Have you experienced something like this?" I answered that once or twice I had had a feeling that something was going to happen, but it was very faint and ephemeral.

2 Mar. 74 - Saturday

During the day, Kashiramji took me to the Hakim for a consultation. Then Jagan and I went to the Ashram. Printed circulars were ready and dispatched — 72 to Indian preceptors and heads of centres, 25 overseas, with 5 more to go abroad — no stamps!

Master called me and discussed all over again about his representation. He said, "Now see, power has started descending into you, and it is also descending into some of the initiated disciples. Saheb, what is to be done when people do not understand that outside this system such things cannot be had. This is Lalaji's work. See, I do not know how power is inserted. This is all His work and He is the only person who can do it. Now I am considering whether I should reveal this matter or not. I shall think about it. I am not afraid of any opposition because the work has to be done and it shall be done. You will see that if X goes on in the same way a great deal of opposition will be created against him. What can I do about it? I had wanted to mention this matter to Y, and I have done so too, but only indirectly. I had told her about it indirectly. It is possible that she has understood something about it. My methods are something unusual. I am always trying to turn people towards me with love. And of course to some extent I am always successful. Now let us see what happens.

"In the beginning, Viraraghavan was very good, but I do not know what has happened to him that he is not working. Really speaking, a man grows only by work. It is a matter for surprise that there are few people who are growing by themselves. In the central region, Raghavendra Rao is progressing very slightly by his own efforts. Kasturi is also progressing but very little. But it is even more surprising that even your father is growing a little by his own efforts! There is not much difference between these three persons, just a little. Now whenever you apply yourself to the work, please think over this thing as to how a person can be made to progress, and what is to be done for it. And now this is all your work."

It was somewhat cold in the evening. Master was feeling slightly off colour, and began to feel what he calls 'palpitations' in the heart. He took three drops of brandy in an ounce of water — which immediately works like magic in calming him. Then laughingly he said, "Look here! It is very cold and if you wish you may take a little brandy. There is some lying with me." I told Him, "You have forbidden alcohol." Then Master answered, "Look here, for the person who has attained contact with Reality, for such a person there are no rules, and he can do whatever he chooses. Now look here! Heat is produced by eating potatoes. Alcohol has the same effect. But for a person who has attained contact with Reality, for such a person there are no rules. But of course we have to be afraid of setting a bad example." .....laughing..... He said, "People should not start saying, 'Sir, my guru is a man who drinks.' Therefore it is a matter of setting the right example. I have also told you earlier what Lalaji told me — do you remember it?"

This refers to a time when Master was asked to eat chicken for his broken-down health. He asked Lalaji for permission to eat it. Lalaji is said to have answered, "Do not ask me such things. If I permit you, others will think they can also do it. But one thing I will tell you. I have assigned you spiritual work, and to fulfil it is your duty. In doing that work, whatever you may have to do to keep your body fit, you may do. Do not ask me further." This he told me some three or four years ago.

Later at night I found Master alone and requested his permission to make a confession. I said, "Babuji, for the past four or four and a half years an idea has been cropping up in my mind that you will make me your representative. I do not know how this had entered my mind, and I did not tell you about this because I was afraid that you may have thought that I wanted to sit in your place, or that I have some greed for your position." Babuji answered, "How could I ever think like that? Look here, good or bad, whatever it may be, you should have told it to me. I knew that this idea had come into your mind."

I felt very foolish when I heard this, and thought of all the occasions, when, sitting in his presence at Shahjahanpur, Madras, Greve Strand and elsewhere, I had struggled to suppress this thought when it came up, lest he should 'read' it and chastise me. I explained to Master that I could sincerely say I have never coveted this 'representation' and that the very thought of it, and the responsibilities carried with it, had terrified me.

3 Mar. 74 - Sunday

At about 8:30 A.M. Mr. Bartariya came from Lakhimpur, met Master, saw Sarvesh, and approved of the proposed alliance of his daughter with Sarvesh from his side.

From 10 to noon I was at the Ashram with Kashiram Agarwal and Shri Krishna Tandon, giving final instructions.

In the afternoon Master disclosed his ideas for Ashram work and finances — he has 3.56 lakhs in the bank account for Ashram construction! He then wrote a letter to Vera Davies, dictated to me and written by me. In this letter he revealed that even when delirious he was active in work! He told me, "Look here. I was of course delirious but even in that condition I was engaged in my work, and whatever I had thought or had said, I remember it all." He cautioned me to keep my tongue under strict control, particularly in blessings, etc., "Keep your tongue under control especially in the matter of giving blessings. If you tell some boy that he will become a saint, it shall happen like that. Of course in your work at your office it does not matter if you become angry with someone, but you should not drown yourself in your heart's condition and say angry things. By your coming, I have been able to stabilise my health in a very short time; otherwise it would have taken a very long time." I asked how this could be. Babuji answered, "Look here, your condition now is such that it is very similar to my own condition, and in such condition there can be an exchange! Have you understood this?"

Received a telegram from Don and Jackie Sabourin to say they will fly to Delhi on 5th evening from Madras and reach Shahjahanpur on 7th morning.

At night, when we were sitting with Master before leaving for Delhi, at around 9:45 P.M., he inter-communed with Lalaji and told me, "Look here. Lalaji Saheb is saying that you are not to be concerned about any special powers. You are to go on doing your work, and your attention should not go towards such powers."

We bid Master good-bye and left for the station at 10:00 P.M. With only one First Class berth between Jagan and me, we managed to sleep comfortably and got to Delhi.

4 Mar. 74 - Delhi (Monday)

Krishnaswamy of Delhi centre met us at the New Delhi Station and informed us that Kasturi had left Delhi for Modinagar only yesterday.

In the evening I took satsangh at Mr. Joshi's house in R.K. Puram. Steen of Denmark was present, but leaves tonight for home.

7 Mar. 74 - Thursday

Returned to Madras by G.T. Express — arrived one and a half hours late at 12:30 P.M. Mr. T.T. Krishnamachari expired at 12:55 P.M., and I had to go to Mr. T.T. Narasimhan's residence for the funeral.

8 Mar. 74 - Friday

At 2:30 P.M. felt a strong vibration on left side of head.

9 Mar. 74 - Saturday (Madras)

My father's youngest brother Shri C.A. Bakthavathsalan expired of a massive heart attack at 8:00 A.M. May Master grant him peace.

10 Mar. 74 - Sunday

Early morning dream at about 5:00 A.M. I am sitting on the carrier of a cycle, and someone, whose face I can't see, is taking me on the cycle; he drives me over a lonely road, wide, well-tarred, but empty of traffic — up and down some rolling countryside. Finally we climb a somewhat steeper hill and go down the other side, free-wheeling. We then come to the foot of a steep, high hill, all rock, where we alight from the cycle and commence walking up. Initially the going is easy, but as the hill steepens, becomes difficult. I then see that the hill surface appears pock-marked with footsteps cut into it, close together, as big as, or slightly larger than, a foot. The surface of the hill is something like that of a 'Sita-Phal', only the surface pock-marks are not raised but are concave, like saucers. I climb up wearily, using these steps and at the summit there is a small wayside shrine, hardly two feet in height. I ignore this. In the distance, I feel, or get the impression, is my destination. I don't see it but 'feel it' in some way. At this stage I woke up.

20 Mar. 74 - Wednesday

Early morning dream. I am in my car with driver Rajan driving. We reach the St. George Fort area of Madras but the whole place is different. Firstly there is no Fort. Only a big restaurant. I go up to the 1st floor and see choice vegetables and fruit displayed. Some 'Rastali' bananas are lovely. I want to buy some, but having no money on me I go to find my driver. I come down, and at the car-park see Rajan. He has no money. I walk up north and find a huge 'welcome-arch' type of structure through which the road passes. It is solid brick, the thickness or width being as much as that of a large house. Inside, on one side, a sannyasi is seated. I pass through and on the other side come to the beach. Here Rajan produces some currency notes, large as towels, for Rs. 2 and Rs. 3 but worthless. The dream ends.

22 Mar. 74 - Friday (Madurai)

At 2:30 P.M. at Valamjee Mansion while on my cot I was transmitting, doing work assigned by Master. After ten minutes or so, I suddenly had a vision of Bakthu's corpse lying on our drawing room floor at 'Gayathri', and as I looked at it, it disappeared and a small, laughing baby, very young, appeared in its place. The impression was of a girl baby, though of this I can't be certain. Does this indicate Bakthu having been reborn? Must refer this to Master.

25 Mar. 74 - Monday

Received a registered envelope from Shahjahanpur containing Master's letter C/269/SRCM dated 19th/23rd March, one certificate, and a letter for Krishna wishing him success at the PUC exam which commences 2:00 P.M. today. Krishna delighted and highly confident now.

My letter is extracted in parts "I have issued a certificate which I am sending with this letter. Preserve this certificate as a valuable document. You start work giving transmission to the East and West and helping the men throughout the world. The work bestowed upon me by

Nature and the Master will be coming to you sometimes after. Your approach is to the Central Region and almost all of these sixty-five points are illumined. Absorbancy is itself coming fastly to welcome you." The certificate, on a printed form like our preceptor's certificate, is dated 23rd March, and in it Master has nominated me to be his Representative and the President of the Mission in his succession.

Posted on the 23rd, it has arrived today, I think almost 10 years to the day since I joined the Mission in 1964, just a couple of weeks after Basant Panchami.

Replied to Master in the evening.

27 Mar. 74 - Wednesday

Letter from Don and Jackie Sabourin from Shahjahanpur. Master progressing after a brief period of spinal pain brought on by an 'old ossification'. Don has revealed that Master's letter of 19th as also the special certificate were both dictated to him by Master.

1 Apr. 74 - Monday

I have been engaging myself in the work given by Master, mainly in the mid-day period from 1:30 P.M. on, and at night. I do it lying on my bed. I seem to slip off into total oblivion almost as soon as I commence, and sometimes when I get back to consciousness say after 20 or 30 minutes, there is no awareness of the time lapsed. It often feels as if I have been 'away' for ages, but on seeing the clock I find it is half an hour and then get on with the work again. Except for the initial *sankalpa* at the commencement, there is no awareness of the work being done, how it is done or even 'when'. I feel much lassitude when I 'come-out' of this condition which, I feel, must be the *turiya* state.

4 Apr. 74 - Thursday

Postcard from Master dated 27 March received today. He writes to say he is generally feeling better though weakness persists.

This was supported by a letter dated the first April from Shahjahanpur written by Don and Jackie Sabourin on the eve of their departure. Don says that Master is taking about three times the quantity of food he used to just before he fell ill, is sleeping for about 11 hours and is generally much better — putting on some weight too — though giddiness on walking is still there. Don writes that Meera's marriage has also been settled and will be in October, followed by Sarvesh's marriage in November.

5 Apr. 74 - Friday

Dream early morning — confused — I only remember a number of people are present, both overseas abhyasis and Indians. Some thoughts about 'automatic' working in spiritual field came to mind — in sub-human creation all is automatic, i.e., 'unwilled', or to put it in another way 'instinctive' — so no sin or virtue! At highest levels like Master's there is certainly will-power but, in a sense **no will** — that is Master has no will of his own, being in a state of surrender to the Grand Master, but the enormous power he has been endowed with is in action, manifested as his will-power. Here too action can be considered 'automatic', i.e., **unwilled** by Master himself in the strict sense of that term. So at highest level too there can be action, pure action, devoid of the concomitants, sin and virtue, success and failure, etc. It is in between where humans exercise their own will that action is not natural or automatic but is personally guided, and it is at this stage of evolution that man is subject to the operation of the law of karma!

25 Apr. 74 - Thursday

It seems I am having insomnia for some time now. As far as I can remember the trouble seems to have started soon after my return from Shahjahanpur around mid-March. I am unable to sleep at nights — previously I used to fall asleep very soon after going to bed — now it takes me a few hours of tossing and turning before I achieve sleep. There is however no discomfort except a tendency to rise late in the morning.

Yesterday morning Kasturi appeared in a dream. She was in bed, covered up to her chin, and when I felt her forehead I found her to be having high fever.

This morning after 6:00 A.M. I had a dream. A new bridge has been completed, I am told (it seems to be something connected with my company) and I proceed to inspect it. Then I find myself in a store-room with B. Ramachandran. Later I find myself outside a large shopping area with B. Ramachandran and B. Rangappa. We go in. Suddenly I find Ramachandran looking green and very tired. I ask him to wash his face and go home. He leaves us. Rangappa and I go on but I find that instead of being in a shopping arcade I am in a very large maze, solidly built with doors, roof, long passages twisting and turning about. Rangappa and I come out at one point which I don't recognise. In the distance the sunlight is playing on a castle or palace-like edifice, all gold and glitter. It is a vision of something sought. Elsewhere it is murky. In front of us there are a large number of peacocks being fed. Rangappa is watching them. I drag him away and enter the maze again, looking for a way back. I hear a door open and close behind me. I look back and Rangappa is missing. There are several doors on both sides of the narrow passage, all closed, and I don't know into which one he has gone. I feel terribly alone and lonely. At this moment I woke up.

1 May 74 - Wednesday

Chitti Shakuntala, my aunt, passed away — of heart attack while I was at Mayavaram. I rushed back in my car just in time for her funeral.

14 May 74 - Tuesday

While at Madurai I had a dream. I am in the verandah of a large house. Just two long verandahs in front of a row of rooms, the two at an angle of say 160 degrees or so, with a central hub-like construction where they join.

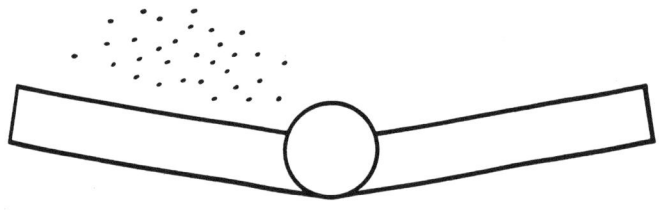

I am on the left verandah. I feel a lot of persons are gathered on the lawn in front. A corpse, covered with a white shroud, is in the right wing. I don't see it but I 'know' it is there. I also know it has to lie there for three days and I wonder how it can be kept for so long. Already a mild stink of decomposition is perceptible. I woke up at this point.

15 May 74 - Wednesday

Dream at Madurai. I am in open country. Facing me is a small hill. It has a tunnel-like entrance at one end, with a door. I enter the door and try to go in and cross through the hillock, but I am afraid and so I come out. Then I find that the hillock has another entrance with a door at the other end. I enter it at that side, walk through for some time, but return.

An idea came that I should write a book on the Master! This came during evening group satsangh which I conducted at the centre.

16 May 74 - Thursday (Madurai)

Dream. I am at the back of a large house. It is late dusk, rather dark and not much visibility. Two other per-

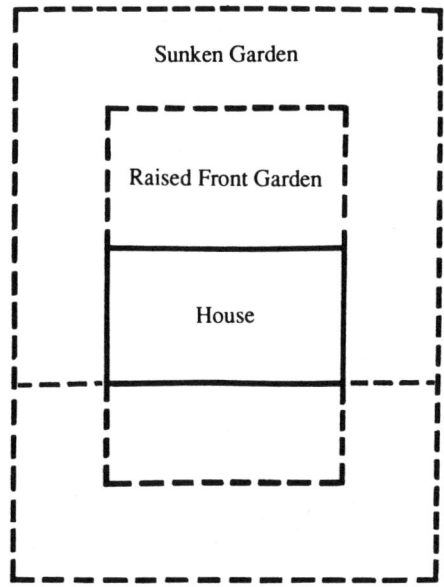

sons are with me. The house is built on a raised area, and there is a sunken garden surrounding it. The house area is separated from the garden area by a wire fence. There is a stray cow in the front garden. We are wondering how to chase it out. Suddenly it runs into the back garden where we are standing. It goes through the wire fence, and enters the sunken garden. We give up the idea of chasing it out. I then find myself inside the house, involved in a party of some sort, eating delicious food.

19 May 74 - Sunday (Coimbatore)

Early morning dream. I find myself on the top floor of a three story house. I am on the landing — all wooden — with my brother Kothand. There is no staircase at all, or ladder or anything — just the bare landing. I have to go down. I wonder how to get down. It is about 20 feet to the next floor below. Some women are there and taunt me, saying they jumped from above. So I too jump, and find myself safe and unhurt.

20 May 74 - Monday (Coimbatore)

Early morning dream. Master and Kasturi are at Madras and I am with them. But the place is neither our house Gayathri, nor Umesh's house at Besant Nagar. I inform Master that Shri K.R. Subramanian, B.E., has been granted provisional permission. He smiles and says, "Yes. Well done."

Actually KRS was granted the permission later at 7:15 A.M.

I have started work on a proposed book *My Master* — the writing commenced in earnest yesterday evening. Actual writing started at Munnar on Friday 17th May.

12 Jun. 74 - Wednesday

Had booked to go to Calcutta by air today in response to Shri Raman Lal Mimani's invitation to the wedding of the daughter of his brother Shri Mohan Lal. Master is to arrive in Calcutta tomorrow. But when I went to the airport in the evening I found that seats were not confirmed, and no seat was available. Returned home disappointed. This is the second time that this has happened. Sent a letter to Master through N.R. Dugar who goes today.

14 Jun. 74 - Friday

Posted long letter to Master to Shahjahanpur along with type-script of first four chapters of *My Master* for approval. I am planning the book in two parts, Part I The Man, and Part II The Master. Let us see how it comes off. I hope to be able to complete writing by August end at the latest.

B. Rajagopal returned from Calcutta in the evening. Says Master is just a bag of bones, and quite weak.

15 Jun. 74 - Saturday

Deep, very deep sleep early morning. Woke up only at 7:30 A.M. as if from out of *samadhi*. Surely Master has done something today! Feeling of depression throughout the day.

Rajagopal told me yesterday that Master has moved him to the 3rd, *agni*, point.

15 Jul. 74 - Monday

S. Sankaranarayanan (formerly of TTK & Co. as NR's PA — now doing business in ground-nut cake) returned from Delhi after a 24 hour visit to Master at Shahjahanpur. He reports Master to be well. Shri Raghavendra Rao of

Raichur and Kasturi, both of whom visited Master for Meera's wedding, have also written to say that Master is now very nearly his old healthy self! Lalaji be Praised for this. Under the circumstances celebration of Master's 75th Birthday as an All India Programme to be held in Hyderabad late October has been authorised.

22 Aug. 74 - Thursday

Appa left for Delhi. He will meet H of Munich at Delhi and take him to Shahjahanpur, reaching Shahjahanpur on 30 August.

23 Aug. 74 - Friday

Completed writing *My Master.* It is in two parts, each containing five chapters. Part I is titled "The Master" and the five chapters respectively are: The First Exposure; The Environment; Tolerance; Duty; Love. Part II is titled "His Teaching and Work" and the five chapters respectively are: The Way of the Spirit; Approach to Liberation; The Role of the Guru; Spiritual Experiences; and the Gift of Liberation. It has come out very well indeed. The chapter on Love, Chapter V, is indeed superb! Even Appa says this is the best book so far written in the Mission, barring of course Master's works.

28 Aug. 74 - Wednesday

My Master goes to press — Kabeer Printing Works — and as matters stand, is scheduled for release next January and during Basant Panchami. Completed typescript, bound, sent to Appa to be handed over to Master.

17 Sep. 74 - Tuesday

Letter dated 3 Sep. 74 from Master (Ref. C/1198) states that on the night of 31st August I have been put in the 3rd

Ring of Splendour!! Re: Chapter on "Love" of the book *My Master*, Master has written, "It is marvellously written."

18 Sep. 74 - Wednesday

Letter from Appa dated 15 September from Lucknow. About the book *My Master* Appa writes, "The typescript corrected by Master is with me and I am to deliver it to you. Master said, 'I had been wanting to write all this down for a long time, but couldn't do so. Now Parthasarathi has done it — I am so glad — this book fills a real need, and will be the best book in Sahaj Marg writings.' He said, 'No preface or introduction is necessary — Judge Saheb cannot write it, S.P. Shrivastav will take months to do it.' I wondered if I could put down his opinion. He said, 'You cannot! You are his father — I cannot write anything like a Preface because I am the subject of the book.'"

21 Sep. 74 - Saturday

Appa returned to Madras.

23 Sep. 74 - Monday

The first 9 galley sheets of *My Master* received from Kabeer Press (31 pages of manuscripts).

6 Oct. 74 - Sunday

N.R. Narayana of Kollegal and R.P. Nanjundiah of Channapatna came to discuss their serious grievances against Shri J. N.R. Narayana wrote to me about 10 days ago and sought an interview, which I gave for today. There was only a hint in his letter of some misunderstanding with Shri J. Now, as a result of today's discussions and letters brought in evidence etc., it appears that Shri J has, since 1966, been using Nanjundiah almost as a domestic servant, and has swallowed nearly Rs. 20,000/- of his money — not as cash but in kind! Shri J is reported to be making demands on Kollegal abhyasis too, and Narayana reports an expenditure of nearly Rs. 1,500/- over the last two years by three persons. According to Nanjundiah, our brother K.V. Abhayahumar was Shri J's first victim. Also Ramachandra Rao of Bangalore. Narayana wrote to the Bangalore preceptor Shri Janardhan, complaining about Shri J, but Janardhan replied that he should resolve the differences himself, and blamed Narayana for the existence of such misunderstandings! Narayana then wrote to Sarnad, who replied in more or less the same way. Then Narayana appealed to Raghavendra Rao of Raichur, whose reply too was of no significant help. Only after all this he appealed to me. Nanjundiah has written a very detailed letter to Shri Raghavendra Rao but no reply was received. It is apparent, however, that Shri Raghavendra Rao has written to Shri J because after some days Shri J came himself to Nanjundiah, pretended great friendship and returned Rs. 2,050/- after asking for accounts. A bad bad case — how am I to take it up with Master?

11 Oct. 74 - Friday

Dream early in the morning — once again of my need to go to the bathroom to clear my bowels — it is dark but I find a large building, with a large bathroom on one side, the side nearest to me. It is well lit up (as against previous dream of this same nature where the bathroom was generally dark) and has a main door, then a pair of flap doors. I enter the bathroom. Then I hear some commotion outside. A man runs into the bathroom, as if to escape something. He is followed by two or three more who want to catch him. Some also jump into the bathroom through a window.

The man puts up a fight. I find a small stool which I pick up and throw at the crowd. I wake up at this point.

12 Oct. 74 - Saturday

Appa received a post-card from Kasturi from Modinagar, where, at the very end, she mentions that Vera Davies has passed away. There is no indication of when, or how.

Dear Vera, such a delicate, pure and sensitive soul which shrank from every contact with the world, while being outwardly so cheerful and active in it. May Master grant her all that she sought, and more, and grant her eternal peace. May Master also grant Elidir, her bereaved husband, solace in this time of great grief and sorrow. Little did I imagine that when Master and I said goodbye to her at London on the 22nd May 1972 we were seeing her for the very last time.

16 Oct. 74 - Wednesday

I had a new experience while conducting satsangh at the Madurai centre at 7:00 P.M. The sitting had commenced. About five minutes later the thought of the Adi Guru of the Mission came into my mind. The transmission was very subtle and blissful. But try as I would, I could not remember the name of Lalaji for fully 10 minutes! The idea kept recurring that 'He' is the Adi Guru, but the name by which 'He' is known was totally forgotten!

17 Oct. 74 - Thursday

Took satsangh at Trichy at 7:15 P.M. — about 8 members present at Ashok Bhavan. I have for the last few months noticed that after giving a sitting, a mood of sadness seems to descend into me. It is a general sadness, without any specific content or direction. This has been there for some months now, I cannot remember how many.

21 Oct. 74 - Monday

Accompanied by B. Rajagopal, I left for Hyderabad by the Express Train at 1:15 P.M. to participate in Master's 75th Birthday Celebrations to be held there on 24th and 25th. Shri N.S. Rao is on the same train as also Shri S.R. Sukaswami, his wife and two daughters, all of Coimbatore. Shri Shastri of Kavali and his wife joined the train at Kavali. Also from Madras are Shri D. Chandrasekhar and Shri Ramanan, both of our Bhavanisagar centre. Also Dasarathan of Trichy centre. These are the people I know of. I am going by train so as to be able to meet Master on arrival at the airport — he arrives tomorrow from Delhi.

22 Oct. 74 - Tuesday (Hyderabad)

Arrived Secunderabad at 8:40 A.M., nearly 40 minutes late. Shri R. Rangappa of Virudhunagar, who preceded us by a day, was there to receive us, along with his brother-in-law Suresh and a car. We proceeded to Abid Road Taj Mahal Hotel, and on telephoning our Mission Ashram, discovered to our dismay that Master's plane arrives at 8:00 A.M. and brothers Kumaraswamy and others had already gone to Begumpet airport to receive him. We telephoned the airport to find that the plane had already arrived. We had a quick wash and rushed up to Domalguda. Master is accompanied by his two grand-daughters Meera and Ninni, who also came by air. His eldest son Prakash has also arrived, by train. Master looked very well — almost his former self. He was, however, rather distant in his manner and after greeting him I moved away. We stayed a few minutes and went back to the hotel to bathe.

In the afternoon we went back to Domalguda and spent half-an-hour with Master.

Mrs. Birthe Haugaard of Denmark, Mrs. Antonietta Bernardi of Rome, and Clara Scramoncin, a French woman working with the F.A.O. in Rome, all came with Master on the same plane. I met Clara for the first time when I went to see Master this morning.

In the evening I took these three, along with Peter Pederson of Denmark who has also come, for dinner at Kwality along with B. Rajagopal and Rangappa.

I asked Master about my 16 October experience when I could not remember Lalaji's blessed name. Master explained that this indicates absorbency, very deep, in one's condition.

I referred to him my melancholic condition after giving sittings, which I have noticed for several months now. Master answered that when a person transmits from a lower level than his own approach, then this melancholy sets in. The proper thing is to transmit from one's own approach.

23 Oct. 74 - Wednesday (Hyderabad)

Large groups of abhyasis have started arriving into Hyderabad. Two spacious halls, the Jain and Kutchi Bhavans in Eden Bagh have been rented to be available from this morning to 26th night. The halls are adequate but the approach is very bad and the halls are both behind a main road, and are situated in an obscure location.

Due to official preoccupations, since as usual I have to combine official and Mission work on this visit, I could not meet Master or talk to him.

24 Oct. 74 - Thursday

All assembled at Kutchi Bhavan at 8:00 A.M. Under Sister Kasturi's leadership the abhyasis assembled prayed for Master's long life and good health for 15 minutes. Then the gathering broke up for breakfast. I went back to the hotel as the next session commences only at 10:00 A.M. When I returned at 9:45 A.M. I found G.S. Mani of Madurai on the stage, singing two of his special compositions on Master in Hindi. The programme had been advanced 20 minutes without notice. Mani was followed by our own S. Narayanaswamy of Madras. Then the address of welcome was read out, followed by Master reading out his own message. After this I was asked to release the Souvenir which I did after a short talk — and received a free copy of the Souvenir (priced atrociously at Rs. 25/-) for my trouble. This was followed by the Chairman's address delivered by Shri Kumaraswamy. A Hindi 'geet' specially composed by Sister Kasturi for this occasion was sung by her. The occasion was embellished by a rather unnecessary stage performance by her brother Prahlad's two sons, and Raju. After this Dr. Chandrika Prasad of Roorkee and some others spoke. The meeting ended at 11:00 A.M.

My personal participation in this celebration was to the extent related above.

I attended the evening session for a brief while.

25 Oct. 74 - Friday

Since my boss Shri T.T. Narasimhan arrived from Madras in the morning I was unable to meet Master. I took TTN to Master at our Domalguda Ashram at 3:15 P.M., and he had a short individual sitting with him. Earlier, I had taken Shri Pidathala Ranga Reddy, the finance minister of this state, to Master, I think on Wednesday morning. He did not start meditation. Shri Ranga Reddy asked Master for advice on how to bring peace and happiness to our people. He had earlier mentioned that he had just returned from the U.K. Master asked him, "You have been to the West. Now tell me, where did you find the people more happy and contented? There or here?" Shri Ranga Reddy answered, "Our people are certainly more happy and contented, Swamiji!" Master smiled and said, "You see this! They are very rich and prosperous materially, but we are more happy and more peaceful! So now you may decide what to do!"

In the evening a preceptors' conference was convened without any prior information to me. When I casually bumped into Shri Raghavendra Rao of Raichur at our ashram at 4:30 P.M., he said the meeting would be held this evening at the Kutchi Bhavan. When I rushed up there at 5:30 P.M., I found all the preceptors assembled in Jain Bhavan with Master presiding.

Shri Raghavendra Rao started off by saying that false and baseless matters were being referred by preceptors against each other to Master, and this was causing Master unnecessary worry and sadness. He claimed that such complaints against one preceptor were made by abhyasis to another preceptor merely to curry favour, so that they could be made organisers, preceptors and so on. He wanted the meeting to decide what should be done, and how to protect preceptors against such vile and untrue attacks.

I realised that the whole thing was precipitated by my referring Jahagirdar's case to Master, on a complaint raised by Shri N.R. Narayana of Kollegal and Shri R.P. Nanjundiah of Channapatna. I told the meeting that though I was a preceptor, I was also General Secretary of the Mission functioning under the powers and authority vested in me by the President, and the Bye-laws and Constitution of the Mission. I stated that no preceptors' meeting was competent to decide on the General Secretary's work or method of reporting — this could only be done by the President and the Working Committee of the Mission.

Shri K. Ramakrishna Chetty, IPS of Anantapur was highly critical saying, "We are talking about strengthening the organisation. I don't think there is an organisation at all. If there had been an organisation, what was it doing when Master was so seriously ill at Lucknow? Why were all centres not notified of his condition and progress? We all love him so much but we were denied any news of him. I knew he was sick only when I received the circular prohibiting visitors till 31 July 74. What was the so-called organisation doing all the time?" And so on. I told him that I had personally written two letters to Shri Kumaraswamy to Hyderabad, and two to Shri Raghavendra Rao of Raichur — and I had expected that those interested in Master's health would refer to these two centres for information. I felt like asking Shri Chetty what he thought of an organisation which tolerated a preceptor keeping silent to at least 25 reminders saying that he owed the Mission Rs. 160/- or so for books purchased by him nearly three years ago? The person was, of course, Mr. Chetty himself, who has not even acknowledged **our** letter so far, and of course the money has to be written off. But I kept quiet as I did not want to make matters worse.

I then told the meeting in a general way that the Mission organisation was doing its best, but was handicapped by the fact that the General Secretary (myself) was a person residing at Madras, far away from Mission H.Q., and the Joint Secretary at Shahjahanpur had not shown his face to Master for almost three years now. I suggested that they select a person to be appointed General Secretary to function from Shahjahanpur itself, and that I be allowed to step down. I added that I had advised Master to do this even when I was with him in Germany in 1972 June.

Shri Raghavendra Rao could say nothing except to halfheartedly say, "Brother you are doing excellent work.

It is immaterial from where you work. You feel the difficulty only when you think Madras is far away from Shahjahanpur."

Kumari Kasturi Chaturvedi was kind enough to add, "However much a person may grow, some childishness always remains in him. There is something remaining even in our Secretary."

The meeting ended on this note.

After this the assembly shifted to Kutch Bhavan where Shri Kumaraswamy took the chair, and formally presented a purse to our Rev. Master — the amount was not disclosed. We then had a sitting for 20 minutes — I meditated standing as I could not enter the hall.

I returned to the hotel after this at 8:30 P.M. At around 9:30 P.M. Mrs. Antonietta Bernardi, Mrs. Birthe Haugaard, Clara Scramoncin, a French lady working with F.A.O. Rome, and a Danish young man Peter Pederson — all came to my room. Birthe and Toni leave tomorrow morning by air for Delhi, and have come to say good-bye. Birthe also apologised to me for her 'attack' on me earlier this evening at the preceptors' meeting. She had then said, "I am very disappointed with having come to Hyderabad. I had hoped to meet the General Secretary and have a confidential talk regarding the Denmark Mission work, but this has not been possible because the General Secretary was not available,"... and so on! I told her not to worry about it. But I did tell her that her attack on me was improper since she had, at no time, asked me to meet her for a confidential talk, or indicated in any manner that she wished to see me. They stayed with me till 11:00 P.M. and left.

26 Oct. 74 - Saturday

I went to see Master at 7:30 A.M. and had 20 minutes alone with him. Yesterday's preceptors' meeting had made me furious and I, in turn, was foolishly angry with Master. I accused him of having put up the whole show to insult the General Secretary in public for no fault of his own, and so on. Later when Master said, "I have made a mistake. Now what should I do?" I felt very sorry that I had said all that I had said. Master left for Raichur by car at 9:30 A.M. but due to official work I could not see him off.

B. Rajagopal, Clara Scramoncin and I left Hyderabad by the 9:00 P.M. flight for Madras, arriving at Madras at 10:00 P.M. Clara stays at the Woodlands Hotel.

So ends my visit to Hyderabad to attend the 75th Birthday Celebrations of our Beloved Master!

27 Oct. 74 - Sunday (Madras)

At our weekly satsangh I gave a short review of the Hyderabad celebrations for the benefit of the Madras centre abhyasis.

1 Nov. 74 - Friday

Revered Master arrived from Cuddapah at 7:00 P.M. by the Dadar Express. He was accompanied by Shri Narayana Rao of Gulbarga, Sister Kasturi, Shri Ramachandra Reddy of Cuddapah, his own two grand-daughters Meera and Ninni, and Vijaykumar Agarwal (Mohan's brother-in-law) of Shahjahanpur. After leaving Hyderabad on Friday 25 October, Master has visited Raichur, Anantapur and Cuddapah centres — and has become very weak as a consequence. He was so weak he could hardly stand up, and couldn't walk. I carried him down from the train and put him on one of the bare, cold concrete seats so kindly provided by the Railways. About 50 abhyasis had gathered at Central Station to receive him. My son Krishna brought a wheel chair. We put Master in it. Krishna wheeled it out to the car. We bodily lifted him into the car and drove him to Umesh's new residence. There we brought a cane chair, put Master in it, and four of us, Krishna and myself included, carried him up to the 1st floor flat and put him to bed.

What is wrong with Anantapur that it makes him so sick? The last time he went there it almost killed him. He was sick at Raichur for almost a month after that, and was on the very verge of collapse! K.R.K. Chetty, IPS, our preceptor there has been back-sliding and is reported to be more keen on the Bhagavata and Ramayana Parayana! He has failed to pay up Rs. 160/- or so due from him to the Mission on books purchased by him while he was at Nellore about two and a half years ago! Twenty or more reminders have been sent, but he has not even cared to acknowledge one of them!

We stayed with Master for about one hour and then got back to 'Gayathri' where Appa had brought Kasturi as she, as always, stays with us. I had taken Clara Scramoncin to Besant Nagar, and she had a private session of 45 minutes with Master — she was radiant when she left even though she has been weeping and sick the last three days. She leaves tomorrow early morning for Colombo en route Rome!

2 Nov. 74 - Saturday

I spent the afternoon with Master. Andre Poray who has arrived from Sanary spent some time, and had an individual sitting for over one hour with Master!! I was sitting outside but watched Master's work and found that Andre had been lifted up to *prapanna* stage!

Master is too weak and spent most of the time in bed — not even sitting up. He was quiet most of the day.

3 Nov. 74 - Sunday

Master was unable to conduct our weekly satsangh. I went to him after satsangh and spent two hours in the morning in his company. Kasturi accompanied us. After lunch I went again and spent the evening with Master. On 31 October, Shri S.R. Sukaswami's daughter Sow. Rama Devi and his wife's sister Rajam, accompanied by our preceptor K.R. Subramanian, all arrived from Coimbatore and are staying at 'Gayathri'. Master approved Appa's recommendation to make Mrs. D. Bhaskaramma, wife of our Kavali preceptor, Shri D.S.K. Subramania Sastri, a preceptor. The work has been entrusted to me.

Poray brought some friends of his to see Master.

4 Nov. 74 - Monday

Could go to see Master only for one hour in the evening due to official preoccupation as a result of Dennis Grove's presence in Madras.

5 Nov. 74 - Tuesday

Master was brought to 'Gayathri' by Appa at 9:00 A.M. for the day. I took leave from 11:00 A.M. and joined him. Earlier this morning Mrs. D. Bhaskaramma was granted provisional permission and Master issued the certificate.

Master is quite weak. He received Mr. Hoffman, Secretary to Rukmini Devi of Kalakshetra for the last 20 years, and gave him a short sitting. Andre Poray brought Mr. Hoffman to see Master again.

4:00 P.M. — a grand tea and snacks for over 150 persons was served.

5:30 P.M. Master conducted satsangh — more than 100 abhyasis were present. Master left for Besant Nagar at 9:30 P.M.

6 Nov. 74 - Wednesday

Andre Poray left for Bangalore en route Hubli. He will come back to Madras on 13 November for a few hours before going on to Colombo.

I discussed my 'reading' of Master's work on Andre on 2 November. Master confirmed that my reading was correct and that he had indeed taken Andre up to 'prapanna' stage on 2 November. He added that on 3 November he had taken him up yet higher to the 'prabhu' stage!

Master gave me an individual sitting for 25 minutes at 4:00 P.M. at Besant Nagar. It was superb! It was extraordinarily deep! When it was over I told Master it was 'near-samadhi' condition. Master called Kasturi (who had come there) and asked her to study my condition. She said that my inside was like a single column of purity and purity alone! Master told her that he had taken my *sukshma sharir* out, divided it into three, and cleaned thoroughly the middle layer where some grossness had accumulated.

This morning Kasturi had given me an individual sitting. Immediately on closing my eyes I felt a shower of light descending on me — a soft light spray, as it were. After some time I felt that the whole of Kasturi had vanished. I did not know who was sitting there. Later the whole world contracted into a ball which was inside my heart. Someone seated on that world was transmitting to me from inside me! I then felt the sun inside my head illuminating the whole system from within me. At this stage the transmission came from my right — from the direction of Besant Nagar (the sitting was at 'Gayathri'). I felt my body dissolving off, leaving the earth and the sun. Then these too vanished and nothing was left. The sitting ended at this stage.

7 Nov. 74 - Thursday

Master, accompanied by grand-daughters Meera and Ninni, and by Vijay Kumar Agarwal, left for Delhi by air. The plane was late by almost two hours — he was lying on a sofa in the airport lounge most of the time. He is very weak and the back pain in the lumbar area has been troubling him.

4 Dec. 74 - Wednesday

I got six calico-bound copies of *My Master* from the press. It has come out wonderfully well — six beautiful photographs of Master included. I gave one to Appa who praised it as the "best book of the Mission" and flabbergasted me by asking for my autograph!!

I left for Delhi by air in the evening.

8 Dec. 74 - Sunday (Shahjahanpur)

Left Delhi by car with B. Ramachandran of ITPT, B. Rajagopal and Ravi Varma of Madagascar who has come on transfer to India. We are bound for Shahjahanpur. Ravi and I have been corresponding for nearly three years now, but we met for the first time on Thursday 5 December when he came to Broadway Hotel to see me and had a sitting — and a couple of hours of talk. We reached Shahjahanpur at 3:30 P.M. Master looks very well — far better than when he left Madras. He was very preoccupied with Sarvesh's marriage preparations. We hardly had 10 minutes with him. I gave him one copy of *My Master*. He praised it and was particularly pleased with the photographs. *Tilak* ceremony for Sarvesh performed.

9 Dec. 74 - Monday

We left for Lucknow at 7:00 A.M. by car. Master was awake but still in bed when I bid him good-bye. Ravi Varma left for Delhi by air from Lucknow.

10 Dec. 74 - Tuesday

After completing my company work at Kanpur and Rae Bareilly we three got back to Shahjahanpur at 6:00 P.M. On arrival we learnt of Umesh's miraculous recovery from an injection which was foolishly given to him, and which almost ended in his collapse! Poor Master, his face has lost its richness and glow. How much he has to shoulder! He looked so wan, forlorn and lonely that my heart was flooded with love for him. I sat with him for some time. He suddenly looked at me and said, "My heart has been impatient for the past one week to see you." He lapsed into silence for a few moments, then smiled quietly and said, "It sometimes happens like that."

Sister Kasturi has arrived in Shahjahanpur yesterday. Others who have come for Sarvesh's marriage are Shri Vittal Rao of Raichur, Ramachandra Reddy of Cuddapah, N.R. Gupta and Ramaiah Meda of Hyderabad, V.J. Chandrasekhar of Madurai, Subramaniam of Rajahmundry, Devram Chavda of Navsari, Architect Chauhan from Gulbarga, Uma Shankar Arya of Sitapur and a few others.

Master gave me a Benarsi silk sari for "elder daughter-in-law" as he calls Sulochana. It appears that as Sarvesh's *bhabhi* (elder brother's wife) she had to perform the *kaajal* ceremony last Sunday — and so she gets a sari in absentia as it were! I gave Kasturi a copy of *My Master*.

It is quite cold today.

11 Dec. 1974 - Wednesday

Delhi is represented by Krishnaswamy, Joshi and Dr. Harnam Singh and his brother-in-law Shri Harpal Singh with his wife (Dr. Harnam Singh's sister) and daughter. I understand that Shri Harpal Singh is a preceptor in Naini Tal. Satya Pal arrived this morning from Pathankot. God Bless him — he is so devoted, simple and sincere — surely one of the very best of Master's handiwork.

The *baraat* left at 1:15 P.M. in four cars, one jeep and a bus. We joined the bus party. At Mohammadi 18 miles away we had a brief stop-over for sugar cane juice — deliciously flavoured with ginger and lime juice provided by an abhyasi. The second halt was at Gola, about 42 miles from Shahjahanpur, where a tea-party in 'high tea' style was provided by another abhyasi. The *baraat* reached Lakhimpur-Kheri, 65 miles from Shahjahanpur, at about 6:00 P.M. Shri Bartariya had made excellent arrangements for the party's stay. We had dinner at 10:00 P.M. and went to bed.

Kasturi and I had a long session this morning. She told me that for quite some time now when she sits in meditation by herself, a total void is created, and **then** she finds me seated in the left, with a covering, like a shawl, around my shoulders. "Brother for some time I have been observing that whenever I sit in meditation first of all there is a blankness in which there is nobody, and there is nothing. But now I am observing this new thing brother that after some time in meditation on this side (pointing to left side of the chest, near the heart) I find you seated there wearing the shawl." I thought that 'you' referred to Master and said, "Oh! Babuji?". Kasturi answered, "No. It is you." I asked her what this meant. She said, "I am thinking about it but so far I have not had an idea. I have mentioned about this to Master too, because it is quite possible that this is because of my peculiar attachment to you. But Babuji Maharaj told me that this is not because of any attachment and that it should be because of something else. He said, 'I shall think about it, and let you know.'"

We then had a sitting. I felt I was on a long walk. I pass a small hillock and find Lalaji Saheb watching me from the top of it. I pass on. It is cloudy and overcast. Suddenly there is a small break in the clouds. The sunlight streams in through it. I find Master seated on a cloud, looking at me from above guiding me.

Kasturi said my condition is now such that nothing from the external worldly life can go **into** me; even if I tried it could not happen! She confirmed my reading of the sitting. She however added, "In the end I saw that you are sitting on one side wearing a shawl or blanket, and from somewhere a voice is heard which says, "Sannyasi Parthasarathi has awakened." She continued, "I do not know what is the meaning of this. It is possible that in some past life you were a sannyasi, and that the samskaras of that life have now been cleaned away."

I told her an experience I had last night. I dreamt I was lying down in the guest house upstairs. Kasturi came in and lay down by my side. I felt she was my mother. She lay down on my right, turned towards me, and put her right arm lovingly over my chest. I grasped her arm with both of mine and went to sleep. Kasturi appeared much affected by this. She said, "Brother, there is certainly some past relationship between us. This is certain; otherwise this sort of attachment could not exist." She then added that whenever Master is unwell, she feels motherly towards him.

Later I was with Master. I referred to him the almost universal personal dislike amounting often to hatred against me. Master said, "Yes. What you are saying is correct. I am seeing in my vision that there is a large lake and you are like a fish in it. All around you there are birds waiting to catch you. Now I shall think about this and you should also think about it." After few moments he smiled and said, "Do you know your present condition? It is the condition of *fana*. I have revealed this to you to please you. I have not yet touched the rings which I shall take up later."

After half an hour he came to me and said that while in my speech and talk there was humbleness, it was somewhat less in my letters. "In all the letters that you have written to me I find only humbleness, but you should also try to have the same attitude in your letters to others." He then ran up to me, patted both my shoulders forcefully, and said, "You will grow tremendously and you will do enormous work." Later he told me, "Your condition is what it is. But in you there is that power which is not to be found in anyone else. Raghavendra Rao is very advanced, and also quite capable, but that thing which is in you is not to be found in anyone else."

Later I told Kasturi about what Master had said about my condition being that of *fana*. She laughed and said, "Brother there are two types of *fana*; one is the *fana* of the disciple and the other the *fana* of the Master. The condition of *fana* in you is that of the Master." I asked her how the two were different. She told me that in the abhyasi's *fana* a beam seems to go up from the abhyasi to the Master, whereas in the latter a shower falls from the Master on the abhyasi.

12 Dec. 74 - Thursday

We left Lakhimpur-Kheri at 6:40 A.M. Master was still asleep so we left without being able to take leave of him. We reached Shahjahanpur at 8:30 A.M. We bathed and had lunch, and left at 11:30 A.M. for Delhi. Sister

Kasturi gave me a sitting before I left. I felt very calm and deeply within myself. We reached Delhi at 7:30 P.M.

13 Dec. 74 - Friday (Delhi)

Ravi Varma, Mahajan, a South Indian couple, a Punjabi couple all came for satsangh. Ravi did not sit but left after a few minutes as he is going abroad tomorrow.

14 Dec. 74 - Saturday

Took satsangh at 9:00 A.M. in Joshi's residence. Some 25 abhaysis were present.

I left for Madras by the afternoon flight.

21 Dec. 74 - Saturday

For the last 15 days I have been feeling that I am totally unfit for spirituality.

Jens Clausen of Denmark was here at Madras for two days. He carries back with him some books (25 calico bound copies of *My Master* and 20 *Voice Real*).

22 Dec. 74 - Sunday

Left for Madurai by car with Appa, Sulochana and Krishna with Sulochana's niece Jayashree coming along. At Trichy I delivered copies of *My Master*. Today I have dispatched copies for Bangalore, Kollegal, Chittoor, Kalahasti, Tirupathi, Vijayawada and Rajahmundry! Copies for Shahjahanpur also go tomorrow.

29 Dec. 74 - Sunday

Feeling of my total unfitness for spiritual life persists.

Reverend Babuji Maharaj inspecting the ashram in Shahjahanpur
August, 1974

1975

1 Jan. 1975 - Wednesday (Madras)

We came back to Madras by 4:00 P.M. Appa, during this tour of South India, visited Madurai, Virudhunagar, Rajapalayam, Trichy and Tanjore Centres, in that order. He is very happy with the progress at all these centres — even Trichy!

My Master appears to be very well received. Those who have already read it praise it highly.

22 Jan. 75 - Wednesday

Ever since I went to Shahjahanpur I have been feeling that I have now become totally useless and unfit for spiritual life. The feeling is growing stronger day by day, and began at Shahjahanpur when I went there to attend Chi. Sarvesh's marriage.

Today I had a 'polypectomy' operation done by Dr. V.S. Subramanian. It was done once in the end of March 1970. The polyps in the left nostril have grown again necessitating a second operation.

26 Jan. 75 - Sunday

Marianne Jepson and Marianne Johnson, both of Denmark, were here at Madras for a few days and left for Shahjahanpur.

This morning our brother preceptor Dr. A. Lakshminarasimhan who has been away at Denmark for more than 3 years, attended satsangh at Madras. He has returned to his job, teaching anatomy at the Veterinary College here. So we have one more preceptor now available for this centre.

My Master is very well received and I receive quite a few letters of high praise for it! Perhaps the first edition should have been printed in 2000 copies instead of 1500.

For the past five or six months, I have been experiencing a fear of death — my own death — which I have never before had in my life. Yes! I have been plagued by fears of near and dear ones dying, and have had sleepless nights watching Sulochana or Krishna while asleep, watching for the rise and fall of their chest to prove that they are still breathing and therefore alive. But I have never before had fears about my own death. Now the twin fears of death by heart trouble for myself, and by cancer for my wife, are obsessing me. I have not written to Master about this because I am ashamed of this new malady. Can this be due to the death by heart attack of my uncle Bakthu and my aunt Chitti both last year on March 9 and May 1 respectively?

2 Feb. 75 - Sunday

9:30 A.M. A sudden overwhelming flood of feeling that I am unfit for worldly life! I then recollect my feeling for the last three months that I am totally unfit for spiritual life. What does this new thought signify? I shall write to Master tomorrow.

13 Feb. 75 - Thursday

A dream early in the morning. I am on a hill road, and on a right hand turn around a spur. A huge African elephant passes me, going in the opposite direction. It has a mahout sitting on it, and the elephant is easily 12 or 13 feet tall. I go on. After some distance I turn and look back, and find the elephant has stopped at the place where it passed me and is now looking fixedly at me. I turn and go forward on my road. I find myself in a large open storage yard with a wire fence all around it. I look around, and see the elephant approaching me, staring fixedly at me. There is a slight apprehension that it may be chasing me. I woke up at this point.

15 Feb. 75 - Saturday

6:30 P.M. The first one hour sitting on the eve of Basant Panchami was superb and immensely deep. About 85 persons present. The sitting was held at our residence 'Gayathri'.

16 Feb. 75 - Sunday

Basant Panchami day. Morning sitting 6:30 to 7:30 — and evening 6:30 P.M. to 7:30 P.M. Evening session followed by talks by M.A. Sayeed (poor), C.S. Ramakrishnan (very good) and N.S. Rao (very emotional — few thoughts). Also some music. Attendance about 100 in the sittings.

17 Feb. 75 - Monday

Concluding sitting 6:30 A.M. to 7:30 A.M. for this year's Basant Panchami. Extraordinarily tranquil and deep.

27 Feb. 75 - Thursday

Charlotte O'Brien of Michigan, USA arrived from Shahjahanpur via Delhi by the Dakshin Express. She came home when we were all out and went to the YWCA.

28 Feb. 75 - Friday

Charlotte came at 11:30 A.M. She stays with us till tomorrow evening when she leaves for Rameswaram en route Colombo. From Colombo she hopes to work her passage home via California if she can get a sympathetic captain to take her! She is just 26 and has come overland from Norway, mostly thumbing lifts — and has spent on an average a dollar a day as she told Appa! And that money she earned while working on a ship in Norway — and she actually has Norwegian seaman's papers. It is astounding what American youth will attempt — and achieve!

1 Mar. 75 - Saturday

Charlotte left at 7:30 P.M. by Rameswaram Express.

4 Mar. 75 - Tuesday

Charlotte O'Brien turned up at around 11:00 A.M.! She was not allowed to board the ferry at Rameswaram as Ceylonese authorities refused to allow her to do so unless she could produce $500, which she does not have. So she is back — and will look for some way to go back home to USA.

6 Mar. 75 - Thursday

I have been passing through a period of physical lassitude, inner discontent and confusion, and general dissatisfaction with life for several months now. The physical lassitude has so taken hold of me that since October 1974, I don't often attend office in the afternoons. When I do go, I am perfectly active, fit and conscious of what I do. Appa's plans to go abroad are crystallising — and he hopes to leave Madras on the 15th of March, go to Calcutta, then Shahjahanpur and leave Delhi on 25th for Munich. His friend H, our abhyasi, is footing the bill —

the trip being ostensibly to have Appa's eyes and teeth attended to! But he is going to Spain for a stamp exhibition immediately on arrival at Munich and returns to Munich only by 18th April or so. All my facts are hearsay as he has not informed me direct so far. It appears that he will attend three stamp exhibitions in Europe. I have warned Appa a fortnight ago that if his arrangement with H is not a definite one of fixed commitment, then their friendship could well run into trouble. Appa will have few qualms about taking advantage of H's enormous generosity. I am quite perturbed over all this. It seems Appa is planning to go to Canada and the USA too — though originally he sought my approval only for one month's stay in Europe. His childish obsession with philately is most distressing to me. And at his age (he completes 70 on 7 April 75!) to go roaming over the world alone is least desirable with half an eye available to him. Anyway there is nothing I can do about the matter.

Nowadays when I read, and then lie down in the afternoon to do the work assigned by Master, I get into a deep-sleep state as usual, but when I get out of this condition I am aware that my head has been full of thoughts going round and round in it. It almost seems as if my other-consciousness has been developing and enlarging upon the thought that the mind had before I entered this condition. If I have read a story, then the story is developed upon, and so on.

11 Mar. 75 - Tuesday

How deep-seated are the normal human tendencies — or rather the lower tendencies — I could see today. My brother Kothand has secured a wonderful job in a company within the group in which I serve. He will probably get about three times the salary that I am getting. Till yesterday I was objective — but alas! Today I have been torn apart by jealousy and depression. This mood lasted the whole day. At night I fervently prayed to Master to rid me of this grossness. I felt some relief. I made a thought as if I am physically removing the jealousy and envy from my heart and went to sleep. This serves as a pointer to the need for perpetual awareness and care to see that baser tendencies don't overtake us — they seem to have this very knack to catch us when we weaken, whatever be the level of spiritual attainment. I was sorely ashamed at this development and pray Master to rid me of it.

12 Mar. 75 - Wednesday

When I woke up my heart was free of all the troubles and complexities of yesterday.

13 Mar. 75 - Thursday

Brother Ramachandra Reddy of Cuddapah came to see Appa for an hour in the evening. There was some talk of the money collected during Master's 75th Birthday celebrations at Hyderabad not being transferred to Shahjahanpur. It seems they are unwilling to send the amount unless Master asks for it. Master, on the other hand, is reported to have remarked during Basant that he was being humiliated by the Hyderabad preceptor. Master wanted to know why he should have to ask for the money. The problem of discipline in the Mission is assuming magnitude, and Hyderabad Centre needs organisational attention. I propose suggesting to Master that either Shri Kumaraswamy should be asked to vacate the ashram premises where he has been living ever since the Ashram was constructed, or he should pay a nominal rent to the Mission. It would have been much better if Master had accepted the suggestions Dr. K.C. Varadachari and I put up to him many years ago when Hyderabad Ashram was still under construction — but Master did not, and so these problems crop up.

14 Mar. 75 - Friday

Charlotte O'Brien's money has arrived. She plans to leave for San Francisco via Bangkok and Manila, on Sunday.

15 Mar. 75 - Saturday

Appa left for Calcutta by the Howrah Mail at 9:00 P.M. He was seen off by a group consisting of abhyasis, friends and philatelists.

16 Mar. 75 - Sunday

Charlotte O'Brien left for Calcutta by IAC morning flight at 10:30 A.M. We saw her off at Meenambakkam airport. She connects immediately at Calcutta for Bangkok.

Accompanied by B. Rajagopal, I left for Delhi by the 6:55 P.M. IAC flight.

17 Mar. 75 - Monday (Delhi)

Called on the Sundaras in the evening and gave them a sitting. Wanted to call on Joshi (R.K. Parum) — the idea was strong and persistent — but due to delay in Sundara's house I could not manage it.

18 Mar. 75 - Tuesday

Went to Modinagar to see Kasturi but found that she had gone to Delhi yesterday and is staying with Joshi! I felt a fool for not obeying the strong and repeated impulses to go to Joshi's house yesterday.

Left Delhi at 10:00 P.M. by Lucknow Mail for Shahjahanpur. Ravi Varma saw us off at New Delhi. He has become very attached and affectionate.

19 Mar. 75 - Wednesday (Shahjahanpur)

Arrived Shahjahanpur 4:30 A.M. The city was plunged in total darkness. Rajagopal and I took rickshaws home. Appa had arrived yesterday evening at 7:00 P.M. by the Howrah-Amritsar Mail. A couple of hours earlier Vibe Erstad and another abhyasi of Denmark, accompanied by Jan of Holland and Tina of Berlin had arrived from Delhi by the day train. Don Sabourin is already here since December end.

Master was sleeping, but when I peeped into his room at 6:45 A.M. he was awake. I sat at his feet. Master said, "Good! You have come! I have been very restless to see you, and if you had not come I would have come to Madras. I have been observing your condition since the day-before-yesterday. The wonderful thing is that wherever I looked into you I only found two, one was you and the other was myself — and both are one. This is Lalaji's work."

Don Sabourin has become immersed in Mission work and is busy preparing proper Registers for Patrika subscribers, both annual and life. It is a labourious job but he has almost completed it. He is looking after Master meticulously with great love and devotion. I learnt from Master that Don is at the *brahmanda*, and only the *yatra* is to be commenced.

Master is looking much better. His health is considerably improved since I saw him last at Sarvesh's wedding. He however complains that thoughts do not come as they used to before his illness of last year.

In the evening Master took all of us in five rickshaws to see the Ashram. It is coming up very well and will indeed be a grand thing when completed. The main meditation Ashram is magnificent in design and proportion. The marble flooring which covers the central area now has come out superbly. A very good job has been done. The two wings remain to be completed. Electrical work is over. Painting is to be taken up as soon as flooring is completed. The flooring of the dais has not been taken up yet. One dining area will be ready by the end of July, and the second area soon thereafter. I expect that by August the main building plus the dining and toilet areas should be ready. Thereafter work will have to be taken up on the construction of 14 rooms atop the dining halls. Our overseas group of four were also much impressed. Vibe expressed her happiness to Master. Master looked at her and said, "It is your work!" Vibe was naturally very very happy. After all she and Thomas have given over a lakh of rupees towards this construction.

20 Mar. 75 - Thursday

B. Rajagopal left in the morning for Lucknow on official work. He will be back on Saturday evening.

Don Sabourin delivered a lecture recently at the Lions Club, Shahjahanpur. It is good. Master instructed me to print it as a pamphlet — and I have commenced the work today.

21 Mar. 75 - Friday

Busy whole day with Mission work. During the day when I was alone with Master, he told me, "Yes. The work of Ceylon is over. Your reading is correct. I did not reply to your letter but the work is over." Then He added, "But as far as the second work is concerned — relating to the egoism of the Brahmins — that work cannot be completed so soon."

I think this was a reminder to me to take up this work, which I have not been doing for some time now.

Appa left by the midnight Lucknow Mail for Delhi. He has decided to cancel his Madrid appearance. He will probably cancel all his stamp exhibits and refrain from participation. He is considerably worried at having to travel alone — I can see that. Master told me, "He will go to Germany and return home. I have told him that he should not apply himself to any work. Yes, as soon as the eye operation is over and the bandages are removed then he could do some work, but only in Germany. I have also told him to inform Robert Koch that he is in Germany."

In the afternoon at 2:20 P.M. Master called me inside for an individual sitting. The sitting lasted one and a half hours — perhaps the longest individual sitting I have had from Master. The shortest was about 40 seconds at Copenhagen airport in 1972! I kept drowning, and coming up briefly for air as it were, again and again, till the sitting ended.

At 5:00 P.M. Master called Vibe and me to accompany him to the Ashram — this was fixed for tomorrow.

22 Mar. 75 - Saturday

Mrs. Sirsikar came in the morning from Chandigarh with her two sons and two young men.

Whole day busy with Don's pamphlet titled "Mind as the Instrument of Liberation". Also spent a long time with Don on discussions about organisational matters.

At 5:00 P.M. Master took us again to the Ashram for some consultation particularly with Vibe who is an architect by profession. We got back at 6:30 P.M.

Parthasarathi standing in his Master's courtyard

Beloved Babuji relaxing with Parthasarathi and others
Shahjahanpur, 1975

B. Rajagopal and Ganesh Viswanathan arrived by the Howrah-Amritsar Mail from Lucknow.

Master has been studying my headaches and says that he finds the bone-marrow in the skull at the two areas, where I generally suffer, to be granulated. He thinks this is the cause and said, "This is my diagnosis. If it is correct then I shall be successful in this work. Brother, it must be successful; otherwise how will the work of the Mission go on?" Later He added, "There is also some complication in the nerves. They appear to be hardening. By Lalaji's grace it shall be all right. You may write to me your condition every 15 days and I shall go on studying it."

I then referred to him my fear of heart trouble which has been coming up in my mind the last several months. Master said, "There is nothing like that. Your heart is strong. There is no necessity to worry about it. I shall remember this matter."

In the evening Master took us to the Ashram as I have recorded earlier. We were able to see the hall with all the lights on! It has come out nicely. Shri Srikrishna Tandon has done a good job of supervision.

After we returned Master referred to the Rishi Agastya. He said, "Whenever he appears in my vision, I see him as a short person with a long beard with a little limp. He is in charge of natural cataclysms! Sometimes it seems to me that Sage Agastya is still in the physical world, but I am not certain about this matter. But brother, I shall tell you one thing — there is one rishi living in the Himalayas whose face resembles Dr. Varadachari's almost exactly. It is a very surprising thing that they both seem to be one. I do not remember that Sage's name but I think he is also in the physical world. He is in charge of the weather and the climate. Whenever it is necessary to do something, then if an order is given to him the climate can be changed. Then the working of nature becomes suspended and the work begins according to my orders but then the responsibility for that work comes upon me."

I recited the names of rishis one by one, and when I came to Atri, Master said, "Yes. He is Atri Muni. It is wonderful how his face resembles so much that of Doctor Saheb. The resemblance is feature by feature. The same complexion, the same height and both seem as if they are one."

At night, before going to bed at 11:30 P.M., Master was in a speculative mood. The talk turned to the phenomenon of inter-communication between Master and disciple. Master seemed to be puzzled that this had not commenced with any abhyasi of the Mission. Master said, "Look here, this thing is present in other *sansthas*, and the surprising thing is that even in the case of persons who have not even crossed the *pind desh*, even in them the condition of inter-communication has opened up, and is present. In our organisation there are many who have approach to the highest but even then I do not find this thing. This thing has not been opened up even in Kasturi. And at least in your case this condition should have been opened up by now. I am unable to understand why it is so. Without inter-communications it will be very difficult. How will the work be done? Aré! I can hardly write about everything to you in my letters. You may also think about this."

I reminded Master about a letter he wanted to address to Brothers Shri Raghavendra Rao of Raichur and Shri Sarnadji regarding the formation of a committee consisting of them and myself to handle Master's work. Master had wanted to write this during Chi. Sarvesh's marriage but there was no time. When I opened this matter now to remind him about it, Master said, "Yes. I remember it.

Sarnad is due to come here in May. I am thinking that I should speak about this to him here, and then write to Raghavendra Rao about it. You please think about this some more and write to me confidentially on how it should be done."

I then mooted two proposals I considered important:

1) To charge abhyasis visiting Shahjahanpur for Basant Panchami a 'delegate fee' of Rs. 30/- per head. I explained to Master that the new Ashram will need approximately Rs. 30,000/- per annum for running and maintenance. By levying such a single delegate fee, assuming 1200 visitors for Basant, the income would be Rs. 36,000/-. Of this say Rs. 10,000/- would go towards the Utsav expenses, leaving Rs. 26,000/- for credit to the Ashram maintenance fund. This is the immediate working. In later years I anticipate larger attendance, and so in three or four years a situation might well arise when out of this delegate fee alone the Ashram maintenance expenses can be covered.

Master said, "You have evolved a very good idea. I like this idea. And your work will also be accomplished by this. I shall think about this and speak to Sarnad also about it. There is however one thing you must remember. The people from our nearby places like Sitapur may complain that their expenses will increase very much. As it is they have to pay some bus charges." I answered, "But Babuji, please think about those people who are coming from far far away like Madras and Madurai. They have to spend a great deal of money. If anyone should complain it is they who should complain." Master laughed and agreed that this was true.

2) I pointed out to Master that Shri N. Kumaraswamy of Hyderabad has been in continuous residence at the Hyderabad Ashram of the Mission ever since it was com-

pleted — which is seven or eight years now. I explained to Master that if a person is in continuous occupation for 12 years without any rent or other charges being paid by him, legally he could claim possession of the premises so occupied. I requested Master to consider charging a rent to Shri Kumaraswamy so that the Mission's legal position as owner of the Ashram was not in any way affected.

Master said, "You have thought about this very well. Look here, I do not know such things at all. It is good that you have thought about it. Look here, Kumaraswamy has even installed a telephone. I do not know whether he pays the charges for it or it is the Mission which pays. It is a very good thing that you have thought about this. You need not do anything further about these matters. I shall think about them and I shall also consult Babu Raghunandan Prasad, because he can give expert suggestions in this matter. You know him, don't you? He is my *sambandhi*."

After this we went to bed around midnight.

23 Mar. 1975 - Sunday

Spent a lot of time just sitting with Master. The old sparkle is missing. He sits mostly silent, and speaks very little, and when he speaks it is only of ashram construction.

Mrs. Sirsikar and children left for Ambala en route Chandigarh by the 6:30 P.M. Howrah-Amritsar Mail.

During my stay here I have had long sessions — two of them — with Jaggan Raizada on Mission work. He will now attend regularly. If Shri K did not interfere in everything, work would go on smoothly.

I have omitted a technique Master taught me which rids one of fear, and also prevents bad dreams and nightmares. Master said, "To me brother this method appears good. You may also try it for four or five days. Before going to bed, meditate on Lalaji Maharaj and say, 'May the Master be victorious.' Do this two or three times. It is very effective. Please experiment on this and let me know."

Ganesh Viswanathan had left for Delhi in the morning. B. Rajagopal and I left for Delhi by the Lucknow Mail. Jaggan saw us off at the station — an unexpected but welcome thing, in view of our reserved berths being occupied by four 'Seths' apparently rich, and obviously under the effect of 'bhang'. We had to wait 30 minutes before the Railway authorities evicted them.

I was calm till the train left. But as soon as the train moved a strange and unbearable sorrow filled my heart, and tears poured from my eyes until we crossed Bareilly — I could not control it.

24 Mar. 75 - Monday

Took Appa to Modinagar to see Kasturi. Kasturi was all praise for my book *My Master*. She gave me a sitting. I felt, or 'saw' a large pipe — about 12 feet in diameter (12 feet!) facing me, and from it came out a flood of crystal-clear water which poured into my heart. It was a strange experience because I have never before experienced such a massive (in terms of volume alone) flow into me. This lasted a few minutes. Then I found a lake on which a beautiful white swan was serenely floating. After this I went deep into meditation and was conscious only of the fact that I was unconscious.

Kasturi was happy. She said, "Yes, whatever you have seen is correct. But brother, whatever I have seen, I have not seen in anyone else till today. I have seen that inside you there is nothing but vacuum — only vacuum. And it is such a vacuum that even if I go on filling it, I am not able to fill it. It appears to me that however much may be given to you it will not be enough to fill up this vacuum. Brother! I have been seeing for many years, that this special thing which is in you is not to be seen in anyone else. Several people are of course there in the central region; but even when your heart region had not been crossed, even at that time the speciality that was in you was not found in anyone else. If an abhyasi only attends to his own making and co-operates with the Master, then let him see what can be done with him. There is nothing in the regions. Master can put a person in whichever region he wishes — but the making of an abhyasi is something else. And it is in this that the speciality of the spiritual life lies."

Later when I was having lunch (alone, as Appa had eaten when I was having my sitting with Kasturi) Kasturi sat by my side and was again and again commenting on my progress and spiritual condition. "There was the Doctor Saheb. There is brother Raghavendra Rao, and there are of course other persons who have approached the central region. But in them this thing is not present. It is not only today but it was so even earlier. Dear brother, your condition is such that to say anything about it is very difficult. I have never seen such a deep vacuum. Dear brother, it appears to me that in you Babuji is preparing a Personality."

After spending three hours with Kasturi we returned to Delhi.

25 Mar. 75 - Tuesday

Appa left for Munich via Damascus by Syrian Arab Airlines flight. It was scheduled for 5:30 A.M. but left at 8:30 A.M.

I left Delhi at 5:30 P.M. with B. Rajagopal and returned to Madras.

27 Mar. 75 - Thursday (Madras)

Mr. Rakotondrainibe of Tananarive phoned to say he has arrived in Madras. He came home at 2:30 P.M. and stays with us at Gayathri.

28 Mar. 75 - Friday

Rako left for Singapore. He has promised to see Master on his way back at Calcutta on 28th April as Master is expected to be in Calcutta for his birthday celebrations on 30th April.

19 Apr. 75 - Saturday (Madurai)

Returned from Virudhunagar to Madurai at 5:00 P.M. Sulochana telephoned from Madras at 5:30 P.M. to say that Salem N.V. Narasimhan had passed away. He was suffering from mouth cancer for just over one year and with the help of imported medicines he had improved a great deal and appeared to be established on the path of recovery. When I saw him last at Madras in January there was a set-back, and apparently the cancer had won in this grim battle. Poor fellow. He was a man of large heart and few people understood that under the lion's skin which he donned so convincingly and often aggressively, there was really only a lamb. May Master guide his soul to its destination.

20 Apr. 75 - Sunday

After conducting satsangh at Madurai Centre I left at 9:00 A.M. by car for Salem, accompanied by B. Rajagopal and Swaminathan. We reached Salem at 2:30 P.M. and spent one hour with Narasimhan's bereaved family. He had passed away on Friday 18th morning after heavy bleeding from the mouth. The atmosphere in his home was quite calm and peaceful. We reached Coimbatore at 7:30 P.M.

30 Apr. 75 - Wednesday

We celebrated Master's birthday by holding two meditation sessions 7:00 A.M. to 8:00 A.M., and again from 6:30 P.M. to 7:30 P.M. The morning session was excellent and well attended too.

Master is in Calcutta at the invitation of that centre. Our S. Narayanaswamy has gone there a couple of days ago. I could not go due to pressure of work.

In the evening meditation I got a flash — I have been wondering why Master does not 'see' lower things. The answer came! When we are in darkness we need a light. Now suppose a candle can speak and is aware of itself, and I tell one, "Please come there, it is dark." The candle comes, but is bewildered. It asks, "Where is the darkness? What is darkness?" Because in the presence of light darkness cannot exist!

4 May 75 - Sunday

Narayanaswamy has returned this morning from Calcutta and attended satsangh. He says Master is well though his memory is very poor and he recalls very little. Several abhyasis from Rajahmundry, Tirupathi, etc., of A.P. are reported to have attended the Calcutta celebrations held at Major Saudagar Singh's residence in grand and elegant style.

12 May 75 - Monday

Left with B. Rajagopal for Delhi by IAC evening Boeing 737 flight at 6:55 P.M. arriving Delhi 9:30 P.M.

13 May 75 - Tuesday

Left by car at 8:00 A.M. for Shahjahanpur, and arrived there at 3:00 P.M. We were welcomed very affectionately by brothers Shri S.A. Sarnad and Dr. A.B. Jajodia who have been here for a few days already, translating Master's confidential diaries, part of which will be published as the second volume of Master's *Autobiography*. Dr. Shyam Rao and brother Gunde Rao are also here. Master was asleep and came out at 4:00 P.M. He was surprised to see me. Evidently my express telegram sent on Friday 9 May to inform him of my arrival has not reached him.

I had a bath, rested a little and had tea. Later we were sitting on the verandah, I by Master's side and B. Rajagopal facing us. Master suddenly spoke to Rajagopal and said:

"Look, I am telling you something which is worth studying. Here Parthasarathi is sitting with us but I am unable to find Parthasarathi. When I look there, I only find myself sitting there. One 'I' is sitting there and one 'I' is sitting here. Please observe this. Such spiritual conditions are not to be found every day."

At 5:30 P.M. Master took us to the Ashram and inspected the work. We returned home at about 7:00 P.M.

Master appears in much better health, though still far from his old self. My bed was by his, in the inside courtyard — just the two of us in the whole place. When we went to bed it was near midnight. After some talk about the Mission he said, "Look here, I wanted to make you cross one more ring but I have not done it. Do you know why? I want to take you up in an absolutely natural way, and Nature is saying, 'Not now,' because you have to become like me, isn't it! You understand? It shall be done. Brother, it is all His work."

14 May 75 - Wednesday

Whole day with Mission work. Hardly any time with Master who is preoccupied with the translation of his diaries — which he dictates to brothers Sarnad and Jajodia. He told me:

"As soon as the work is done you will get a copy. I shall not print it fully because there are so many things which I do not wish to reveal now. But you will receive a complete translation because after all you have to work. There are so many things as to what work I did, and how I did that work; what were the orders of Nature, what I did and what work was achieved — all these things will appear there."

In the evening Master and I attended the marriage of Madhu Tandon at Khattri Dharamshala. While there, the Allahabad Bank Manager came to pay his respects to Master. Master sent me to the bank to get a letter drafted, addressed to the Bank, giving me authority to operate on the General Account of the Mission at Shahjahanpur. He signed this in the Dharamshala and said, "This work has been delayed for a long time and it is good you have now come. Who knows what will happen and when? Now you can also operate the account, and if something should happen to me the work will not stop. Of course the construction account is a temporary account, and as soon as the work of the Ashram is over it will be merged with the General Account. Is this all right? That is why I did not think it necessary for you to operate that account."

Master gave me a copy of the letter for my files. I met Jaggan Raizada at the marriage. He took me aside and confided to me that even though he was eager to continue working for the Mission, Shri K had hounded him out. When I pressed him for details he reluctantly told me, "Shri

K has told me that either I should stay here or he will stay here, but that both of us cannot stay in this house together. 'If you keep coming here, then I shall have to leave the house and go.'" Therefore Raizada has not come for work for the past several months. I did not discuss this with Master — I couldn't!

Mr. Tandon has been seriously ill, and was actually in bed in a room here. We met him for a few minutes. There was scant courtesy shown to Master — no one even came near him. No dinner was offered. Even Shri Shri Krishna Tandon was absent till we were about to leave — then he appeared and greeted Master. We left the Dharamshala at 10:00 P.M. without dinner.

15 May 75 - Thursday

Rajagopal and I left for Delhi at 9:00 A.M. Master leaves for Lucknow this morning and goes on to Assam via Calcutta tomorrow for a marriage there, and is due to return here to Shahjahanpur on 22 May 75. From Moradabad (3:00 P.M.) to Delhi (7:30 P.M.) was a solid gale, with a wall of dust all the way.

16 May 75 - Friday (Delhi)

Some satsanghis of Delhi started coming for satsangh from 7:30 A.M. and this went on till 11:30. Actually I could bathe only at 11:30. Then Ravi Varma joined us for lunch. Brother S.C. Kishore, Mission Auditor, came and spent one hour with me discussing Mission Accounts and related problems. Rajagopal and I left by the 6:30 P.M. flight and arrived at Bombay at 9:00 P.M. We left by Air India at 1:00 A.M. for Cairo.

19 May 75 - Monday (Cairo)

Went to Casino Sans Souci at 4:00 P.M. Met Mme. Dina Joannides and her husband Niccola there. Surprisingly one of our abhyasis Mrs. Amenophis Acer, was also present with her husband Mr. Amenophis. We spent two hours or more, and went back to the Sheraton Hotel where we are staying.

20 May 75 - Tuesday (Cairo)

Madame Dina Joannides came at 8:00 A.M. to the Hotel Sheraton and spent three hours with me. She related her problems — how she has been with a faith healer for nearly one year now trying to get herself in condition to have a baby — how things have gone from bad to worse — the fear of death haunting her — how she is unable to be alone in the house and can't sleep in her bedroom where a near-relation died recently, and so on. She was afraid to receive a transmission but I gave her a mild transmission without her knowledge. In fact this was commenced by me ever since I left Delhi. She was also transmitted to yesterday evening when I was with her at Sans Souci — without her participation — and this morning all tension lines which made her look haggard and beaten down yesterday have disappeared. She looks radiant and spontaneously told me, "Chari! I feel so much better since your visit yesterday — I cannot tell you but I feel so 'free' and all my pains have gone. Only some slight pain in the head is remaining there now. Please help me Chari, and ask Master to help me. I so need help. I thought I would die, but when I was thinking that now there is no hope, your letter came about your visit and now you are here. I know Master and you help me. But you are so far away and I need you here to help me. Do you think Master will come to me? I need him so much. Maybe he thinks I am no longer following his meditation and so will not help me. What do you think Chari?"

I assured her Master's help would never be withheld from her. She was very grateful and tears welled up in her eyes. She has a lot of problems, the foremost being her husband Niccola. Secondly she has been frantically wanting a baby to inherit her property. I told her it was unnatural to want a baby just to leave money to. If she wanted a baby for its own sake, that was natural — but this desire of hers was unnatural. She agreed and said, "Maybe that is why God does not give me a child, because my desire is unnatural. I see your meaning correctly. Thank you for explaining this to me, Chari!" She also wants to sell off her business and go back to Greece but the Egyptian laws are very restrictive on transfer of assets out of the country, and she is afraid that she will lose all her money. Her greatest fear is what would happen if Niccola, her husband, were to suddenly die, because under Egyptian law the widow has no independent status and in such cases all property left reverts to the state. In such an eventuality she could not even get a residence permit as only males get permits, and wives automatically are permitted to reside where the husband resides — but women cannot get separate residence permits. This is perhaps her greatest fear. I tried my best to give her calmness and bring some tranquillity into her. By Master's grace she was almost her normal self when she left.

31 May 75 - Saturday

I left Cairo for Bombay. Rajagopal goes on to Libya and then on through several countries of Africa before returning from Mauritius at the end of June. During my 13 days at Cairo I met Dina about four times, and I believe she is far better now. I am sorry I could not meet her just before I left.

1 Jun. 75 - Sunday

Arrived at Bombay at 2:30 P.M., having over-flown Delhi where the plane could not land due to a severe dust storm. Left Bombay at 5:30 P.M. and came to Madras at 7:30 P.M. and so back home.

8 Jun. 75 - Sunday

Conducted satsangh at Madurai Centre and inspected their books of accounts. There are no accounts — only some receipt books and loose cash — all very very slipshod. Receipts have been issued without collecting cash — and I found three receipts where the amount had been changed from Rs. 101/- to Rs. 10/-!! One preceptor still owes the Mission Rs. 30/- for which receipts were issued months ago. I have found during my last few visits to Madurai that this particular preceptor has been playing off preceptors one against the other, and is utterly unpopular with the abhyasis — all of whom complain that he is a liar, and denies sittings to most of them while giving sittings to a couple of his own *chelas* — Vicchu, Mahalingham, etc. I had to speak rather bluntly to Shri Thasma Swami, head of the centre, for the deplorable state of accounts as well as for the low morale and total indiscipline in the centre.

11 Jun. 75 - Wednesday

Sat with Ponniah of Madurai Centre for three hours and prepared accounts, opened new books, obtained opening balance for 1 October 74 and posted entries up-to-date, and also prepared half-yearly statements of account for the centre up to 31 March 75 — tallied accurately — and handed over to Thasmaji. In the evening conducted group satsangh at the centre.

13 Jun. 75 - Friday

Have been busy with a great deal of correspondence which I have completed at Virudhunagar. A long letter from Jens Clausen of Denmark required an equally long reply. Hyderabad Centre's closing of accounts relating to the celebrations of Master's 75th Birthday last year also has been delayed due to a purse presented to Master. Have consulted our company auditors and written to Shri N. Kumaraswamy and to our Mission auditor brother S.C. Kishore. It is a pity preceptors don't ask or consult before they act.

Conducted group satsangh at the Tirunagar house of Shri W.H. Srinivasan. Good attendance. This sub-centre at Madurai is coming up well.

15 Jun. 75 - Sunday

Conducted weekly satsangh at Madurai.

16/17 Jun. 75 - Monday/Tuesday

At Coimbatore. The centre is developing well. Gave a number of individual sittings on Monday, followed by a group sitting at 8:00 P.M., all at Shri Sukaswami's residence, where our centre operates. Started Shri Sukaswami's *yatra* by Master's Grace.

On Tuesday, a few individual sittings between 11:00 and 12:30, followed by a group satsangh from 1:00 to 2:00 P.M. Then left for Madurai.

18 Jun. 75 - Wednesday

Back at Madurai, conducted the evening satsangh at our centre.

20 Jun. 75 - Friday

Visited Rajapalayam from Virudhunagar. Shri B. Ramachandran of ITPT and my wife Sulochana also came. Conducted satsangh at Rajapalayam Centre 5:00 to 6:30 P.M. Back to Madurai 10 P.M.

22 Jun. 75 - Sunday

After conducting Sunday satsangh at Madurai Centre, on behalf of Master I granted provisional permission to Shri W.H. Srinivasan of Tirunagar, and to Shri P.K. Venkatesan of Virudhunagar.

25 Jun. 75 - Wednesday

Mission problems have been worrying me much. Unable to sleep, I have been meditating for guidance the last two nights.

2 Jul. 75 - Wednesday

Conducted group evening satsangh at Madurai Centre. Mission work is posing more and more problems. Brother Dhond Rao of Kalahasti has referred to me his sorrow and bewilderment at some remarks that Shri Kumaraswamy of Hyderabad made about late Dr. K.C. Varadachari while lecturing at Nellore and Kavali Centres. Complaints also regarding Shri J, alleging involvement with abhyasis in financial areas; demanding physical service from abhyasis in his garden; not giving sittings to abhyasis, etc.

I have handled a great deal of correspondence from Madurai this trip.

6 Jul. 75 - Sunday

Conducted Sunday satsangh at Madurai Centre and then left for Madras by car.

13 Jul. 75 - Sunday

Appa returned from Germany (via Delhi and Shahjahanpur) after a stay away from home of nearly 4 months.

14 Jul. 75 - Monday

Attended the wedding of Sow. Seethalakshmi, daughter of Shri S.R. Suhaswami, at Coimbatore, and gave a lot of sittings throughout the day up to 10:00 P.M. right there in the Kalyana Mandapam.

15 Jul. 75 - Tuesday

A number of individual and group sittings at Coimbatore. Shri Sukaswami has done good work in introducing Sahaj Marg to a large number of his relatives, and since most of them had come for the wedding, attendance at group satsangh exceeded 30.

16 Jul. 75 - Wednesday

On Master's behalf granted provisional permission to Shri S.R. Sukaswami at Coimbatore (the 14th preceptor thus granted provisional permission so far).

17 Jul. 75 - Thursday

Appa has received a letter from Mrs. R.P. Nanjundiah of Channapatna to say that brother Nanjundiah has passed away. She has sent Appa a copy of Nanjundiah's letter of early 1974 addressed to Shri Raghavendra Rao. I have written to Shri Raghavendra Rao about this.

19 Jul. 75 - Saturday

Shri D.S.K. Subrahmanya Sastri of Kavali came to Madras. Advised him suitably on future conduct, and the need for caution in moulding his relationship with abhyasis.

22 Jul. 75 - Tuesday

Wrote a four page letter to Master putting before him all my problems. I have drafted a "Code of Conduct for Preceptors" and have sent it to Master along with my letter. I hope he will approve it so that it can be printed, and his signature obtained, and copies issued to all preceptors. My idea is to have a perforated detachable printed undertaking printed at the bottom of the "code" which a preceptor should tear-off, sign and send to the H.Q. to be filed.

I have forgotten to record what I find to have been a significant dream. It was on Wednesday 16th July night as I was in the train, alone in an air-conditioned coupe compartment, returning from Coimbatore to Madras. I dreamt that I was in a large hall, maybe 60 feet by 40 feet, with a high ceiling of over 20 feet. Along the wall was a row of pillars, forming part of the wall but protruding — with flutes (a fluted column). At the top was a decorative overhang, supporting the ceiling. I saw there were five pillars, and on the top, hanging suspended from the decorative support, were five monkeys, one on each pillar. Then I saw a man standing next to me holding five large dogs on leashes. He said something and let the dogs loose. They ran to the walls, and by sheer momentum seemed to scale up the wall, and each dog caught hold of a monkey and came down. When I looked down I saw pieces of torn flesh which I kicked away. That was the end of the dream.

I couldn't interpret the dream. Suddenly on Saturday 19th early morning, when I was in a semi-sleep condition, the idea came to me that the five monkeys represent my five *indriyas* (*karmendriyas*) and the dogs represented the *gnanendriyas* — and the significance of the dream was that my five *indriyas* have all now been destroyed! I have to refer this to Master for verification.

25 Jul. 75 - Friday

Woke up as from deeply drugged sleep. I woke up once at night and felt drugged. When I woke up in the morning the condition was still the same. It took half an hour to clear up!

29 Jul. 75 - Tuesday

Dream early in the morning. A large gathering of our abhyasis is there. It is either dusk or dawn. Most of the abhyasis are our overseas brothers and sisters. Some function is going on and I seem to be sitting in an easy chair, all alone presiding. The feeling comes to me that I am sitting in the Master's chair. People are milling around but I am alone, and feel lonely.

18 Aug. 75 - Monday

The Jahagirdar episode has come up again with the receipt of a letter from Mrs. R.P. Nanjundiah (addressed to Appa) to say that brother Nanjundiah passed away. She seeks redress for the alleged monetary loss through Jahagirdar. I have written to Shri Raghavendra Rao of Raichur emphasising the need for an early and fair settlement of this issue — his reply was a bland statement that such letters have been sent out by the widow of Shri Nanjundiah not only to Appa but to all preceptors in the South!

I wrote to Master but he has not replied. I also drafted out a "Code-of-Conduct" for preceptors which I sent to

Master, along with copies to brothers Shri Raghavendra Rao and Shri Sarnad. The former had no comment to make except to say that if Master approved it, it could be circulated to all preceptors. Shri Sarnad has not even acknowledged it. My letters to Master remain unanswered and so I get no advice from him too. All this has been between the middle of July when Appa returned from Germany and today.

Brother Kamalesh Kumar of Bangalore had been to Shahjahanpur and returned today to Madras. I had sent a letter to Master through him — no reply! So what do I do now?

23 Aug. 75 - Saturday

Shri S.C. Kishore, auditor of the Mission, arrived from Vijayawada by Circar Express at 7:30 A.M. He was met by Umesh and taken to Besant Nagar. He came to the office at 11 A.M. We started audit of the Mission's Madras centre accounts at 11:40 A.M. and completed the audit for 1971/72, 1972/73 and 1973/74 at 5:40 P.M. No errors, no complaints! This is the first time Shri Kishore has come out to South India. He has been at Hyderabad where he audited the accounts of that centre for three years, as well as the accounts of the Raichur centre. Then he was at Vijayawada where the audit for that centre was concluded, and now he is here. He goes on to Bangalore and Channapatna and will finally leave for Delhi on Wednesday 27 August. He is accompanied by his wife.

31 Aug. 75 - Sunday

Our brothers S. Sankaranarayanan and G.S. Mani, with the latter's family, have all been to Shahjahanpur and returned last Friday to Madras. Sankaranarayanan gave us a report after this morning's satsangh on Ashram work at

Shahjahanpur. He reports near-completion of the main Ashram building. The work will surely be completed by the end of September.

No letter from Master — nor have brothers Raghavendra Rao and Sarnad commented on the preceptors' code. So much for co-operation!

I have started compiling a card-index of preceptors, and the printer delivered the cards last week. About 40 cards have been posted so far with name, date of birth, date of joining the mission, date on which provisional permission was granted, date on which full preceptorship was granted, and the photograph pasted on each one. When the job will be completed is anybody's guess. I have to receive all the information and photographs from all the preceptors, and then only can the work be done.

I am revising *Efficacy of Raja Yoga*. It goes to press for its fourth edition next week. The third edition was printed at Madras in 1968. Now that Kabeer Printing works has closed down, this, and all future work, will be given to G.S. Press.

26 Sep. 75 - Friday

At Calcutta. To Major Saudagar Singh's residence in Ballygunj to conduct evening satsangh at 7:30 P.M. Shri R.L. Mimani, three of the Bhattar brothers and about seven others were present. Good sitting. The Major is a deeply devoted person.

30 Sep. 75 - Tuesday

At Nagpur — arrived by car from Jabalpore at 2:30 P.M. Shri P. Rama Murty, newly created preceptor here, came at 6:30 P.M. and took B. Rajagopal and me to his residence where we had a long talk on his work as a preceptor. Then a young man, Dr. Lakkad, PhD in Sanskrit, came to be introduced to me and I had a long talk with him, after which all of us had dinner, before leaving for my hotel at 10:30 P.M.

Shri Murty is very enthusiastic. He confided to me that some abhyasis are receiving 'long-distance transmission' from Shri K.C. Narayana at Hyderabad and Dr. Swamy at Tirupathi. These abhyasis don't attend satsangh here. There has developed a craze for this 'long-distance transmission' and ever since I came across it (N.S. Rao at Madras being the most blatant example, with a whole week's 'schedule' of such transmissions from preceptors like Shri G.S. Mani of Madurai, Dr. V. Parthasarathi of Vijayawada, etc.) about two years ago I have written to Master about it — NO RESULT! The craze is growing. I believe Sister Kasturi to be responsible for this development — she has been fixing up with abhyasis all over India for such sittings, and the disease has caught on!

1 Oct. 75 - Wednesday (Nagpur)

8:00 A.M. — Conducted group satsangh at Smt. Tara Kaley's residence for 40 minutes. About 25 were present.

2 Oct. 75 - Thursday

Returned to Madras at 7:00 P.M. by the Link Express from Nagpur. Appa told me that Chi Umesh has become the father of twin boys, Amita having been delivered of them yesterday morning at Lucknow. It appears Master reached Lucknow on 29 September!!

8 Oct. 75 - Wednesday

After a long time Master appeared in my dream just before I woke up, at 4:30 A.M. The dream: It is twilight. I am with two persons probably B. Rajagopal and one other.

We are sitting on what appears to be sand near a cottage of some type. Suddenly Master appears, dressed in a dhoti and kurta. He is pulling out a piece of paper from his kurta pocket and is walking away from me. He suddenly stops, turns around to face me, smiles as he takes something out of his pocket and says, "Have you seen this picture? Your father gave it to me." He gives me a photograph. I look at it. It is a photo of Master which appears cut off at the forehead. I then see that it is not really cut off but is folded back. I open it out. I don't like the picture at all. I tell Master, "This picture is not good," and I crumple it and throw it away.

My interpretation. The photo 'represents' Master. It is not good — as I say. Originally the picture appeared cut off at the forehead, but on examination I found that the picture had been folded, hiding the rest of the head behind the face. What does this mean? That which represents Master is NOT a real or true representative! But it is not as bad as it seems on first sight. It does not lack brains (the cut-off at the forehead) but only the brains have been 'pushed back' or 'folded away' indicating the fact that His 'representative' is behaving unwisely or with lack of wisdom. "Your father gave it to me," — the meaning is obvious. It points a direct finger at me! So it is a direct criticism from the Master of my unwise way of existence. I have to do what is necessary to effect the required changes in myself — my inner self is conscious of the 'lack' as witnessed by my emphatic rejection of the picture and my throwing it away.

15 Oct. 75 — Wednesday

Master has at last agreed to a special donation of Rs. 30/- per head to be collected from all abhyasis visiting Shahjahanpur for Basant Panchami 1976 (5 February 76)

— his instructions for the Utsav celebrations incorporating this were received recently, and cyclostyled circulars sent out to all preceptors.

Efficacy of Raja Yoga fourth edition goes into print as of today. Copies should be ready by the end of this month.

We have commenced a collection of donations at Madras Centre under the head "Donations for Madras Ashram Construction Fund". Recently both Swaminathan and Vijayaraghavan have been to Shahjahanpur. Both said that Master has stated that, "The next ashram must be in Madras." So on this basis this collection has been started. A nucleus of funds is available — the profit from the Lalaji Birth Centenary celebration amounting to over Rs. 80,000/- being earmarked for this purpose under Master's instructions.

23 Oct. 75 - Thursday

At Virudhunagar. Went with Sarvesh and his father-in-law Shri Bartariaji to see Sarvesh's wife Aneeta at the nursing home. Their baby boy was born on the 21st. The baby is healthy and fair, and somewhat resembles Prakash's son Sanjay. Spent half an hour there.

2 Nov. 75 - Sunday

Deepavali day. At 5:00 A.M. I was getting ready for my bath when a telegram came from Coimbatore — "Sukaswamy expired, Anasuya." The telegram was dispatched at 3:55 A.M. A great shock and a very sad shock to us all. Shri Sukaswamy was not at Coimbatore on the 29th and 30th October when I was there. He was due back from Baroda on the 31st. So I missed him. Actually I arrived back at Madras on 31st morning and so we must have crossed each other near Salem. He was made a preceptor only recently, on the 16th of July, and his certificate was sent hardly 10 days ago through Swaminathan. The poor family will be deeply hurt by this bereavement. He leaves behind his son S.S. Ramakrishnan, a preceptor of the Mission, three unmarried daughters Anasuya, Rama and Shobhana, a married daughter Seethalakshmi, Mrs. Sukaswamy and her elder sister. A very devoted and loving family. I pray to our beloved Master to guide his soul to its destination without further rebirth.

21 Dec. 75 - Sunday

Appa and Krishna left for Delhi (en route Shahjahanpur) by the Grand Trunk Express at 19:40 hours. They reach Delhi on 23 December at 11:15 A.M. and leave, almost immediately, at 2:30 P.M. by the Delhi-Varanasi "Kashi Vishwanath Express" which reaches Shahjahanpur at 9:30 P.M. H, his wife Inna, and two other German abhyasis join them at Delhi for Shahjahanpur.

Saw, and heard, the Dalai Lama at the Theosophical Society Centenary celebration.

22 Dec. 75 - Monday

Andre Poray arrived in Madras by air from Delhi at 22:30 hours. I met Francis Brunel at the Theosophical Centenary celebration. He was at Paris — a past General Secretary of the Theosophical Society of France — when Master and I went there in 1972. He showed a lot of slides prepared under a title "In the Footsteps of the Master of Wisdom". A lot of colour and good photography, but otherwise meaningless. He didn't recognise me — naturally — but even after I introduced myself he appeared unwilling to make contact and was quite abrupt, even after I told him about Master!

23 Dec. 75 - Tuesday

Andre Poray spent two hours from 5:00 to 7:00 P.M. with us at home.

24 Dec. 75 - Wednesday

Andre took general satsangh after giving a talk. About 80 were present. Tea and snacks were served later, and the meeting closed with devotional songs by Jayashree and G.S. Mani.

28 Dec. 75 - Sunday

Andre left for Bangalore en route Goa to visit a large camp of Tibetans. I left for Madurai after morning satsangh. We are preparing for sale printed reproductions of Lalaji and Babuji — full size 11 1/2 inches by 9 inches, picture size about 9 inches by 7 inches; copper blocks were received a few days ago. I am carrying proof copies to be shown at Southern Centres for order-booking @ Rs. 5/- per pair. The printing will be on Japanese Real Art Paper of 100 lbs.

31 Dec. 75 - Wednesday

Took satsangh at Virudhunagar. About 30 were present. After P.K. Venkatesan was granted provisional permission this centre has picked up well. B. Rajagopal has not taken to the work as expected — in fact for the last two years he has neglected it and so PKV's appointment became a necessity.

Beloved Babuji Maharaj

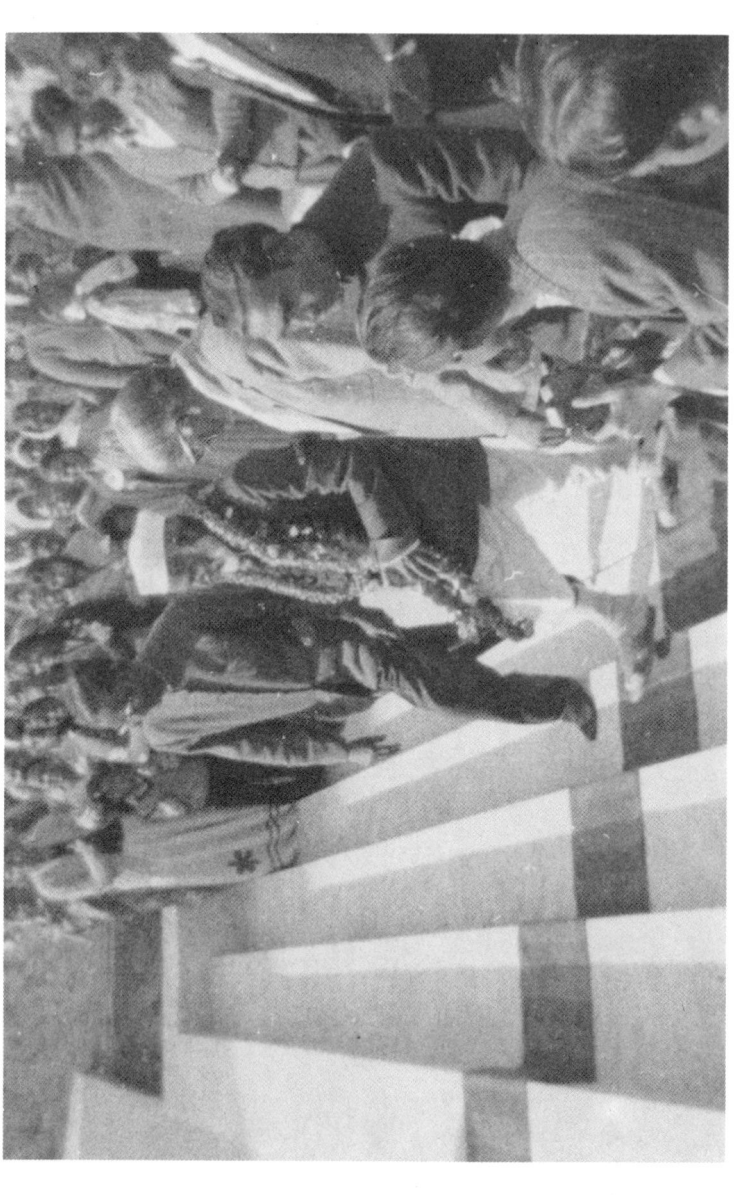

Reverend Babuji and Parthasarathi ascending stairs during ashram inauguration in Shahjahanpur, February 1976

1976

1/2 Jan. 1976 - Thursday/Friday

I am at Madurai — giving sittings to such as come to Valamjee Mansion. On Friday the 2nd took evening satsangh at Tallakulam Centre. About 10 present. On the 1st quite a number of people came to Valamjee, morning and evening, for satsangh including J.R. Doreswamy Iyer. After the evening sitting he became quite emotional and wanted to praise me for the work of the Mission I am doing.

On January 3, after satsangh, I left for Madras at 9 A.M.

4 Jan. 76 - Sunday

Judith Ann Polston and her husband came for satsangh. They have recently got married at Denmark, went to see Master, and have come here for a short stay. They will go back to Shahjahanpur for Basant.

Krishna returned by the evening IAC flight at 21:30 hours after spending nine days with Master at Shahjahanpur and after a visit to Agra. He said Master had given him one special sitting, and that he had also joined three general sittings.

5 Jan. 76 - Monday

H of Munich arrived in Madras, and telephoned. He had been to Shahjahanpur but fell sick and returned to

Delhi after a mere two days stay. Subsequently his wife Inna has gone back once again to Shahjahanpur.

6 Jan. 76 - Tuesday

Appa returned from his trip — last halt being two days at Rajahmundry.

The printed photographs of Lalaji and Babuji — 2000 sets — have been received from Gnanodaya Press — good work. The first standard printed photographs offered for sale by the Mission.

7 Jan. 76 - Wednesday

I gave dinner to H, Judith, her husband Neil and nine others including Dr. A. Lakshminarasimhan and his wife, as also my uncle Mr. Bhadran, Aunt Gouri, etc., at the Chola Hotel.

11 Jan. 76 - Sunday

We have been having three sessions of discussions with H regarding *Efficacy of Raja Yoga* which he will shortly translate into German and publish in Germany. This morning after a marathon session we completed the discussion on it.

16 Jan. 76 - Friday

Left by IAC flight leaving Madras at 6:00 A.M. for Delhi en route Shahjahanpur. Met C.E. Gupta at the airport and gave him a talk; he did not know when Basant is to be celebrated, nor did he want to attend it after I gave him the date, and he is a preceptor! — and asked him to be devoted to the Mission! Sulochana and T.K. Narasimhan saw me off. Landed at Hyderabad at 7:00 A.M. — delayed departure due to fog over Palam — we finally took off at 10:30

A.M. to arrive at Palam at 12:30. TTK & Co. car met me and the driver gave me my train ticket for Shahjahanpur. I drove straight to the External Affairs Hostel on K.G. Marg (Curzon Road), met Ravi Varma, had lunch with him, and then caught the Kashi Vishwanath Express at 2:30 P.M. from New Delhi, arriving 10 minutes before time at 8:38 P.M. at Shahjahanpur. Jagdish met me on arrival. Went to Master's house to find I am the sole visitor on the premises.

Since Gunde Rao Nagnoor of Gulbarga is now permanently a resident at Shahjahanpur, he has become Master's companion and sleeps in his room. So I was allotted a room in the guest-house block — the only resident — and felt quite lonely there. It is not very cold here.

17 Jan. 76 - Saturday (Shahjahanpur)

From 3:00 P.M. to 6:00 P.M. inspected Ashram in the company of Master. Much work remains to be done. The main residential block, even, is not yet ready. Floors have to be done up. Plumbing is just half-way through. Bathrooms and lavatories are not yet ready. Electrical wiring is in progress. Even doors are not yet in position! A separate external block of ten latrines and five bathrooms on the northern side has been started. Shell of brick is ready. That is all. I wonder if it will be ready for the Utsav. On the north-east corner the septic tanks (two large ones) are ready, but much work is yet pending. Connection (drainage) of latrines to septic tanks is yet to be given, even from the main Ashram Block. Trenching is in progress. Barbed wire fencing work is going on. All land is being "dressed" by layering with sand and compacting. The meditation hall is more or less ready but marble floor polishing is not complete. I think another 20 days work definitely remains to be done.

On return to Master's house I found Shri Ram Chandra Saxena, preceptor, retired Assistant Registrar of Co-op Societies from Moradabad, now settled in Shahjahanpur, waiting for me. He is doing much of the work done formerly by J.R.K. Raizada, but has no official designation. He is in charge, or has assumed charge, of the Utsav work. We spent two hours discussing necessary arrangements till 9:00 P.M. He appears to be capable and efficient, though perhaps easily irritated — I had no evidence of this, but surmise this from his face. He has not considered a great deal of things necessary to be done. We set down a list of things to be done, and set a timetable for achievement, to all of which he has agreed. I have left him in charge as I don't want any friction to develop at this stage and hamper the Utsav arrangements.

18 Jan. 76 - Sunday

There was some discussion about *avatars*, about liberated persons, etc. Master said, "Ramanuja has been liberated, but Sankara has not been liberated. Now look here, I have thought a great deal as to how Christ earned his liberation. He did not have the necessary approach for it but nevertheless he got liberated. I have not been able to understand this till now, and I will think about it further. I will tell you one thing. Shri Ramachandra is accepted by all as an *avatar* and I have thought about this quite a lot. I am not prepared to say that he was not an *avatar*, but even today I have some doubt about it."

Later I asked Master about my condition. He replied, "There is a good condition of merger, but there is some heaviness in it."

19 Jan. 76 - Monday

I had a long confidential session alone with Master. I put up to him the question of my donation of the cost of one room in the Ashram in memory of my mother. Yesterday, on our daily inspection visit, I found that Major Saudagar Singh, the Bhattar brothers of Calcutta, the Harnam Singh brothers of Delhi, etc., had donated one room each. Master himself has donated one room, and a large marble slab inscribed suitably in memory of his father Shri Badri Prasad, has been installed over the door. Master first demurred. He said, "No. I shall not allow you to spend so much money." But I kept asking him for permission again and again, reminding him that she had been liberated by him, and so it would be a fitting thing. Finally he agreed but conditionally. He said, "Look, the cost of this will be approximately Rs. 15,000/-. But I had announced it at last Basant as Rs. 12,500/- because I had urgent need for money. I like your idea but I shall take from you only half the amount, ie., Rs. 6,000/-, which you may send to me. That is enough. I shall not take more than that from you because you are the General Secretary of the Mission, and you are doing a lot of work for the Mission. Today I shall take you to the Ashram. You can select your room so that I can have the marble stone made. Please write on a piece of paper what you want inscribed on it and bring it to the Ashram. I shall select your room for you myself. I will tell you one more thing. I also paid only half the amount." (laughing)

I finalised the inscription on the marble slab to be fixed. It will read:

IN LOVING MEMORY OF
SRIMATHI R. JANAKI
BELOVED MOTHER OF
P. RAJAGOPALACHARI
GENERAL SECRETARY
SHRI RAM CHANDRA MISSION

In the afternoon we went to the Ashram and he selected my room for me. It is the same room as his. His is on the southern wing, mine on the northern wing. They are identical in all respects. Both rooms have long verandahs opening out in front and so have a view of the meditation hall, etc., which none of the other rooms have. Both are on the first floor where all 14 rooms are built.

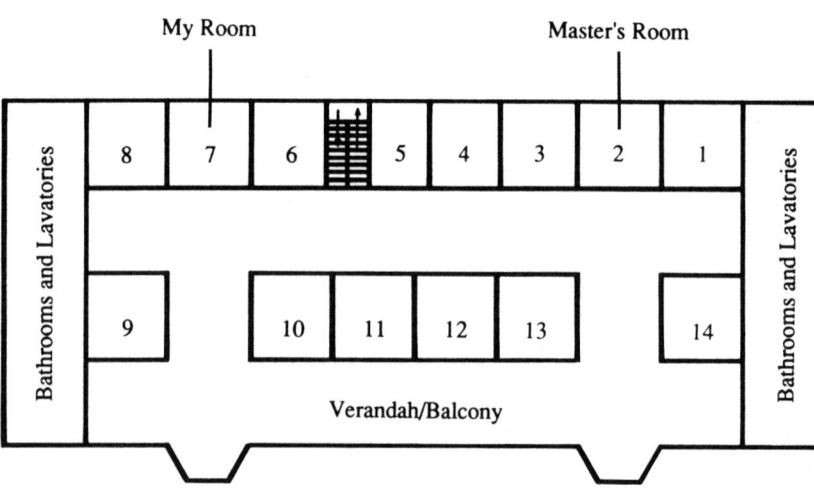

The rooms had not been assigned numbers. This posed a problem as Ramesh did not approve of any scheme which came under the 3 - 13, 8 - 18 scheme which they superstitiously avoid. Finally the rooms were numbered as shown, by which Master's room became No. 2 and mine became No. 7. The stone-cutter was called and given instructions for the slab to be fixed. Master enjoyed the visit to the Ashram and was immensely pleased with the room he had selected for me, and was as happy as a child.

I later discussed the need for a preceptor in Coimbatore, since the demise of Shri S.R. Sukaswamy leaves that centre without a preceptor. Master said, "Make a careful selection and make the preceptors yourself. You may do the work yourself but study the persons carefully."

I then asked about Shri Sukaswamy's condition when he left the body. Master answered, "Peaceful condition was there when he left, but there is no liberation. Yes. He took something else with him; he took some light with him but it is not liberation. There is one more thing. There was not the idea in him of coming towards me. Perhaps that idea may be formed but it has not occurred so far. Aré Saheb! What shall I tell you? For good souls it can even take 1000 or 2000 years. They keep wandering around this world, and if they are able to find a personality who can do their work for them then of course that work can be done in two or four minutes. All that is necessary to do is to make a will that such and such a person shall be liberated, and it is done!! Brother, if such a personality can be found then of course the work is possible. The personality can do this work for anybody whether he be good or bad, but to liberate a bad person can be considered to be against nature, if you look at it in one way. But brother, for one who has the Master in front of him no one can touch him, even if God himself is upset with him. (laughing boisterously)"

This discussion made several things amply clear:

1) A Personality can grant liberation to anyone of his choice. The person's character or his fitness or stage of attainment have nothing to do with this.

2) In the absence of a Personality, even a good soul can take thousands of years to achieve the point of liberation, if at all.

It was also clear that unless Shri Sukaswamy turned voluntarily toward Master, his future progress would be uncertain. This indicated the paramount need for 'awareness' on the part of the soul even after leaving the body behind. If awareness was lacking, then the inevitable conclusion is that the samskaras could drag one down. So, even after death, the soul MUST retain its longing, and have what amounts to a conscious approach towards the Guru, seeking merger in him. This point was later (a few minutes later) proved or clarified when Master referred to the late Vera Davies. He said, "Look here, Mrs. Davies is one such case where the person wanted to reach me alone. What devotion there is in her! I do not know why this is not found in everybody. This thing is found more among the foreigners."

Master asked me to take the weekly Monday evening satsangh. About 22 persons were present. Satsangh from 7:00 to 7:40 P.M. It was good.

After dinner Master was telling me about Lalaji, and how Lalaji had prepared detailed notes on the methods of performing miracles. Master said, "He had done research on all these things, and all these matters are present in His writings. But one servant maid sold all His writings thinking them to be waste paper and this has resulted in a great loss."

I asked him whether he knew about any miracles performed by Lalaji. Master said, "What was there that he could not do? Everything that he did was a miracle. He used to go for a walk sometimes and he used to keep his close disciples with him. On one such occasion one of his disciples stopped on the way and maybe he was absent for some time because when he looked he found Lalaji Saheb had gone ahead a considerable distance. A thought arose in the mind of the disciple that Lalaji had gone away very far, and at that very moment he was back with Lalaji."

I recall another instance, miraculous in a similar way, concerning Lalaji. Once someone brought news to Lalaji that a relation of his, in a village about 18 miles away, was seriously ill, and requested Lalaji to go to his assistance. It was already evening. Lalaji managed to find an aged Hakim to go with him. The Hakim worried about going so far, and that too with no conveyance to take them where they had to go. Lalaji merely told the Hakim to hold his hand and stop worrying. And 20 minutes later they were at the village by the sick man's bed without the Hakim ever knowing how they got there!!

20 Jan. 76 - Tuesday

I am busy with Utsav plans. Shri R.C. Saxena, formerly Assistant Registrar of Co-op Societies at Moradabad, now retired, a preceptor of 20 years, and an associate of Master for over 40 years, is the chief man here now. He is assisting me. He seems to have stepped into the gap created by the exit of J.R.K. Raizada, and is assisting Master even in correspondence.

This evening Master and I went to the Ashram on our usual inspection tour. I found my marble stone for the room with inscription finely cut thereon ready. It has to be fixed on the wall of the room assigned. Ramesh and Shri

Krishna Tandon were given suitable instructions before we returned.

Don Sabourin of Canada arrived by the Kashi Vishwanath Express at 9:15 P.M.

21 Jan. 76 - Wednesday

Master by himself started discussing my condition with me. He explained that my *layavastha* is good, or rather that his mergence in me has come to a good stage. He said, "Look here, whether I go to the Emperor's palace or whether the Emperor comes to my house, there is a very great difference in this!"

He said he has, or had, a book which explains how death can be brought about. He praised the book, which he said was in Urdu and published very long ago. I asked Master how Bhishma withheld his own death till the *Uttarayana*. Master answered, "Look here, we think the Uttarayana (northern path of the sun) to be of higher approach, and we think the *Dakshinayana* (the time of the sun's southern path) to be a lower approach and this seems to be all right in my opinion, and it must be correct. What it means is that he did abhyas and when he had acquired the higher approach then he gave up his life."

I then asked Master again how Bhishma was able to hold on to his life from the time he was mortally wounded till the time of his actual death. Master replied, "Perhaps his death was untimely, or it had come at the wrong time, and because of this he got the time to correct his approach, or make his own approach. Ordinarily when the time comes one has to go. Perhaps his death came before time — untimely death — and perhaps he had been practising some yoga by which he could postpone it. In my understanding nobody can delay death. Of course if there is transfer of life then that is another thing."

Later there was some reference to Swami Vivekananda. Master said, "In the beginning there used to be a lot of inter-communication between us, but not now. Of course occasionally if there is need for it then that is another thing. And perhaps now there is also no need for it. I will tell you one thing. You of course know that matter concerning evil spirits when there was an attack upon my life cell. At that time I had requested Shri Vivekananda to control their attack upon me, but then Saheb, the reply came, 'You do it yourself.' This did not appear to me to be correct. Aré Saheb! If I got Lalaji's order in this way that I should do it myself, that would have been another matter. He is the Master."

Then he suddenly changed the topic and said, "You have got a good man in Europe and that is Mr. Poray. Look here, in Denmark there are several persons who have so much love that it is not possible for me to describe it. It is present in all of them, and side by side they are also improving. You will get even more persons like this in Denmark."

He was silent for some time after this. Then suddenly he said, "I want to give you a cap. It will of course be old and torn because it must be a cap which I have worn. But Lalaji Saheb is saying "Not now." Yes. I wish to have you perform an initiation so that you may understand how it is done, but then people may suspect what it is all about, and therefore I shall wait a little."

At night Shri R.C. Saxena (Ramjibhai) came to my room and spent nearly one hour with me, voicing his concern for the future of the Mission, and his worries about Shri X's behaviour. He repeatedly spoke about the fissiparous tendencies developing, and the noticeable lack of discipline. I gave him a patient hearing. He was very outspoken and generally attributed the deterioration in morale to Master's unwillingness to give a proper lead to affairs, and to step into administration matters wherever necessary. He is terribly worried about Shri X and his belligerent, and often violent attitude to workers of the Mission. He openly stated that Shri X was responsible for throwing out J.R.K. Raizada, then Krishna Murari Saxena and finally Radha Raman Saxena. He is afraid that Shri X will pounce upon him next, as Master is entrusting more and more work and responsibility to him (Ramji). He wanted me to be aware of these problems and take a firm stand in vital matters for the good of the Mission. I was surprised to hear Ramjibhai say that Shri X has even threatened to wreck the ensuing Utsav if he is not given over-all responsibility and control. It seems he has even boasted in public that he would set up a parallel Mission and would attract "lakhs of people" to it!!

22 Jan. 76 - Thursday

At about 9:00 A.M. I was sitting with Master alone on the verandah. He said, "Last night I did a great deal of work upon you. I removed all the heaviness. Now you tell me how you are feeling."

I told Master that from the time I woke up I have been feeling joyous, and extremely light, with a state of something like intoxication, but extremely light, which is still present. It is not really intoxication but something like it in subtle form. Babuji said, "It is called *khumra*. When someone drinks wine there is intoxication. Afterwards when the intoxication is gone there is a certain condition present which is called *khumra*."

Sometime later there was some general talk about heredity, etc. After some time Master and I were alone again. He looked at me and said, "Look, I have studied one thing; your mother was a very good person. But the surprising thing is that her tendencies have not come down to you. All your tendencies have come to you from your father. This is a surprising thing. What is the reason for it?" I laughed and said, "What do I know about these things? Perhaps I had no control over these things and it is a question of heredity, and that is how we have to understand it." Master was quiet for a few minutes. Then suddenly he said, "Yes, but there is definitely one thing, her heart was very soft, and your heart too is very soft. This much is surely there. Maybe there are some other things also which have come from her in you but I have not studied that yet."

I then asked Master about my father's condition, explaining that he continues to be highly irritable, indeed increasingly so, and is still obsessed with childish hobbies, etc. Master said, "Look. There is a great deal of grossness, and he is also creating more and more. I am going on removing it, and he is going on creating more. It is very difficult to change in one's old age, but by Lalaji Saheb's grace, his approach has been achieved and that will be stable. But the surprising thing is that his grossness is having an effect upon you — I mean in spiritual matters. I have been observing this since the time we were abroad, and I have been noticing that grossness and heaviness are descending upon you from him. Of course I am pulling all of it out. Let me see what is going to happen in the future. But you need not worry about this. (laughing)"

Later I had a long talk with Master on organisational matters. He has been speaking highly of Ramjibhai and hinting that he would be an asset in any capacity in the Mission. Yesterday I had suggested to Master that Shri Gunde Rao Nagnoor, who is now permanently here in Shahjahanpur should be made Superintendent, Publications Department, which post remains vacant since Raizada's exit. Master has agreed to this. Now I suggested

Ramjibhai for the post of Joint Secretary, and added that even if he has to be remunerated for this we should consider this. Master readily agreed to this. He said, "Your suggestion is a very good one. I am also thinking on the same line but one big problem is Shri X. He will not allow this person to become the Joint Secretary, because he is totally against him, I don't know why. Now I shall think about this because the Mission's work is not being done, and I shall have to do something about it."

I took a bold step and told him about my own fears, and suggested that a time could soon come when Shri X might attack my own position. I told Master bluntly that Shri X had systematically thrown out workers at Shahjahanpur one by one, and told Master that all this was only because Shri X wanted the position of Joint Secretary to start with so that he could gain official control over Mission affairs. I told Master that only he (Master himself) could solve this problem, and that he must act soon before the situation deteriorated further. Master agreed and said, "Whatever you are doing is all done well and correctly. I also know that Shri X wants to have power in the Mission, but I don't want to do anything in a hurry. Confidentially I will tell you that if I make R.C. Saxena the Joint Secretary, then Shri X will become ready to take extreme steps — do you understand what I am saying? It is of this that I am afraid."

Just then Shri X came there, dressed to go to his office. Master called him and said, "Look here, I want to make R.C. Saxena the Joint Secretary. What have you to say about it?" Shri X said, "If you do this the Mission will be broken into bits and pieces. I shall never allow this to happen. I am looking after all the work and so what is the necessity for this? All the work that is there is being done by me, and if you give him the post then nothing but bad can come out of it."

Master replied in an irritated tone, "The work of the Mission is not being done, and things cannot go on this way. I have given you my opinion and this alone appears to me to be correct."

I told Master, "Now it is very clear that Shri X wants some position. What are you going to do about it? I feel that it would be best if you do not consult Shri X about Mission matters. What is the necessity to consult him? He is not even in the Working Committee." Master said, "Yes, whatever you are saying is correct. I am afraid that there may not be a fight between him and myself. You know that he is capable of taking extreme steps. Nothing will happen, but nevertheless I have to think carefully before I do anything."

I cautioned Master against giving him any official position in the Mission. Master replied, "I shall never do that. The Mission will be destroyed."

23 Jan. 76 - Friday

Don Sabourin left early morning for Lucknow to consult Dr. Agarwal regarding Master's treatment.

S.S. Ramakrishnan of Coimbatore turned up around 8:00 A.M. It appears he arrived last night from Lucknow, came to Master's house, saw everything dark and quiet and so went back to the station! Don came back at 8:00 P.M. with one month's supply of medicines for Master.

I have been giving sittings to Bhabhi, Y and Z almost daily. They all seem to be very keen to have quick spiritual progress. Today when I gave them a sitting, I had a new experience. In Bhabhi's heart I found thorns, thousands of them, pointing all ways, and choking the inside of the heart completely. It was very vivid.

Later I consulted Master as to this experience. He thought for a moment and replied. (1) The person would be of a very jealous nature, and (2) the person would be completely unreliable, and would let down a person precisely when assistance or support was needed. Therefore such a person should not be trusted.

24 Jan. 76 - Saturday

In the morning at about 10:00 A.M. Master asked me to go in and sit in meditation in front of Lalaji's couch. He came in some 15 minutes later to terminate the sitting. The first experience as soon as I sat in meditation was of something like total confusion. This lasted some time, perhaps five minutes. Then it was very deep, calm and peaceful, but there was no intoxication.

Speaking of thoughts, Master said, "It is only after the *sookshma sharir* (subtle body) has been broken that the formation of thoughts is stopped — that is after death. To my understanding the mind is like wet soil, and however much it may dry, there will always be some wetness in the ground, and if there should be rain again it will be soaked up immediately. Thoughts are also formed like this. Mind is of course there, and I have given you the example of the wet earth — if there is any such thing in the environment then thoughts arise."

In the evening when I went to the Ashram I found the marble slab had been installed in place but not yet set — it is held in place by bamboo poles — but looks nice and appropriate.

Ashram work is going on apace but nowhere near completion. The outside permanent latrines are not ready. Only walls and roofs erected. Flooring to be done, pans to be set in place, plastering to be done. A lot of work is left, so much of it that I wonder if these latrines will be ready for the Utsav. The main block too is incomplete. Leveling of the grounds where tents, *shamianas*, etc. will come up is in progress. Wash places on the outer ends are not ready. Plumbing is way behind.

26 Jan. 76 - Monday

At 10:00 A.M. Master gave Don Sabourin and me a sitting. It lasted about 25 minutes. It was very very deep. At one stage I felt as if the skull was about to split open longitudinally. Then, for the first time as far as I can remember, I felt vibrations in the region of the occipital prominence.

When I discussed my experience with Master, he said that he was going to break up a bondage. He did not elaborate.

In the afternoon I spent two hours at the Ashram with Don measuring all places and areas, and planning the location for temporary lighting, placement of tents and *shamianas*, location of PAX loudspeakers, etc. I made a map and handed it over to Ramjibhai. Y.K. Gupta of Bareilly came and the map was handed over to him subsequently as he will carry out this part of the work.

Satyapal from Pathankot and N.R. Gupta (Poultry Gupta) from Hyderabad arrived today. Uma Shankar Arya along with Smt. Jageshwari Devi, Daksha Rani and one other lady are here since 23 January. Work on cleaning of wheat and rice, dal, masala, etc., has been going on at a fast pace. Now the place is beginning to feel busy, and the old Utsav atmosphere is coming up. Master conducted the evening weekly satsangh.

29 Jan. 76 - Thursday

Tuesday 27th and Wednesday 28th, I have been in bed with what appeared to be a mild flu attack. It started with a chill, shivering and body ache, after which fever came on. I was attended upon by Dr. S.B. Shyam Rao of Gulbarga who arrived, I think, on the 26th together with his wife Nalini, Mrs. Shantabai Jahagirdar, and one Mr. Heble, a chartered accountant of Gulbarga who has been in the Mission for three months now. Don Sabourin has been nursing me most affectionately. This illness has had one direct benefit. Dr. Shyam Rao has become very close to me, and I believe quite affectionate too! He told me, "I have always been believing you to be a most proud and reserved person, but I find you to be so nice and friendly! It is a revelation to me." We spent a great many hours together in my room with myself doing most of the talking. I think he has been deeply affected by his talks with me, and I can count on having added him to my very short list of friends. Heble is very friendly too. Judith McKinney and her husband Neil have arrived a couple of days back, and Judith, too, has been looking after me, giving me leaf and herb teas etc. On the whole I have been excellently looked after, and I must say I have enjoyed my two days rest in bed. Satyapal has also been a frequent companion. But even though I have been in bed, I have done quite a lot of work too — what with meetings, conferences about Utsav arrangements, and long talks on Sahaj Marg, all in my room from my bed! Life is getting hectic now. Utsav-fever has caught on, and there is a lot of running around by everybody.

31 Jan. 76 - Friday

I am back in circulation. We had a long talk with Master on finances needed for Ashram maintenance which

I have estimated at minimum Rs. 30,000/- per year. Master has agreed that he will not undertake any further construction at Shahjahanpur during 1976. He will review the financial position of the Mission in 1977 and then decide on further work to be taken up.

When the others had left, Master suddenly looked at me, smiled and said, "When you came into the Mission at the same time the Goddess Lakshmi also came in with you. Now there is no shortage of money, nor will there ever be. It is all Lalaji's grace."

Ever since I came to Shahjahanpur, I have been taking ginger (about a 1/2 inch piece boiled in water and strained) with honey on the advice of Kashiram Agarwal — thrice a day, hot, — and I think it is helping me.

1 Feb. 76 - Sunday

N.S. Rao, his wife, and S. Narayanaswamy, all three volunteers from Madras Centre, arrived this morning. G.S. Mani and family also arrived, though the rule stipulates that they should not arrive before the 3rd! He (G.S. Mani) has not been amenable to discipline, and even the delegate donation was not paid in at Madras Centre but was telegraphically remitted to H.Q. just a few days back. The entire volunteer force arrived today from all over India and all are staying at the Ashram, accommodated in the two dining halls of the ashram building. Cooking starts from this morning at the ashram, the work being done by our own volunteer force, since the contract cooks will take over only on 3rd morning. Shri Uma Shankar is in charge of the kitchen and stores.

As I came out of the inner quarters in Master's house after having my lunch, I found Master sitting on the open courtyard in front of his verandah, sunning himself! Master called me to his side and said, "The sun is shining, and the moon is displaying its glory!" Having said this, he smiled intimately! I understood that he was referring to my condition and was hinting that he was happy with it.

At 1:20 P.M. Master and I were sitting alone, still on the paved courtyard. Suddenly he said, "Come, let me give you a sitting, but not here — let us go to your room." So we went into my room. He sat on the bed and I sat on an armless chair facing him. He transmitted to me, the sitting lasting for just about two minutes. I felt as if he was coming into me through my head — trying to enter in, feet first, through my forehead! When Master asked me how I felt, I told him this experience. He was very pleased, laughed with great pleasure, patted me on my shoulders and said, "Sabash! This was the thing! I was transmitting my condition to you. Now look here, it is on such special occasions that the mastery of the Master can be known. Such a person is called the Master. Lalaji Saheb was here — patting the bed on his side, indicating the place. Brother, it is a very important thing. It is rarely given to human beings."

Later at 2:30 P.M. or so I felt something crawling down my spine, halfway down the back, clutching the spine and making it chilly. The grip was a very real feeling. I reported it to Master. He did not seem to think much of it. In the evening *prasad* was offered on behalf of Chi. Umesh at his request through Narayanaswamy, by Don and myself. The sitting brought tears to my eyes. Narayanaswamy stayed the night in my room.

2 Feb. 76 - Monday

To the Ashram in the morning. Conducted a thorough inspection and found most things ready. The trench latrines — 26 in number — are getting ready on the north-eastern corner. Plumbing is almost complete. The residential block is ready including floor polishing.

At 10:00 A.M. I addressed a meeting of all volunteers on the Eastern court of the Meditation Hall, and spoke to them for 20 minutes. I then distributed badges and left it to Ramjibhai to do the detailed briefing.

From 2:00 P.M. the tents were put up. About 75 small ones were up by 6:00 P.M. These were supposed to be able to accommodate eight persons, and 10 at a pinch, but on inspection I found that they were meant for a couple, and could with the greatest difficulty accommodate perhaps just five persons! I had a long chat with Y.K. Gupta and asked him to put up 50 or 60 more by tonight and he has agreed to do so. Groups will start arriving tomorrow morning.

3 Feb. 76 - Tuesday

Sister Kasturi, Sister Kesar, Prahlad's wife Uma, and children all arrived this morning. About 790 abhyasis arrived in total till midnight, including the Madras group, which came by a special bogie leaving Madras by Link Express on 1st morning, arriving Delhi 3rd and connected, after marathon efforts, to the Kashi Vishwanath Express.

Master was to shift to the Ashram on the 1st. I had kept postponing it till today. This morning he wanted to move. I suggested to him that he could go to the Ashram each morning at 6:00 A.M. and come back to sleep at night, thus avoiding a lot of strain. For one and a half hours he held out. Then while we were sitting on the verandah, he suddenly smiled and said, "Look here, there is now inter-communication going on with Lalaji Saheb. He is saying 'When I am here, why do you get worried?'"

He then laughed and agreed that my idea was a good one and that he would sleep at home and not in the Ashram. Then he walked up to the well to wash, and I went with him. At the well he said, "I don't know why, but Lalaji Saheb is accepting everything that you say." Master decided that he would come to the Ashram in the evening. I took permission to go. Master said, "Yes, you may go there. When I am not there it is necessary for you to be there."

So I packed up and brought my things and was just beginning to load them in Captain Moorthy's car when Master came out to me and said, "Where are you going?" I told him I was shifting to the Ashram. He said, "No. Why have you to go there? It is unnecessary. You may sleep here with me. Yes, you may stay there the whole day and that is right. How can you leave me here and go there?" So I put back my luggage in my room and went to the Ashram. The whole day I was there, getting the routine fixed in everybody's mind — the volunteers — helping with tents, shifting the volunteers into tents etc. Today contract cooking commenced and by midday the planned processes were going like clockwork.

Master came at 4:00 P.M. He went round on a tour of inspection and was visibly relieved to find all essential things ready. I gave him dinner at 8:00 P.M. and brought him home by 9:00 P.M. He told me that I should take the next morning meditation, the first sitting of the Utsav, but that I should not announce it in advance.

When we left the Madras group had not yet arrived — they came much later around midnight due to a slip-up in our bus transport arrangements.

4 Feb. 76 - Wednesday

I left home at 6:00 A.M. drove to the Ashram with Captain Moorthy, and conducted the 6:30 A.M. group satsangh in the dining tents — one single *shamiana* 240 feet by 60 feet. About 1200 abhyasis were present. The sitting lasted 50 minutes or so. It felt very good to me.

Master came at 10:00 A.M. He told me, "Your transmission was very good. I have asked some other persons, and they also said that it was very good. There are of course many advanced persons in our *sanstha*, but in your transmission the people will find something special which they will not get from anyone else. You will be now transmitting from my condition. Isn't it? It is all the result of the transmission that I gave you two or three days ago."

The sales counter, the canteen, everything functioning ship-shape. Extra tents were put up. The Madras group was put up in a large tent capable of sleeping 100 persons! I was on my feet the whole day, going round and round the campus. I estimate I walked 10 miles today! Everywhere there was something I had to attend to, some instructions to modify, or some gap to step into briefly. The volunteers are working with enthusiasm and a will to get the Utsav conducted in grand fashion. The canteen is a novel innovation! It has been let out on contract and the Mission makes a small profit from it. The abhyasis are happy as the canteen is open 24 hours, and their general needs are fulfilled. I inspected the stuff in the canteen — tea, coffee, samosa, sweets, etc. — and found the standard good!

Master took the evening satsangh from 6:30 P.M. to 7:25 P.M. Later we had early dinner at 8:00 P.M. and I whisked Master home at 9:00 P.M.

At around 9:30 P.M. a highly agitated Ramjibhai telephoned to say, "Brother, I have had some trouble with Shri

X. I was sitting with my wife and children and some friends when he suddenly came up to me and said that all arrangements were breaking down, and that his friends felt insulted, and so on. Then he called me names in front of my family and insulted me badly. My daughter started weeping and is still weeping. My son was about to beat him but somehow I managed to stop him. I wish to be relieved from my responsibilities immediately, and you may make such arrangements as you wish."

I pleaded with him but he was terribly upset and agitated. So I told him I would call him back. I went to the verandah, called Master inside, and told him the whole thing. Master became very worried. He spoke direct to Ramjibhai on the phone. Master said, "Parthasarathi has told me everything. What do you want from me? Please tell me what you think is right." I then pleaded with Ramji that he could not ditch Master like this at an awkward moment in the middle of the Utsav, and with great difficultly prevailed upon him to continue. He made a very reserved statement, "I shall be here till you come in the morning and then decide finally."

The Working Committee of the Mission had met earlier today at 3:00 P.M. The meeting was presided over by Shri R.L. Mimani. We had decided that the post of Joint Secretary should be filled up soon, and the committee had so resolved, adding that a remuneration could be paid if necessary. I suspect that the Assistant Secretary, Dwivedi, has given this news to Shri X and this has caused this eruption.

I went to bed very upset myself — and prayed to Lalaji Maharaj to set things right. What will happen to the Mission if this person behaves like this?

5 Feb. 76 - Thursday

Got up at 3:00 A.M., fired the hot-water boiler, got ready by 4:00 A.M. and then woke up Master at 4:30 A.M. While I was going back to my room Shri X came out to go to the bathroom. He stopped outside my door and said, "Yesterday all your arrangements broke down." Then he went on to talk of Ramjibhai and his mismanagement. He went on for about 20 minutes ranting away and finally he said, "I have heard that you are going to appoint R.C. Saxena as the Joint Secretary." I denied that any decision had been taken as yet. Then he said, "No, I have heard that yesterday the decision was taken by the Working Committee. Look here, Saheb, if you appoint him then the Mission will be split into two. Nobody is there to accept him. Here without my permission no Secretary or anybody else can remain. If they will not go away when I order them to do so, then they will be thrown out by the power of bullets."

I took this as a direct threat and told him, "Look here! Nobody can chase me away, even if they shoot me. Of course, if I go by myself that is another thing. But no one can remove me from here!" He laughed and said, "Aré Saheb, nobody can say anything about you. Whatever you have got, you have got by your work. But I was only saying all these about Ramji. You may certainly take work from him, but do not give him any position. This is all that I have to say." Then I assured him that there was no decision to appoint Ramji as Joint Secretary at the Working Committee meeting, and clarified that the Committee had recommended to the President that the post should be suitably filled up. Anyway that there is a nigger in the wood-pile — the Assistant Secretary Dwivedi — is now certain as only he could have reported the deliberation to him. So begins Basant Panchami morning!! Master, Don and I left for the Ashram at 6:00 A.M. I gave a gist of Shri

X's conversation with me to Master. Master conducted the Basant Panchami meditation from 6:30 to 7:30 A.M. He then went to his room to rest, to await a call at 9:30 A.M. for the inaugural celebration.

With the assistance of Captain K.K. Moorthy and other volunteers I got things organised, the main Ashram and its external platforms on all sides cleared, volunteers posted at the four entrances, the red carpet laid etc. At 9:30 A.M. Captain Moorthy went and escorted Master to the Ashram, bringing him along a pre-specified route. Many cameras at work, including two movie cameras! As Master came up to the steps of the Ashram and stepped on to the red carpet I garlanded him on behalf of the Mission. I escorted him to unveil the two marble plaques, and there garlanded him once again. Then he was led to the entrance (NW) where I handed him a pair of silver scissors on a silver salver, which he took and ceremoniously cut the ribbon, declaring the Hall formally open. After a third garland, I escorted him inside, and seated him on the dais.

Then abhyasis and invitees were allowed to enter. It was an overwhelming surprise to see the hall jam-packed, and about 300 persons waiting outside on the platforms surrounding the hall. On the opening day itself the hall was full! The proceeding began with a speech by Shri R.C. Saxena (Ramjibhai) introducing the Sahaj Marg system to the invitees. Printed copies of this were also distributed to invitees. Simultaneously tea, and snacks were being served to invitees in the front *shamiana* specially erected for this purpose.

When Ramjibhai's speech ended I was supposed to read Master's message, "Love Universal", but I persuaded Master to read it himself so that the assembly had a delightful surprise. After this there were four speeches, the first by Sister Kasturi, the next one by Don Sabourin, the third by Shri S.A. Sarnad and the concluding talk by Sister Judith McKinney. The celebrations ended at 11:30 A.M. I escorted Master out to the front steps, put him into a waiting car (by prearrangement) and sent him home with Don.

3:00 P.M. meeting of the preceptors of the Mission. Shri Raghavendra Rao presided. Meeting till 4:30 P.M. No significant decisions emerged. About 50 preceptors were present, including Judith who was 'at sea', since everything was in Hindi!

Master returned at 6:00 P.M. and conducted the evening satsangh in the main Ashram — the first meditation sitting there. It was a superb sitting. This was followed by talks by Shri Raghavendra Rao and others, a very moving devotional music programme by Kasturi, some English songs on Master by Mari-Ann Johnson of Denmark, etc. The Secretary's Annual Report was read out. Master had early dinner at 8:30 P.M. and we left for home around 9:15 P.M. I have taken 'leave' for tomorrow and Master has instructed Shri Raghavendra Rao to take the final meditation sitting tomorrow morning. So for me Basant Panchami has ended.

6 Feb. 76 - Friday

Abhyasis kept coming to Master's residence the whole day for *darshan*, and were very well-behaved on the whole. Master was busy discussing income tax matters with some of the abhyasis. I went to the Ashram at 9:00 A.M. for a two-hour inspection round. Half the crowd were departing and, by 11 A.M., the place looked bleak and forlorn. The Madras bogie leaves tonight by Kashi-Vishwanath Express for Delhi.

Along with Brother C. Raghavendra Rao, IPS, I left by 9:00 P.M. for the station and returned to Delhi by the

Kashi-Vishwanath Express. The Denmark group leave tomorrow and Don on 11 February. I had no time for any separate talk with Master except for five minutes at about 11:30 A.M. when he called me inside and said, "You know that room outside which a marble slab has been put by you — you need not send any money for it. I will not take any money from you." I reminded him that he had decided I should pay 50% of Rs. 12,500/- and requested permission to remit this sum. He laughed and said, "No, you may forget this matter. You have done a very great deal of work for the Mission and you are also the Secretary and therefore I cannot take anything from you." So that is that! My mother's memory is firmly carved out in marble as a gift from my Master.

7 Feb. 76 - Saturday

Arrived at Delhi — stay at Broadway Hotel — spent most of the time with Ravi Verma who came at 6:00 A.M. to New Delhi to receive me!! Left by evening flight for Madras and arrived home at 10:00 P.M.

8 Feb. 76 - Sunday

Distributed 'Utsav' prasad brought from Shahjahanpur to our abhyasis of the Madras Centre and gave them a brief account of the Shahjahanpur celebrations.

20 Feb. 76 - Friday

At Bangalore. Yesterday the *Upanayanam* of my brother's two sons Chi. Sudarshan and Chi. Narayan was celebrated with Narayan under my ritual tutelage.

This evening Appa and I went to Mr. Hegde's residence (the same one, where J.R. Doreswamy Iyer used to stay) for satsangh. Shri Raghavendra Rao of Raichur had arrived. Appa and I were taken to see the Ashram site and the construction work in progress. It is an impressive site, large enough for our future needs too, on an elevated level, quite near the Mysore Road on its west and Basavangudi to the north. Then we came back to Hegde's house for satsangh. After satsangh I had an in-camera talk with Shri Raghavendra Rao for about 30 minutes on Mission matters, the need for discipline, etc.

21 Feb. 76 - Saturday (Bangalore)

Appa, Krishna, Sulochana and I had lunch with Col. S.C. Tandon and his nice family at their residence. Later we went to Malleswaram for satsangh where once again I met Shri Raghavendra Rao and Shri Jahagirdar. The Tandons have been coming to Appa frequently for sittings these 10 days (since the 17th February) that we have been here. They are a devoted couple.

16 Mar. 76 - Tuesday (Bombay)

Held satsangh in Room No. 3612 of the Oberoi Sheraton Hotel. Shri C. Rajagopalan had arrived this morning from Ahmedabad at my request. I am preparing him for provisional permission and he has had three individual sittings. In the evening sitting Dr. A.B. Jajodia and Mrs. Jajodia were present along with some seven others.

17 Mar. 76 - Wednesday

On behalf of Rev. Master I granted provisional permission to Shri C. Rajagopalan of Ahmedabad at 9:00 A.M.

At 2:30 P.M. I checked out of my hotel, and was driven by an abhyasi brother Shri Desai (of Chika) to the Ville Parle residence of Dr. Jajodia. About 20 assembled for satsangh including the veterans Bapubhai Desai, Mr. and Mrs. D.B. Motiwalla, Radhakrishna formerly of Chittoor, and others. After satsangh I was dropped at the airport at 5:00 P.M. and I returned to Madras.

24 Mar. 76 - Wednesday (Madurai)

Conducted group satsangh from 7:00 P.M. to 7:45 P.M. at Madurai Centre. About 45 abhyasis were present. I find the transmissions here at Madurai have something special about them which I generally don't notice elsewhere.

25 Mar. 76 - Thursday

Group satsangh at Valamjee Mansion from 7:00 P.M. to 7:45 P.M. It was an excellent sitting. About 22 present including Shri J.R. Doreswamy Iyer. A long question answer session followed.

26 Mar. 76 - Friday (Virudhunagar)

R. Varadhan of Coimbatore arrived at my request. I have started work on him this morning to prepare him for provisional permission. I think this is the 16th case that I am personally handling under Master's overall permission to me to "create preceptors anywhere".

Conducted evening group satsangh at the Virudhunagar Centre from 6:30 P.M. to 7:15 P.M., 28 persons were present. This centre has picked up after Shri P.K. Venkatesan was granted provisional permission. It had been sliding for some time under the stewardship of B. Rajagopal.

27 Mar. 76 - Saturday (Madurai)

Conducted group satsangh at Valamjee Mansion from 6 to 7 P.M. Nearly 25 present. Good sitting.

28 Mar. 76 - Sunday

Took group satsangh from 7:30 A.M. to 8:15 A.M. at Madurai Centre.

At 8:30 A.M. at Valamjee Mansion, on behalf of Master, I granted provisional permission to Shri R. Varadhan of Coimbatore. This has become necessary following the sudden demise, on last Divali day, of Shri S.R. Sukaswamy, preceptor of that centre. Coimbatore Centre has been falling back since then as S.S. Ramakrishnan is at Suratkal. I hope Coimbatore activity will now pick up again.

7 Apr. 76 - Wednesday

Long discussion with Shri Y in my office for over one hour. He is very bitter about the behaviour of Chi. L.S. after his marriage, and also about Babuji. I advised him and finally Shri Y said, "See, I do not want any wealth from Babuji, but I am not even getting that thing which I should get as a disciple. If he will give me a guarantee that I shall not be reborn again, then I shall never again open my mouth about property, nor will I ever make any complaints about it."

I laughed and said, "Is that all! It is not necessary to ask Babuji for your liberation. I give you this guarantee that your wish will be fulfilled. And I shall also say this that if ever it is a question of whether I am to be liberated or you, because both cannot be liberated, then it shall only be your liberation that shall take place, not mine. I give you this guarantee on behalf of Babuji Maharaj." I shook hands with him. Swaminathan was witness to this conversation.

9 Apr. 76 - Friday (Madurai)

Group satsangh from 6:30 to 7:30 P.M. at Valamjee Mansion. About 15 abhyasis were present including J.R. Doreswamy Iyer.

11 Apr. 76 - Sunday (Virudhunagar)

Group satsangh at Virudhunagar Centre from 8:30 to 9:15 A.M. About 25 abhyasis present.

In the evening conducted group satsangh at Valamjee from 6:30 P.M. to 7:30 P.M. Gave a talk on preceptor's duties in relation to their responsibilities to see that people who came into Sahaj Marg were treated with love and thus made to continue our *sadhana*.

Master's European Tour

(Full details are given in my book *Sahaj Marg in Europe*. Here only confidential matters, and such matters as could not be published in that book, are noted.)

4 May 76 - Tuesday

I left Madras at 6:30 P.M. by Indian Air Lines flight 440 for Delhi. Seen off at Meenambakkam by family members Sulochana and Krishna, and two or three abhyasis including S. Narayanaswamy and B. Ramachandran. Ganesh Viswanathan met me at Palam and we drove to Mr. Sundara's residence, where Master and I stay. On arrival there at 9:40 P.M., I found Master had arrived just a little earlier by car from Shahjahanpur, accompanied by brothers Y.K. Gupta of Bareilly and Gunde Rao. Master looked quite fit though tired after a long car journey in this summer heat.

After dinner there was a long discussion about the *kundalini*. One particular sanstha headed by a lady guru came up for notice, as all the abhyasis under her are said to have their *kundalini* awakened. Master commented on another *sanstha* which made a similar claim, and laughingly stated that according to his own reading, even the guru of that *sanstha* did not have his *kundalini* awakened — what to say of his disciples! Master added his usual statement that the *kundalini* had nothing to do with spirituality or liberation. He said, "Yes, there is a great deal of power, and when it awakens, or is made to awaken, then the power can be used in performing the work of Nature, and it can also be used in work on other worlds. But it is of no other use. Look here, there is also the danger in this, and if one tries to awaken it himself then there is a very definite danger. When my *kundalini* was awakened I began to experience a great deal of pain below the navel and I could not get rid of it. No doctor could do anything, nor did any medicine prove beneficial. But as soon as I attained my spiritual condition then the pain stopped by itself. Now look here, later on when I awakened the *kundalini* of Kasturi I asked her whether she was feeling any pain in her abdomen or in her navel. Kasturi answered that she was not feeling any pain. I watched her very carefully for one or two months. Now this is what I call experience. Now I have understood that the pain comes only when someone tries to awaken his *kundalini* by his own efforts, but when it is awakened by the guru's grace, then there is no danger of any kind. And as I told you there is no doctor or medicine which could help in this. There are two or three more persons in our *sanstha* whose *kundalini* has been awakened. In all these cases there was no pain."

Master later referred to the *kundalini*, and said much havoc had been wrought to the human system by ignorant attempts to awaken the *kundalini*. "Permanent harm can be done to the person," Master said, speaking to Mr. Sundara.

When Mr. Sundara queried whether this damage could be repaired, Master said, "Yes, of course it can be done but with great difficulty. The method is the same. Please make the will that the same conditions as prevailed before the *kundalini* was awakened may now prevail again. Then make an effort to create the necessary circumstances. It is of course very easy to say it, but very difficult to do it."

Master later laughingly revealed how he and Pt. Rameshwar Prasad had tried to demolish a wall between a temple and a mosque. The wall cracked but would not fall — and they discovered that they had been transmitting from opposite sides!

5 May 76 - Wednesday

Kasturi arrived from Lucknow accompanied by Shri Nasib Chand. She conducted the morning satsangh at 9:30 A.M.

2:00 P.M. — Kasturi gave me an individual sitting. At first I felt as if large banks of dark clouds were surrounding me. Then I became spherical, like a ball, which became brighter and brighter until it became so bright that the surrounding clouds became radiant, like burnished silver. Then this ball started moving, and wherever it went it made things luminous. At the next stage I felt as if I was the same inside and out. At the third stage I felt as if I and my condition were two separate things, and that a third entity was studying both. Sister Kasturi confirmed the readings.

4:00 P.M. Master presided over a Press Conference which ended at about 5:30 P.M. Master conducted the evening satsangh at 7:00 P.M. — over 60 abhyasis present.

6 May 76 - Thursday (Denmark)

Master and I left Mr. Sundara's residence at 11:30 A.M. for Palam. About 50 were present to see Master off. Due to delay in flight we were in the departure lounge for nearly 40 minutes after checking in and other formalities were completed. SAS flight SK 988 on a DC-8 aircraft finally took off at 2:00 P.M. — 50 minutes late! The first halt was Frankfurt, after a steady nine hours flight. We landed at Frankfurt at 6:20 P.M. local time (10:50 P.M. IST) took off at 7:00 P.M. and landed at Copenhagen at 8:30 P.M. (0100 hours IST). Jytte Gravesen was in the baggage enclosure to greet Master. We were soon joined by Judith Polston McKinney and Henrik Babu. About 60 abhyasis were present outside to welcome Master. We were driven home by Ole in Birthe's car to the home of Mikala and Palle Kousgaard in Ehlersvej.

7 May 76 - Friday

The accumulated mail awaiting us included a copy of the French translation of *Voice Real*, printed in Etoy by Stella Jaquerod-Davis. She is also the translator.

Master told the abhyasis, "Denmark is growing richer, both materially and spiritually. By Master's grace I want that the whole world should grow like that. It is not only that Shahjahanpur may grow or that India may grow — the whole world should grow, and in this you all must assist. I am telling you Parthasarathi can do as good work as I can. There is only one difference. I am very assertive in my talk, and in this he is wanting. This is only due to lack of experience and nothing else. It is necessary to understand how to exercise the will, and that is an art. Experience alone can teach this, and words are useless to describe how it should be done." I was somewhat shocked by his reference to me as I had always imagined that I was very assertive!

Master conducted group satsangh at 10:30 A.M. It was a fantastic sitting, sending me deeper and deeper. I also experienced a constant physical push to the left, even though I kept righting myself again and again. This sitting of 35 minutes duration was superb.

Don Sabourin and his wife Jackie arrived from Canada. They will accompany Master throughout his European tour. They brought a heavy load of books for me.

At noon Master gave Thomas Mogensen a special sitting and asked me to sit and observe his work. The sitting was for about 20 minutes. I found Master cleaning the upper chest area thoroughly. Thomas's condition appeared to have crystallised into a solid ovoid in the area of the heart. It was quite bright but solid, and like an egg in shape. Master spread the condition out again. After this I had a suggestion of cleaning of the astral body and then the sitting ended.

Master confirmed my reading, with the following corrections. (1) The solidified condition was spherical in shape and not ovoid, as I had seen it. (2) He had actually not cleaned the astral body, but the suggestion I had received was correct. Master said, "Look, I have of course not cleaned the astral body, but you have had the right suggestion. It was necessary to clean it. See, you have read the conditions correctly."

Just before the sitting ended, Thomas appeared to me like a bent and shrivelled old man, with head bowed down. Master said this was because Thomas was "carrying a load of worries". With a mischievous twinkle in his eyes Master asked Thomas, "Shall I tell you the truth? You are overburdened with worries and so you have become dull in your work. It is noticeable particularly in your relationship with Vibe, who is also under strain. These things are telling upon you. Now it is in your hands to correct the things — and you must do it. I have thoroughly cleaned you. The rest is now your work and you have to do it." Thomas confirmed all that Master had said, and promised to work upon himself.

The Danish preceptors have formally represented to Master regarding Bent Ruus, requesting his removal from preceptorship. Master discussed this with Birthe and Thomas, Jens and me. It was decided to withdraw the provisional permission given to him in 1972 as of date, and a letter was issued accordingly.

After lunch I was alone with Master. Master said, "Look here, you have prepared some persons for the granting of permission for the work and you have done good work. But in one or two cases there has been something lacking. Not in all cases of course. I am only mentioning those cases which come before me in my vision. Perhaps you did the work in a hurry because I find that the cleaning was insufficient. You should try to do more thorough cleaning. Of course you have done the work well, and I see that the power is present in all of them, but the beauty is not there. Whenever you prepare someone please do thorough cleaning, and then make this thought that there is a beauty being created in them, and try to spread that beauty throughout their system."

This is the first time Master has referred to this aspect of my work — the preparation of persons for provisional permission.

Master developed a mild diarrhoea. He conducted the evening group meditation from 8:30 to 9:20 P.M. About 100 abhyasis were present. The food preparation is in charge of Leela Srinivasan and Jette Smith. Leela is the wife of Raja Srinivasan cashier at the Sheraton Hotel here. They are a nice couple with a one year old daughter. They are helped by Mikala and Leif's Kirsten.

8 May 76 - Saturday

Master better, but complained of a "tendency" to diarrhoea. As the first hookah was under way, Master told me, "I had mentioned about the inter-communication for you, but he (Lalaji) said that when the work grows that condition will automatically open up in you. It is not necessary to do anything now. Look here, I have already placed you in the position of *Dhurvathipati*. The next stage is that of *Parishad*. Lalaji Saheb told me, 'Let it be for the present. The preparation has not been completed.' And after *Parishad* there is *Maha Parishad*. What should I tell you about it? There can be only one such person in the whole universe. Lalaji Saheb has told me, and I have also written it down in my notes somewhere, that if this condition is transferred during my lifetime then it is possible, otherwise, after I pass away it will leave me from one side (pointing from heart to the left side out of the body) and pass off. When Lalaji Saheb took me up to that condition, he praised me very much. He said, 'That thing which does not come down in thousands of years has now descended upon you. And it is possible that even after you there shall be one who shall occupy this position.'" Master continued, "Now let us go forward and see what happens in the future."

Master was tired and complained of increasing weakness. He took the 10:30 A.M. group satsangh and later gave Jens Clausen a special sitting.

At 4:00 P.M. all preceptors present assembled before Master. Addressing them, he said, "I am glad that you all are working so well for the public good, or good of the people, whatever you may call it. Today I want to give you all a special sitting so that you may all become energised to do even more and better work." Preceptors present included Birthe, Vibe, Thomas, Elsebeth, Jan and Jytte, Henrik Carlsen, Judith, Hans Knakkergard, all of Denmark; Jan Van Den Beemt of Holland, Jackie, Don and Christine of Canada, and Fred Weinstock of the U.S.A. Jens, though not a preceptor, was allowed to join. I felt the transmission begin from the *brahmanda mandal*, and 'saw' Master equalising the condition of each person over his entire system, spreading it out and activating it. The sitting lasted 20 minutes.

This was followed by a preceptor's meeting which Master presided over. It was over by 5:30 P.M.

9 May 76 - Sunday

Master better. He conducted morning satsangh at 10:30 A.M. — 100 abhyasis were present. At 3:30 P.M. we all went to the deer park 'Dyrehaven', where Master and about 30 abhyasis enjoyed a charabanc ride for almost an hour. On the return journey Master went home with Mikala while I went with Don to Vibe's house before going home.

10 May 76 - Monday

Master a bit weak. Yesterday's brief outing seems to have affected him somehow. No morning satsangh — in future there will be only one per day. I conducted the 8:30 P.M. satsangh with over 100 abhyasis present. Apart from this I gave all the individual sittings during the day.

F.O. Petersen of Auckland, New Zealand, a Dane living in there for over 35 years came to see Master at 3:30 P.M. Seems to be interested in this system.

Some questions and answers:

Q: What were you in your past life?

A: What is the proof, if I say something?

Q: I don't want any proof.

A: "I was born in the Vaishya community. I was poor. I had a long, thin wife and five children. I was doing some small business." Master then laughed and added, "Look here! That tendency of the *Baniya* is here in this life also!"

Q: Have you come into this life out of compulsion or of your own free will?

A: Midway between the two.

Q: Was Lalaji born before this life?

A: With emphasis, "No! That is impossible!"

Q: What is life?

A: Well, there are so many definitions. But I tell you my definition. Life in life is the real life!

11 May 76 - Tuesday

Today I conducted the 8:30 P.M. group satsangh, a separate group satsangh for 12 university people, and 14 individual sittings.

Master was badly constipated — has had no bowel movements since leaving home. He was forced to use suppositories and had relief at 11:00 A.M. He rested the whole day. After the evening satsangh a group of our sisters sang Kasturi's songs in Hindi for about half an hour. Delightful!

The first week of absence from Madras ends. Fourteen percent of tour over!

Parthasarathi and Babuji Maharaj
Copenhagen, 1976

G.L. Saravanamuttu, Reverend Babuji, Parthasarathi
Rome, 1976

12 May 76 - Wednesday

At 10:00 A.M. a lady, wife of Eric Kircheiner, came to see Master. She is a disciple of a guru near Poona and is on the *shakti* path. Violent emotional behaviour almost upset the hookah! She was with Master for half an hour. She appears to be sincere and in need of help but does not want to leave the old *shakti* method, which, she said, has already endangered her life by putting her into a trance-like-fit or seizure while driving a car!

I conducted the evening 8:30 P.M. group satsangh but gave only four individual sittings as Master wants me to rest!

13 May 76 - Thursday

Good night's sleep — the first night so far during which I have been able to get seven hours sleep! Thanks to a cloudy sky no early morning sunlight (the sun rises here at 4:00 A.M.) was there to disturb my sleep.

At 10:55 A.M. Master granted Jens Clausen provisional permission.

At 11:30 A.M. Master presided over a meeting of the U.S. and Canadian preceptors — Don, Jackie, Christine, Fred and Judith. Master unhappy about the U.S. No work done there. Spoke plainly to the sole U.S. representative present in no uncertain terms! Said it was up to them to make use of him for spiritual development if they wanted it!

2:00 P.M. to 4:00 P.M. I was with Jens and Thomas auditing the accounts of the Danish Mission for the past three years. They have a very good system, flexible while being exhaustive.

Conducted the 8:30 P.M. group satsangh. Mikala, Palle, Birthe, Leela, Jette Smith all had dinner with Master — all of them were overjoyed.

14 May 76 - Friday (Germany)

Till yesterday it was all sunshine and fine weather. This morning it is heavy clouds, rain and cold winds! We left Mikala's house at 9:30 A.M. for the airport and found 25 abhyasis grouped there to say 'farewell' to Master as we leave for Germany. Vibe in tears all the time, far away in a corner. She is getting more and more emotional instead of less and less.

Accompanied by Don and Jackie we left by LH-015 scheduled to leave at 11:30 A.M. but left late at 12:10 P.M. We arrived in Hannover at 13:00 hours, attended to immigration formalities, took off at 13:55 and landed at Munich at 2:40 P.M. Having Don and Jackie has been a help as Don goes ahead to get good seats, which I can't do if Master and I are the only ones to travel. Then we are invariably the last to board. Now Don goes ahead, gets seats in the smoking area and we go in a leisurely manner, and board last, and yet have good seats. A decided help.

When we got off the plane at Munich I was stunned to see a welcoming crowd of 15 at the foot of the mobile staircase, right by the plane, headed by Inna and her husband! I found Zora Tuner too has come from Yugoslavia and was waiting, self-effacing as usual, in the background. A red carpet welcome to Master in every sense! Inna presented Master a huge bunch of roses and lilies. Master was very tired, but revived in spirit amazingly. H drove us to the Hotel Garni Eisenreich where Master and I have a double room on the 1st floor. We rested till 6:00 P.M., then went with H to his house in Schuleinplatz for supper, and came back to the hotel for Master to preside over the first public meeting of this tour held in the hotel dining room at 7:00 P.M. The room was full. H told me Inna had been doing all the organising for this meeting.

H spoke for 10 minutes in German introducing Master and the Sahaj Marg system. Then I spoke for about half an hour on "Purification and Regulation of the Mind by Sahaj Marg Yoga" — and H translated simultaneously, doing it very well too!

One person I saw at the meeting — sitting on the floor right in front — impressed me much. Later I was introduced to him — Rolf Muller, a young boy trying to get into medical college — will be good future 'preceptor' material! Another person, a goateed young man also very impressive — Jean Marie Bottequin — a Belgian.

The whole group had a sitting after my lecture ended at 9:00 P.M. Then as all wanted to commence our system, Master transmitted again to them. The meeting ended 9:30 P.M. Master was taken up to his room by Don while I spent half an hour with H discussing the rest of the Munich programme. An exhausting day but a rewarding one too.

15 May 76 - Saturday

H picked us up at 9:15 A.M. and took us home. Master conducted group satsangh for half an hour — about 30 present including Zora of Yugoslavia. She is strangely silent, and refuses to be drawn out. She is watching everything keenly. When I told her that she could have a special sitting with Don she laughed, rather sarcastically, and said, "I cannot be a spiritual prostitute. If I am to sit, I shall sit only with you or Master!"

After satsangh I spoke to the group for about one hour. After lunch I spoke for about 40 minutes. These talks could not be included in *Sahaj Marg in Europe* as I had no tape recordings available.

H asked Master — "Master! I have given you this house and everything in it. Is there anything more that I can offer you?" Master, while washing his hands replied, "You can give me yourself." H did not follow this. I explained to him that he should offer to take up Master's work. He did so at once. Master agreed to grant him provisional permission and also to Inna, "whose condition is better." We had lunch and dinner with H and Inna and got back to the hotel around 8:00 P.M.

16 May 76 - Sunday

I conducted group satsangh at 9:30 A.M. at H's house — about 20 were present. The sitting was 40 minutes in duration. In that time Master took up the cases of H and Inna and both were granted provisional permission. After this we all were driven to the Stadtische Krankenhaus to see Antee Graune, a girl abhyasi who is hospitalised there. Master spent 15 minutes with her and then we all drove back to Schuleinplatz. Irene Brant Ramierez took a lot of pictures of the Master. She is 'going' with Rolf, and is a Mexican girl settled here in Germany.

At Schuleinplatz we found a young Yugoslav girl — Mirjam Zupancic. Looking for someone — she did not know whom to look for. Then by enquiry I discovered that she had met Tom Whitlam who had asked her to go here, presumably to meet Master. I spoke to her in Serbo-Croat, which astonished her considerably, and told her to wait there. We all had to go to meet a group of Freemasons at the home of Mannfried Giesel, who is already our abhyasi. So too is Jean Marie Bottequin. But about 12 others are not, and they wanted to meet Master separately as a group. We spent about two hours there and then came back to

Schuleinplatz for lunch. Mirjam started our puja with Don. We now have two abhyasis in Ljubljana!! And only this morning Zora was in tears, discussing her personal predicament in her country and bewailing her fate at being alone! She has not come back yet after she went off this morning after satsangh.

2 P.M. to 4 P.M. a hectic session of question and answers. No record available with me. Master hilarious. Just then Zora turned up, was introduced to Mirjam, and hugged her with joy.

Master said, "Philosophy is the way of thinking; Yoga is the way of doing; and Realisation is the way of undoing." Master discussed this and referred to the Sanskrit term *akarta* for 'undoer'! When I asked Master to explain this he said, "When something is put before the sun — S U N — that is undoing!" I said I still did not understand. He then referred to the conversion of hydrogen to helium in the sun and referred to this 'undoing' for the creation of light! I then suggested to him that the phrase, "Can it stand the light of day?" is used to mean precisely this. If it can, it need not be 'undone', but if it cannot then it has to be 'undone'. I also suggested that Sahaj Marg cleaning is such a process of undoing!

Some questions and answers followed. Then Master spoke about the real goal of our system. He said, "The goal is to achieve the original condition that was prevailing before this creation came into being." Mirjam who was sitting on the floor close to Master, almost hugging his knees, asked what was the use of all this knowledge if it, the condition about which he was talking, could not be experienced. Master tried to put her off but she was insistent on the need for actual personal experience. Master laughed and said, "All right! I will give you an experience of that condition but it will be for just a minute, and it is possible you may not feel anything." He transmitted for about two minutes. Mirjam said she felt very calm. I had felt a palpitation in the heart. Master verified that the feeling was correct but not in the heart — it must have been in the mind! He said, "Look here, there is a great deal of power. And when it is used in the lower regions then jerks are felt."

Saravanamuttu and Clara Scramoncin came from Rome at 6:00 P.M. having driven all the way.

8 P.M. to 9:15 P.M. another lively session of questions and answers. Then we came back to the hotel. Referring to Mirjam, Master said, "I have shown people that I only adopt a practical approach. Now let me teach you too something! Fixing the thought upon the heart, I created this condition from the central region. There is some danger, and therefore one has to keep a watch on one's heart. I had given this up but today by Lalaji's grace I have shown this to this girl. She will at least carry away some impression about this with her!"

A hectic day on the whole!

17 May 76 - Monday

Master was in a very affectionate but deeply introspective mood in the morning. He said, "Look here, little by little I want to teach you all the work. I have been thinking that I should have one initiation done by you, so that you may know the method of doing it. After we return to Madras I shall perhaps have you take up the case of Krishna for this. If I take up anybody else's case, the whole secret may be revealed, and that I do not wish to happen now. Anyway let me tell you the method. Take the hand of the abhyasi in your hand — I hope you remember what I did in your own case — and then make an effort to pass one drop of your spiritual wealth into the abhyasi.

That is all — but only one who has earned something can do this. (laughing) I shall think over this matter in Madras and decide whether I should have you initiate Krishna or not."

Then there was a long discussion about *Dhruv Pad, Dhruvadhipathi, Parishad* and *Maha Parishad*. Master said, "In the whole Universe, there can be only one *Maha Parishad*. He is next in position to God, and there can be only one such. You of course know who is occupying that position now!" I answered that he was there. Master smiled and said, "Yes, I do not wish to speak about this openly but nevertheless I am now occupying that position. It is Lalaji's grace that he gave me this position. Now the position of *Parishad* is vacant and there is no one in that position. Everything happens according to the requirements of Nature. In the *Dhruvadhipathi* you alone are there, and Viraraghavan is there. I do not remember whether there is anybody else or not. The position of *Maha Parishad* cannot be transferred to anybody else during my lifetime. It can be only after my lifetime. Whatever other positions there are can of course be given to anyone, and they can also be withdrawn. I am now occupying the position of *Maha Parishad*, but after this, I mean after myself, it will be your turn."

Inna took the morning group satsangh. Master gave Zora an individual sitting.

In the evening Master related a Sufi story about a parrot's way to freedom which I related in English to the abhyasis. Then there was a short session of questions and answers.

Q: Where does man come from? What is the purpose of his existence? And where does he go?

A: He comes from the Source. His final destination is the Source, and the purpose of this existence is to go back to the Source!

This was my answer. Master appreciated it very much.

Clara Scramoncin of Italy has agreed to work as a preceptor. We left H's house at 9:00 P.M. after saying goodbye to all, as we leave tomorrow for Switzerland.

18 May 76 - Tuesday (Switzerland)

I missed seeing Zora. Evidently she had packed off either late last night, or left this morning very early for Ljubljana.

We got packed early. Master well rested and cheerful. H picked us up at 8:00 A.M. and took us home to Schuleinplatz where Master had a glass of orange juice and spent five minutes with assembled abhyasis before leaving for the airport. On the way to the airport Master told H of his disturbed night — disturbed by lascivious thoughts — which he attributed to his bed linen. He could sleep only after he cleaned it at 3:00 A.M. or so!

About 15 abhyasis saw Master off.

We left Munich by SR 551 scheduled to leave at 9:35 A.M. but took off 9:40 A.M. and arrived Zurich at 10:10 A.M. We had to change planes there. Don and I did some window-shopping and then, as we were going down the stairs to the departure lounge, Master stumbled at the last step and had a minor fall. We took flight SR-242, scheduled for 11:35, but it only took off at 12 noon due to some extra passengers having been taken on for whom there was no accommodation.

We landed at Geneva at 12:30 P.M., and passed out of Customs at 12:55 P.M. to find Stella Jaquerod-Davis, her husband Roland, a Dutch group of six and some Swiss abhyasis assembled to welcome Master. Stella had two garlands. One she garlanded Master with. The other I garlanded Master with, on behalf of all Swiss abhyasis!

Master rested for half an hour and then we drove off to Etoy, 50 Km. from Geneva, almost 45 Km. being on the autoroute. Master had been very apprehensive of this road journey — he has been threatening to cancel his Swiss tour ever since we came to Germany — but the drive was uneventful and pleasant. He was also moody on the plane, as he remembered that the hookah basket was lost in 1972 in Switzerland.

At Etoy, Atonietta Bernardi came to see Master, accompanied by Marie Louise and two sisters from Latina, Anna-Maria Rizzo and Rina Rizzo. Elidir Davis and Kathleen Burke Collis of U.K. also arrived, followed by Ron Mendelsohn and his wife Pauline with two children. Fred Weinstock came in at 6:30 P.M. having come from Copenhagen by train. We all had outdoor lunch on the lawn at 3:00 P.M. I received a letter from my son Krishna written from his N.C.C. Camp at Ooty, the first letter from India!

Master conducted group satsangh at 7:00 P.M. — 26 were present. Toni spoke to Master about Italian Sahaj Marg and proposed the two Rizzo sisters for provisional permission.

19 May 76 - Wednesday

I gave preparatory sittings to Anna-Maria and Rina. Master conducted group satsangh at 10:00 P.M. Andre Poray, Birthe, and Vibe all arrived today. At 2:30 P.M. Master granted provisional permission to Clara Scramoncin of Rome.

7:25 P.M. we left for Geneva for a public meeting over which Master presided — well attended — I gave a lecture which Master liked very much. He suggested the title "Need for Need" for it. Back at 10:15 P.M. to Etoy and bed at about midnight.

20 May 76 - Thursday

No morning programme at Etoy. We left Etoy at 9:00 A.M. for Morges in heavy rain to attend the meeting of all European preceptors convened for this morning there at the Hotel Du Mont Blanc. Master presided and I officiated as the Secretary. The meeting began at 9:30 A.M. Those in attendance were:

Master
myself

West Germany:
H
Inna
Rolf Muller
Irene Brandt Ramirez
Renate Baumann

France:
Andre Poray

Italy:
G.L. Saravanamuttu
Clara Scramoncin
Antonietta Bernardi
Anna-Marie Rizzo
Rina Rizzo

UK:
Elidir Davies
Kathleen Burke-Collis
Ron Mendelsohn

Holland:
Bernadette Van Steven

Denmark:
Birthe Haugaard
Vibe Erstad

Switzerland:
Stella Jaquerod-Davis
Roland Jaquerod

USA:
Fred Weinstock

Canada:
Don Sabourin
Jackie Sabourin
Christine Langstaff
Tom Whitlam

Total 26 present representing nine nations apart from India. U.S.A. and Canada representatives have 'observer' status only. The others are grouped as European members.

I started the meeting by laying down broad parameters of functions and objectives, and proposed the formation of a European Council. I spoke for about half an hour outlining the historical background of the Mission, and explaining the need for a European body for integrated planning and guidance. Then H delivered his inaugural address. The subject was then thrown open for discussion by all. There was a great deal of discussion on why an organisation was needed at all! Elidir and Ron were particularly and vehemently critical of organisations! Kathleen supported them but not so vociferously. After this I spoke again, re-emphasising the historical background of Mission work and its development in India. I spoke quite at length about this, seeking consensus.

Master intervened to say, "I don't want disorganisation. So we go towards organisation. We come from infinity. So we feel lonely here, and search for others to help us, or to be with us. This is natural. So organisation comes into being."

Immediately all agreed to the formation of a Council for Europe.

1) Name will be "Shri Ram Chandra Mission European Council". The heads of national Mission Organisations in Europe would be members of the Council (Birthe, Jan Van Den Beemt, H, Stella, Andre, Sara and Elidir). They may be accompanied by aides of their choice from their respective countries. Initially the Council will meet once a year or oftener.

2) It was decided that national heads should try to have the Mission registered in their countries as early as possible.

3) Translation of Mission literature — to be reviewed by editorial groups for each language before publication.

4) Choice of preceptors to be Master's. We may **suggest** where we feel a person may suit.

The meeting ended at 12 noon. Master rested for an hour in Don's room in the hotel with Sara, Clara, Don, Inna, H, Birthe, Jackie and Chris in attendance. Then we all had lunch together which Master enjoyed. We got back to Etoy at 2:45 P.M.

At 4:00 P.M. Master granted provisional permission to Anna-Maria Rizzo and Rina Rizzo of Latina, Italy.

At 8:00 P.M. Roland projected a film he had taken of Master. Very shaky and poor in quality.

21 May 76 - Friday

Master severely constipated. He was unwell and in bed the whole day. All were in his room throughout the day. He had his meals served to him in bed. Stella loves fussing over him!

The morning satsangh was taken by Don Sabourin, while Birthe took the evening satsangh.

22 May 76 - Saturday

Woke up early at 5:30 A.M. and packed up for departure for Nice. But when Master woke up he complained of much pain and weakness. He looked very tired and weak, and at 7:00 A.M. I decided to cancel our journey. Spoke to Don at Morges and requested him to tell Andre Poray of this and also to cancel our Geneva/Nice flights and request fresh reservations for tomorrow etc. Andre goes on to France as planned today.

8:00 A.M. Master said, "Look here, I have just got an order from above 'Postpone travel for today.'"

A doctor was called at 9:00 A.M. Master was examined thoroughly and medicines prescribed. Urine samples were taken. At noon, in view of Master's weak condition and continued pain, I decided to change travel plans as under:

Tuesday 25/5   Geneva - Nice

Sunday 30/5   Nice - Rome

Saturday 5/6   Rome - Copenhagen OR Rome - Delhi depending on Master's physical condition.

Master approved this. It was decided to cancel Sanary and St. Come as involving long car journeys.

At 3:30 P.M. I telephoned Andre Poray at Nice and gave him the revised programme. He was very upset as he has made a lot of arrangements and fixed three lectures for Nice. But I could not help it. I requested his help and co-operation, and secured it by promising to go to Sanary if train travel could be arranged. He agreed to this and the phone call ended amicably.

The doctor came again at 4:30 P.M. and examined Master all over again. He said Master's condition was primarily due to exhaustion, and that he should "eat double, sleep double and rest double!"

5 P.M. - 6 P.M. with Don at Morges. At 8:00 P.M. we decided to cancel our visit to Denmark and go back to India from Rome. Wrote to Mikala and my father accordingly indicating return to Delhi by 6th June.

H, Inna, Rolf and Fred are still here. Irene Brandt and Renate left for Munich this morning. The two Van Steven sisters have also left. Albert and Francoise and the baby are here.

Don and Jackie have been planning to do Europe a second time by car after Master left. Today they are thinking of accompanying him to India!

At night Master spoke about a spiritual representative and said, "He must be very straightforward and he must also be quite handsome. There should be no deformities in him such as can repel others."

23 May 76 - Sunday

Telephoned Jens to give him a possible schedule including a return visit to Denmark. Master had an oil massage and a bath followed by a light breakfast. He is very fresh this morning. He decided that as he is getting old and may not be able to come outside India again, he would complete the present trip as planned!! It was therefore decided to go on as per original plans, making changes only when necessary.

Andre telephoned to confirm France travel and other work plans from Nice.

I went at 4:15 P.M. with Roland and his son Pierre-Edouard to Caux to leave the son there at school, and got back at 7:30 P.M. Master well. Doctor visited again and certified him as fit as he can ever be. H said goodbye to Master as he leaves for Sanary by car with Rolf tomorrow early morning. Christine Langstaff had gone to Nice but returned to spend a few hours with Master. She left at 9:00 P.M. to return to Canada.

Stephan Peter Brander has been chosen to be a prefect to assist Stella in her work. Roland too has been considered for this at Stella's request.

24 May 76 - Monday

Master didn't sleep much last night but is looking better generally. After an early bath he 'exercised' for some time in the lovely rain-wet garden and lawn for half an hour and spent two hours with abhyasis in the downstairs drawing room. Franco Giusti and his secretary Marielli Gniechhi who had come from Milan to meet Master left for Milan today.

Jens telephoned and I confirmed that Master will visit Denmark again as planned. He was naturally very very happy to hear this. Don and Jackie have decided to go back to India with Master — though not on the same flight — and I requested Jens to arrange for their travel.

2 P.M. - 6 P.M. with Roland, Don and Jackie for a shopping spree in Lausanne.

I gave a morning sitting at 8:30 A.M. and a second one in Master's presence at 3:30 P.M. to Stephan Brander to prepare him for provisional permission. Later, after the second sitting, Master congratulated me on my work. He said, "You have done very good work. This case was a very difficult one. Normally in preparing this case it could not have taken less than three months, but you have done this in just two sittings. You have done very well. Now I am convinced that you will do my work well because now I have the proof of it. Haven't I seen you work myself?"

In the evening I conducted group satsangh at 9:45 P.M. This is our last evening at Etoy!

25 May 76 - France

Got up at 5:00 A.M., packed up and ready by 6:30 A.M. Left Etoy at 8:00 A.M. for Geneva. Caught AF 1693, left at 10:16 A.M. in a Caravelle aircraft with Don and Jackie in attendance, and landed at Nice at local time 11:53 A.M. (1 hour ahead of rest of Europe) after a 37 minute flight whereas schedule is 55 minutes! Nice was bathed in bright sunshine and was quite hot too. Andre Poray, Jean Michel Piquemal, Roger Voue, Mme. Bon Jour, H and some others met Master at the airport. Master and I were driven to 'Mariadis' in Parc Liserb to the house of Mme. Bon Jour, while Don and Jackie went with H to the nearby hotel where they stay. Immediately on arrival we had lunch. Master then rested for an hour. At 2:00 P.M. we assembled in the 'ashram' at the back for a welcome by 30 abhyasis assembled there. Tom Whitlam, H and Rolf were there as also Jim Metz of Boston whom I met for the first time, along with Sonia Anderson of Jamaican origin and Barbara Jeanne Levin, also of Boston, who have come here with Jim. Master gave a brief transmission for five minutes and then we returned to his room. The hookah was brought into service at once.

3 P.M. to 5 P.M. a long talk with Andre on Mission work in France. He wants 15 more preceptors for France! Master later agreed to this and H, Don, Jackie, Andre and Jim Metz were asked to take two cases each of a panel of 10 selected for thorough cleaning!

7:00 P.M. group satsangh at ashram taken by Master — 35 wonderful minutes! I later gave a talk on the specificity of our methods and the absolute need to follow the three elements of our *sadhana* meticulously — prayer, meditation, and cleaning. Back to Mariadis at 8:30 P.M. for dinner. Then again to the ashram for a '*darshan*' of Master for the selected invited public at 9:00 P.M. After this we went to the residence of Mme. Ythier, a hundred yards away, to sleep as there is no accommodation here at Mariadis. Bettina played a solo violin for Master before we retired at 11:00 P.M. Preparatory sitting for Roger Voue.

26 May 76 - Wednesday

Master resting at Mme. Ythier's residence. I conducted the 9:00 A.M. group satsangh at the ashram — then gave individual sittings to Roger Voue, Brigitte Michaud and Maguy Olivier to prepare them for provisional permission, which Master granted to all three, one after the other, between 9:30 A.M. and 10:30 A.M. After issuing the certificates Master told me, "Look, you have of course done the work but one mistake has occurred — you have given too much power." He laughed and said, "Look here, even I make mistakes. When I was giving this person permission I found that you had given him too much power. As soon as the thought 'too much power' arose in my mind, then I too gave him more power." Laughing happily, "Now these people do not have to meditate for three months."

Later, a Frenchman living in Canada, Jean-Claude Robolay, a film maker, came to see Master. Master gave him a short sitting and was greatly impressed with his condition. He told me, "This person's soul is very good. If he should commence the meditation I can give him direct help."

At 12 noon we had lunch with Mme. Ythier, Andre, Jean-Michel, Marianne and her daughter Bettina. Andre left for Toulon by car at 12:45 with our baggage. We left at 1:00 P.M. with Jean-Michel, drove with Roger Voue to Nice station, and left by a fast train at 14:05. Jim Metz, Sonia Anderson, Barbara Jeanne Levin and Tom Whitlam travelled with us. Don and Jackie have gone by car with H and Rolf. We arrived at Toulon at 3:40 P.M. (140 km.). Andre and several abhyasis met Master on arrival, and Andre drove us home to Sanary (15 km.). Master is tired and complained of stomach ache. Letters from Swaminathan and Narayanaswami give me first information of a recent serious illness Sulochana has undergone — and Krishna too away at Ooty NCC Camp!

Andre took me to the Centre Azur (YMCA) for group meditation. Elidir Davies, Kathleen, John and Ose Wadlow, were all there along with the three from Boston, as also H, Don, Jackie and Rolf. I conducted the group satsangh from 6:30 to 7:00 P.M. Just before we left the Centre Azur, Irene Pignatelli arrived by taxi, having taken 12 hours to arrive from Naples via Rome — thanks to airline strikes in Italy. Irene De Marle from Paris has also arrived. Over 40 were present for the satsangh.

Elidir is trying "spiritual healing" on Master.

27 May 76 - Thursday

Master slept well and so did I. Andre's bedroom is conducive to general peace. Elidir's work on Master has helped him to sleep naturally without recourse to His *'kriya'* for sleep. I went to the Centre Azur at 9:00 A.M. and conducted group satsangh from 9:30 A.M. to 10:05 A.M. with about 50 abhyasis present. Then back to L'Hippocampe.

Between 10:30 and 11:30 I granted provisional permission on behalf of Master to the following whom I have been preparing for the past two or three days: Stephan Brander (Switzerland), Guy Voue (Epernon), Yvon Combe (Roquebrunne), Jean-Francois Mincet (Paris).

Irene De Marle and H had lunch with Master at Andre's residence. Long discussion between Andre and H after lunch. Andre's main problem seems to be 'tolerance' for all and everything, which he interprets as a commandment (almost) not to propagate any single system! I gave a long talk on this 'tolerance' and explained the 'active' and 'passive' aspects for almost one hour.

At 3:00 P.M. Master was escorted to Centre Azur and conducted group meditation. 50 abhyasis present. The sitting was very deep. After this sitting Master rested till 5:00 P.M. and went back to L'Hippocampe. I remained behind to give preparatory sittings to five persons proposed for provisional permission. I also gave an individual sitting to Pierre Faideau of Paris.

After this I accompanied H to the Hotel De La Tour at Sanary where Don, Jackie, Stella are all staying. I gave them a group sitting and then came back to L'Hippocampe for dinner. Andre, Martine and her husband Michel came in briefly to greet Master.

After dinner, Master sat out with his hookah for over an hour, and told me that he had adopted two techniques in this afternoon's transmission. He had used very subtle transmission and then, after some time, potentised it so that potency may develop in the abhyasis. He said, "Give a light transmission, and after some time have this thought that the abhyasi is becoming potentised. It depends on the dosage of the transmission. And if you are able to come to the base of it, then it will become the central region! There is also danger in it. The work can be completed in one second. How can I ever praise Lalaji Saheb sufficiently! If there is a guru he must be like Him."

Later we had a long discussion with Andre on French Mission work, and methods to be adopted here. Elidir Davies came at 9:30 P.M. to do his healing work on Master. He spoke at length to Master about his work in U.K. He says he has a large group of persons with him, mostly healers etc., "people who use their hands to touch other people to help them", as he put it! The sum and substance of his long monologue was that he is no longer doing anything even faintly resembling Sahaj Marg meditation — though for himself he claimed to still follow Master! When he told Master about psychic and spiritual healing techniques, Master taught him a yogic technique of recouping one's lost energy! Master said, "Stand facing the sun with your hands upraised, palms facing the sun. Do not look at the sun, but gaze at the tip of your nose. Feel that energy is coming into you through the palms of your hands, while mentally counting from one to seven slowly. Repeat this seven times." Then, characteristically, Master added, "I can charge you with energy in a second!" Elidir failed to grasp this. Master then added, "Of course, if a person has the necessary approach, he can draw energy direct from the Cosmic. But your approach is not to that level yet." This too Elidir ignored in his anxiety to talk about himself.

After this Andre spent half an hour with Master in our bedroom. Master confirmed Andre's approach to be *prabhu-prapanna*, and said that after taking him through a few of the 64 points, he will pull him up to the central region! Master told Andre, "Outside our *sanstha* there is no person higher than you in India and the whole world!" Lucky Andre!

28 May 76 - Friday

Master slept well. I went to Centre Azur and conducted the morning satsangh at 9:15 A.M. — about 60 were present. Good meditation. Then I spoke for about half an hour to the assembled abhyasis with Andre translating in French. Back to L'Hippocampe at 11:30 A.M. Master ready after his morning ablutions. Left at noon for Sanary for Master's lunch with Don and Jackie. Others present totalled 19! Lunch at the 'Au Roy D'Ys Creperie' — we had 'Crepes Indienne'! A sort of rava dosa stuffed with champignon etc. Back to L'Hippocampe for an hour's rest for Master, and then to Centre Azur at 3:00 P.M. From 3 P.M. to 5 P.M. Master devoted to the English group exclusively. Master developed pain after this and returned home. I conducted the evening group meditation at 6:00 P.M. Then, on behalf of Rev. Master, I granted provisional permission to Patrick Fleury, and his mother Paule Fleury.

H drove me back home. H and Rolf said good-bye to Master as they leave tomorrow early morning for Munich.

Master is in considerable pain. Jim Metz did some healing work on him.

Centres Functioning in France:

Nice — 25 abhyasis; Golfe Juan (15 km. west of Nice) — 15 abhyasis; St. Laurent du Var (5 km. west of Nice) — 10 abhyasis; will be attended to by Jean-Michel, Jean Francois Mincet, Yvon Combe and Brigitte Michand.

Toulon: Maguy Olivier.

Cannes: Roger Voue.

Paris: Pierre Faideau, Irene and Guy Voue.

Figaniers (4 km. from Draguignan): Mme. Paule Fleury, Patrick Fleury (also part Paris).

Sanary: Andre Poray.

Vallauris (25 km. west of Nice): Marcel Fievet and Pierre Fievet.

Lyon: Irene Arago.

Total abhyasis strength at all centres is about 150. It is spread-out considerably, unlike Denmark where all abhyasis are concentrated.

29 May 76 - Saturday

I conducted the 9:30 A.M. morning satsangh at Centre Azur — 50 abhyasis were present. Then I gave a second sitting to a small group — Stella, Irene Pignatelli, Irene Di Marle, and Toni Bernardi, who arrived this morning. Then took up a third group — Barbara Jeanne, Sonia Anderson and Irene Arago for preparation to provisional permission. Back home at noon.

After lunch Master sat out with his hookah, and somehow the talk veered to the subject of death. Master talked about Yama the Lord of Death and confirmed that such a cosmic functionary does exist, according to his own experience. He said, "Look here. This is a private conversation, but if you reveal it to Poray Sahib there will be no objection. It was the time of the death of Umesh's mother, and it was only a question of a few hours more. Pandit Rameshwar Prasad was with me, and brother, how may I tell you? When I looked at Umesh's mother I was wonderstruck to see a ring like thing around her neck. I was not able to understand what it could be. When I thought over it, I understood that it was the noose of Yama.

I became enraged. Aré! My wife had Yama's noose around her neck. I began preparation for the destruction of Yama. At that moment, I heard Lalaji's voice from above. He said, 'Yes. You can destroy Yama and there is no doubt about it. The necessary power is there in you. But please think over one thing and then do his destruction. If you destroy Yama, then you have to look after his work.' Now look here! This was Lalaji's grace, that He did not say 'No' to it. But my anger immediately cooled off. If I had to do this work, I mean Yama's, who would do my work? However, with my will power I destroyed the noose around my wife's neck. Now you can see that Yama is there, and the noose of Yama is also there, and this is a matter of my personal experience. Now you can tell this to the Sahib."

At lunch we were joined by Marga, and Jean-Michel. Master praised Jean-Michel's devotion and work highly, and appointed him Secretary of the Mission in France.

To Centre Azur at 2:30 P.M. Master took satsangh — 105 present. 25 wonderful minutes. Then a large number of group photos were taken.

Between 4:00 P.M. and 5:45 P.M. on behalf of the Revered Master I granted provisional permission to Barbara Jeanne Levin and Sonia Anderson, both of Boston, Mass., and to Irene Arago of Lyon.

Then I interviewed a group of persons proposed by Andre for future preceptorship — the Sahaj Marg Bank as Andre laughingly called it. Got back home at 6:30 P.M.

Stella, Stephan and Sonia came at 7:00 P.M. to say good-bye to Master as they leave for Switzerland tomorrow early morning. After dinner, Elidir came and Andre, Elidir and I had a long talk in Master's presence about Mission work. I gave them my open mind and Master remained silent. Later Elidir did his healing work on Master and left.

30 May 76 - Sunday

Mid-point of tour in terms of number of days elapsed.

To Centre Azur at 9:00 A.M. I conducted the group meditation at 9:30 A.M. for half-an-hour. About 100 abhyasis present. Then between 10:45 and 11:30 A.M. on behalf of Revered Master, I granted provisional permission to Marcel Fievet and Pierre Fievet.

Master came to the Centre at 12 Noon and sat with the group for half-an-hour. Then there was a grand lunch for all together with Master — 115 were present for this lunch. After lunch Master rested till 3:00 P.M. I sat with the group, telling them stories of the parrot's way to freedom, the *yaksha prasna*, etc. Master came back to the hall at 3:00 P.M. and conducted group satsangh for 30 minutes. Then from 4 P.M. to 5:15 P.M. we had a preceptor's meeting. Present: Andre Poray, Jean-Michel, Roger Voue, Guy Voue, Marcel Fievet, Pierre Fievet, Mme. Paule Fleury, Patrick Fleury, Irene De Marle, Irene Arago, Jean Francois Mincet, Yvon Combe, Maguy Olivier, Brigitte Michaud — all 14 representatives of France! (Pierre Faideau, the 15th is absent, having left for Paris). Others present: Elidir, Kathleen and John Wadlow — U.K.; Jim, Barbara Jeanne and Sonia — U.S.; Don and Jackie — Canada; Irene Pignatelli — Italy. Total 23 preceptors!! Not bad for a European meet of preceptors! Master occupied the chair and gave a personal message. Then I spoke for one hour. Then group photos were taken. Master left at 5:40 P.M. I stayed till 6:40 P.M. giving more sittings.

Post dinner talk with Master:

1) *Avatars* come **only** from *mahamaya*. The story circulated by preceptor R. Seshadri that Sri Krishna came from the central region or near-about it is **NOT** correct, said Master. Master confirmed this by inter-communications with Sri Krishna himself.

2) A Special Personality is higher than an *avatar*. He can draw spiritual power unlimited, **as also** power from the region of *mahamaya*. Avatars come with specified powers for a specified job.

3) Sri Rama, the *avatar*, built a foundation of culture and ethics for society. Sri Krishna built upon this foundation and introduced *bhakti* into *sadhana*. Therefore Sri Krishna is considered a greater *avatar*.

4) Master said that there is a point in the heart which, if one's will is applied upon it, then the Master **MUST** come!

5) For provisional permission only the *atma* region is filled with power. For full permission the full heart is filled with power, and then the full system is filled with power.

Master related a humorous story of how he gave a transmission of 'spiritual wine' to a Kayastha friend during the Holi festival — and how Lalaji reprimanded him for it.

The day ended with Elidir's healing session on Master.

31 May 76 - Monday

Master's constipation relieved by bowel movement. I conducted the 9:30 A.M. satsangh at Centre Azur — only 60 present, all the rest have left. Then I gave a number of sittings. Saw Kirlian Effect with Guy Voue. After lunch to Centre Azur with Master, who took 3:00 P.M. satsangh. Then sat for two and a half hours with all the abhyasis. Questions and answers. Piano session by Jean-Marc Roosz of Toulon followed by the playing of Schumann's 'Requiem', and then a Shiva dance by a Malagasy abhyasi,

Rajohnson. Then Master bade farewell to all and left for L'Hippocampe. I stayed on till 6:15 P.M., gave one more group sitting and then went home. Elidir came at 9:00 P.M. and stayed till 10:30 for long discussion with Master on karma, samskara, etc.

1 Jun. 76 - Tuesday (Italy)

Left at 10:15 A.M. for Toulon with Andre, and took the 11:32 fast train for Nice — departure 11:50 and arrived Nice at 1:50. Many abhyasis travelled on the train with Master. At Nice we stayed briefly for about one and a quarter hours for rest for Master in the basement room of Y's book-shop on the Boulevard Victor Hugo. Irene Pignatelli, Yvon Combe, Brigitte Michaud, Mme. Bon Jour were all there with Roger Voue to help Master. We left for the airport at 3:15 P.M. The Boston trio — Jim, Sonia and Barbara Jeanne left for Rome by an earlier flight. Andre was due to leave at around 3:00 P.M. for Barcelona and so had already said good-bye to Master at Toulon. Our group of five, Master, Irene, Jackie, Don and I, left by Air France 2642 at 4:32 P.M. — 12 minutes late and arrived Rome, Leonardo Da Vinci Airport at 5:20 P.M. Irene went off from the airport to Naples. Sara and Clara met Master on arrival. Later, just as we were about to drive off, Toni and Anna Maria rushed over from Latina. The Australian girl Carol Williams was with Sara. Sara lives in a different place now, not at Casal Palocco but in Rome. We again had a basement room, and not too convenient at that. It was chilly and scantily furnished. Master relaxed with two quick hookahs, had a good dinner of dal and roti cooked by Sara's maid Shiblim, and was up till 10:45 P.M. telling stories of Swami Naradananda.

2 Jun. 76 - Wednesday

Master rested well though he suffered from acid pains in the stomach. He took group satsangh at 10:30 A.M. with about 14 present. A very powerful transmission, I felt completely intoxicated, and this condition lasted till 6:00 P.M. Tom arrived at noon by train from Nice. Fausto Russo and Dino Evangelista of Naples, proposed for provisional permission by Irene, came in the evening. Toni's sister Anne and some others also came. None were present from our old group! I conducted the evening group satsangh at 7:00 P.M. Master well and cheerful — spoke to abhyasis till 10:30 P.M. and went to bed at 10:30 P.M. He spent a painful and very restless night.

3 Jun. 76 - Thursday

Master had a bad night. Frequent doses of milk and one of Gelusil gave him some relief. At 7:00 A.M. he told me, "Lalaji is full of praise, and nothing but praise, for you. I will give you something now but I won't tell you what it is!"

He laughed in a teasing way, full of mischief in his eyes! Later he said, "One divine post has been lying vacant for many years. And Lalaji is telling me to fill it up, but not now. It shall be done when I reach Madras. I shall tell you the reason for it. When I do this work upon you, then I cannot take work from you for three days, and here you have to do a great deal of work and therefore this work cannot be done on this tour. There is also another thing. When this work is done you will start getting work — small and light work — during my presence here on earth only the smaller jobs will be given to you." A little later Master again spoke and said, "This post cannot be given to a woman, however much advanced she may be. A woman cannot undertake the work of destruction because in their nature destruction is not there. Yes! They can develop as much as man, or even beyond, but they cannot be given this post."

I think he is referring to the post of *Parishad*.

Yesterday evening Master agreed to grant provisional permission to Dino and Fausto. At 10:30 P.M. last night, Albert Holtslag of Holland saw me alone and spoke of his great longing to do Master's work. What a transformation there has been in his case! He was so cantankerous and cynical when I met him first in Denmark on this trip. He is an unbeliever, and but for Francoise's influence he would have gone home the day he came. After one sitting with me in Denmark, he asked me, "Chari, Do you really transmit, or do you pretend to transmit." I asked him, "Do you really receive transmission, or do you pretend to receive it?" That floored him and he became friendly thereafter. I spoke to Master about him, and Master smilingly agreed to his being given the work too. At 8:00 A.M. I took up the work of preparing all three and gave them individual sittings. Master is very happy with Toni. "I am restless to see her," he said. Lucky Toni!

Toni, Anne-Marie and Rina came at 10:30 A.M. because their car broke down. Master laughed and said to Toni, "See! I wanted to see you. I was restless for it and here you have come!" They left at noon for Latina.

Between 11:15 and 12:15, on behalf of Rev. Master, I granted provisional permission to Fausto Russo, Dino Evangelista and Albert Holtslag.

Master did not leave his room the whole day. A visit to the Vatican, planned for this morning, was cancelled as he was not for it. But in the evening he was better. To bed at 11:00 P.M.

4 Jun. 76 - Friday

Master had a bad night — considerable pain which milk helped to alleviate a little. He has also been having trouble in emptying the bladder. I had little sleep last night — slept at 5:45 A.M. and woke up at 7:45 A.M.! Master weak and depressed. Referred again to his death. Then he told me of a past occasion when he had urine-retention. He had been suffering for a couple of days with severe pain. He had been lying on his charpoy when suddenly he felt a "push" which Lalaji had given in the back, in the lumbar region, "from above". This made him run to the bathroom to relieve himself! He told me he has been lying on his side as he did on that occasion, waiting for Lalaji's push, but nothing happened. Later he passed urine and became cheerful and happy again.

From 3:00 P.M. rain commenced and went on the whole evening. At 5:00 P.M. we went in Sara's car to the F.A.O., 'C' Building, for the public meeting fixed for 5:30 P.M. held in the German room. Sara spoke to introduce Master. Then Don Sabourin gave a short lecture after which I delivered the main lecture for about half-an-hour, simultaneously translated into Italian by Toni. Master transmitted to the full hall and we left at 6:50 P.M. for home. Toni went off to Latina. Master said he had transmitted the *samadhi* condition. The sitting was wonderful.

Master went to bed early after dinner as we are to go to Latina tomorrow morning.

5 Jun. 76 - Saturday

Master had a very bad night — and naturally I had a bad one too. He wanted to cancel the Latina trip but at 7:00 A.M. he told me that Lalaji had asked him to go. We left in Sara's car at 9:55 A.M. with Leela and Carol Williams, arriving Latina 75 km. away at 11:00 A.M. It rained right through, and on till 3:00 P.M. We found a group of four abhyasis from France had arrived including Maguy Olivier and Jean Francois Mincet. Also here are the Boston trio, Don and Jackie, Albert and Francoise, Victoria Checa and five abhyasis from Naples. Master is in pain and went to bed with a hot water bottle. Public meeting at 6:00 P.M. I spoke for about 40 minutes and then Master transmitted — it was superb! Meeting ended at 7:00 P.M. Master up with abhyasis till 11:00 P.M.

6 Jun. 76 - Sunday

The first night of full sleep for me since leaving Madras! Master slept through the night and did not get up even once for milk. Master gave me a sitting for 13 minutes in the morning. No transmission — only cleaning! Master in fine form. Group satsangh at 10:30 A.M. for 22 abhyasis present. More have arrived from France — Paule and Patrick Fleury, Jean Marc and his sister Anna — the group from France now totals 12. Sara, Leela and Carol came at noon from Rome (they had gone back last night after the public meeting). We all went to Prato Di Coppolo — the Rizzo residence, for lunch. Fifty abhyasis were present for lunch. I gave first sitting to Evaldo Covalloro of Rome and three others including a girl from Firenze.

5:00 P.M. — meeting of preceptors. Eighteen present including myself: Paule Fleury, Patrick Fleury, Maguy Olivier, Jean-Francois — France; Don and Jackie — Canada; Anna-Maria, Rina, Toni, Dino, Fausto, Sara — Italy; Jim, Sonia and Barbara Jeanne — U.S.A.; Albert — Holland; Carol Williams — Australia. Master did not attend this meeting but rested in Rina's room with a few abhyasis and the hookah.

Meeting ended at 6:00 P.M. I took 6:15 P.M. group satsangh. Forty-two abhyasis present. Back to Toni's house at 8:30 after dinner.

7 Jun. 76 - Monday

Master slept well the whole night and woke up at 7:00 A.M. He said, "I am quite well now. Toni's house has a good atmosphere. There is a great deal of grossness there — the person living there is like that! See how much rest I am able to get here!" Left Toni's house in Latina at 9:15 A.M. and reached Rome at 10:30. Rain all the way.

Discussion on reincarnation. Master told two stories, one about a Brahmin whose spirit continued to be seen and felt until opium was offered to it, and the second about his own son who, after death, asked for puris in a dream. He also quoted Swami Ram Tirth on death! Then a quatrain from the Sufi Sarmad:

"The Pain of Love is like the butterfly
Wafted on a breeze;
Going hither and thither without purpose.
But the moth is able to immolate itself in the flame!"

Some of the French group — Maguy Olivier, Jean-Francois, Anne Roosz — all left for France in the afternoon. The Fleurys and some others will be in Rome till Master leaves. I went out shopping with Don, Jackie, Anna-Maria Rizzo and Toni Bernardi. I bought myself a blue suit and one fawn jacket.

8 Jun. 76 - Tuesday

Individual sittings to Arul Pragasam and Carol Williams. Master said he would soon awaken in me a state of miracles — a state where miracles would happen in a natural way without my even knowing that they are occurring — but yet they would happen! But I would have to fast three days for it! He could not say when he would take up this work but felt it would be soon. Irene Pignatelli came and spent the whole day with Master. I conducted evening group satsangh from 6 P.M. to 6:40 P.M. for about 25 persons. Master slept from noon to nearly 6 P.M.

9 Jun. 76 - Wednesday

Master up at 7:00 A.M. well refreshed. Shri Mahinda Silva, Secretary, Ministry of Agriculture, Sri Lanka, arrived. We had gone to the Vatican at 9:00 A.M. accompanied by many abhyasis. Master saw the Pope at about 4 feet distance. I gave a special sitting to four French abhyasis of Toulon who leave this evening. Second public meeting at FAO. Full hall.

10 Jun. 76 - Thursday (Denmark)

Master woke up refreshed. Mr. Mahinda Silva had a private session with Master. I gave six or seven individual sittings in the morning.

We left Sara's house at 2:15 P.M. for Leonardo Da Vinci airport. Victoria Checa took an earlier chartered flight to Copenhagen. We left at 3:35 P.M. by a DC 9 aircraft on SAS Flight SK-682 and arrived in Copenhagen at 5:05 P.M. local time after a two and a half hour direct flight. On the way there were big thunderhead formations which the pilot skillfully avoided. He announced that the flight would arrive late at destination but we actually landed at 5:05 against a scheduled arrival of 5:20 P.M.!!

Master said, "Look here, somebody told me that the plane will arrive 20 minutes late, but we have come 20 minutes before time! This matter is worth studying. When I heard that the plane was going to be late, I began to think that the people who will assemble would be much inconvenienced. Look here, my thought has had its effect — and maybe it is not its effect also — but the plane has nevertheless come 20 minutes early. You may think about this."

After we had waited 20 minutes, the welcoming abhyasis came. We drove to Mikala's home.

Group satsangh at 8:00 P.M. taken by Don. Wavered for five minutes and then steadied up. Later it was superb! Charlotte O'Brien is here with her baby. Fred is here, and his mother has come over. Judith and Neil are already here. The Boston trio stayed behind at Rome to go back home. Rolf Muller and Irene Brandt of Munich have also arrived.

After dinner, Master told me of his serious concern with the total loss of character in India, and said he would have to take up the work of destruction of evil forces if necessary. "Look here, whoever you may send here should be a person of character. Please remember this. Here a person can be spoilt very soon and it is very necessary that whoever may come here should be a person of character."

11 Jun. 76 - Friday

Master had a poor night and suffered much pain. Today was a rest day for him. A quiet day for me too. It is sunny but fresh and cold. Received a letter from P.D. Gaekwad, giving Sister Kasturi's tour programme - Delhi - Bangalore - Vijayawada - Vizag - Calcutta - Assam - Lucknow, commencing 6 June 76. Master commented:

"I do not know why people keep inviting her. I have been thinking about this for some time now. What is the speciality in her that people keep inviting only Kasturi and no one else? Once I had asked this question of some abhyasis of Assam, and they had replied that she gives very good speeches, and also gives them sittings. And this is of course true. But often she says the wrong things! Now I tell you one thing. Kasturi is no doubt capable, but she is not advancing. She is perhaps in the second ring of splendour and maybe she has advanced so much (making a space with two fingers, showing a minute space). Your father is also in the second ring but he is advancing a little more than her, and Saheb, in the case of Kasturi I had to work a great deal because she was incapable of advancing by herself. Now I shall think over this matter as to why they invite only her."

There is a letter from Prakash pointing out that preceptors are going on tour without formal approval and asking for action on this as appropriate. I felt he was making a veiled reference to Kasturi's proposed (in fact already commenced) tour. I took this opportunity of asking Master whether he had given approval to her tour. He answered, "No. This is the work of the Secretary. I have not given her any permission."

In the evening at about 4:00 P.M. Master asked me whether I felt any heaviness near about the sternum. I asked whether it was so. Master said, "Whatever it may be — you may tell me whether there is heaviness or not."

At that time I couldn't feel anything and said so, but just a few minutes later I felt a grossness or heaviness down from the hollow of the throat to the tip of the sternum along the right. I reported this to Master. He said, "That is correct. Now keep observing and tell me tomorrow morning." Later in the evening I felt the blackness falling like the mercury in a thermometer till it was about halfway down between the throat and the bottom end of the sternum. To bed at 11:30 P.M.

12 Jun. 76 - Saturday

Woke up very late at 7:00 A.M. No shave or bath! At 8:00 A.M. Master asked me how I felt. I told him my observation. He said, "Look, I had forgotten it — but the thought had been made and its effect was there. Now let me see what is the matter." After a few moments he smiled and said, "Yes, now I understand it. Reality has descended into you!" He beamed with pleasure, patted me on the shoulder and said, "Sabash! Sabash! Come near me," — and patted me again heartily on both shoulders and said, "You are the best among my sons." He then reverted to the matter of Kasturi's tour and said, "Nothing will go wrong because the Supporter is there, but I am having only this concern that the Mission may not be split up. In any case with me present here such a thing cannot happen. Sarnad is a very good person and I will tell him something about this. Now brother there are very high powers in you, and other than you such powers are in no one else. Now little by little you will have to take over the work. I would like to retire but Lalaji is not permitting it. He is saying, 'Not now.'!"

I gave 13 individual sittings through the day. Hans Jorgen Hvid came to see Master — wants to give up his preceptorship. I spoke to him and he has agreed to continue to work. Stella phoned from Etoy to say she will arrive on Tuesday.

At 5:00 P.M. Master called me to him and said, "I want to tell you a rare experience I had. Please note it down. You of course know Karuna Shankar, and perhaps you have also met him. It is about two years since he passed away. He used to be in Pilibhit. I was just thinking that it is more than two years since he has passed away, but I have not been able to know whether he has been liberated or not. He did not have much of a higher approach — perhaps it was up to *para brahmanda mandal* — but of course there was no question of his taking rebirth here. But this question kept coming up in me as to whether he had been reborn in some other world. Once or twice I had even thought over this matter but did not get any answer — my heart was not giving a confirmation. Now look here, just now I have got a telegram (pointing upwards to its source) that he has been liberated. It has taken two years! Now such a person is to be called 'Master' (meaning Lalaji). Even after his (Karuna Shankar's) death Lalaji has been working upon him. Otherwise such a thing could not have happened." I asked why Lalaji had to do this work himself. Master replied, "Karuna Shankar was His direct disciple. Therefore his work was done by Him. Now look here, how much time it has taken. Today liberation has become very cheap. Please note this because such experiences are rarely to be had."

At about 8:30 P.M. Mr. Krishnamurthi of Geneva and his wife arrived at Mikala's house. Birthe took group satsangh while Master was alone with the Krishnamurthis. Late at night just as I was going to bed, Master told me that Lalaji had confirmed that Shri Karuna Shankar's liberation had been done just this afternoon. Master said, "See, it has taken more than two years." He laughed and said, "Karuna Shankar has gone to see the Ashram." A little later, just as I was about to switch off the lights, Master said, "It will be good if you do not take any food tomorrow. Today you have got a very very big thing — accidentally! Or you may think this to be Lalaji's work. You will have to offer *prasad* when you reach Madras."

13 Jun. 76 - Sunday

Yesterday Master approved Palle Kousgaard for work and I had given a first preparatory sitting. This morning I gave him another preparatory sitting. Master took group satsangh at 10:30 A.M. It is a cold and windy day. Left at 2:15 P.M. for the Kunstakadamiet in Copenhagen for the public meeting at 3:00 P.M. Birthe spoke in Danish, followed by Thomas, also in Danish. Then Jackie Sabourin spoke in English and lastly I spoke. The meeting ended at 4:45 P.M. with Master's transmission. We returned to Ehlersvej at 5:00 P.M.

14 Jun. 76 - Monday

At 7:00 A.M. on behalf of Master, I granted provisional permission to Palle Kousgaard. This was followed by about 10 more individual sittings to abhyasis during the day.

At 12:15 P.M. Master called me into his room and when we were alone said, "The post of *Parishad* is vacant and this you already know. Now Lalaji Saheb wants this post to be filled up soon so that it should not be given to anybody else!"

I asked Master how this could happen, that the post be assigned to someone without his knowledge/approval. Master said, "There can be direct orders from above. I had thought of doing this work after returning to Madras but, dear brother, this matter has now become urgent." Then suddenly he said, "Look here. Now the work has begun — just a little part of it but now you may think that the post is reserved for you." (laughing happily)

Just before this conversation, Master had asked for a copy of *Reality at Dawn* to read page 113 where he has written about the cosmic positions of *Maha Parishad* and *Parishad*, and also dealt with the other posts such as *Dhruv Pad, Druvadhipati*, etc. He called all the assembled abhyasis in and then read out the relevant paragraphs to them too, to "kindle their interest by creating aspiration for such posts," he said! Later Master told me about Babu Madan

Mohan Lal and his craving for this position of *Parishad*. He was not given it — and it appears that this position has been vacant for many many years. Master said that according to needs of the times these posts were filled — and anyone could be selected for them. He said appointment or removal was a second's matter. Then he suddenly added, "Lalaji Saheb says that whoever is sent to the West you should ensure that it is a person of character. Here the people are so fallen that I cannot even describe it. Our people can be easily spoiled here. Please remember this, that if you send anybody here, he must be a man of strong character."

At 1:15 P.M. we went to 'Magazin Du Nord' in Copenhagen for shopping. Birthe took the evening satsangh at 8:30 P.M.

15 Jun. 76 - Tuesday

At 8:45 A.M. Master said that he was going to continue the *Parishad* work on me, and gave me a sitting which lasted four minutes! I felt as if I was in total darkness but it became progressively brighter, and finally brilliant. At noon I felt a state of intoxication, what Master calls "lost condition". I gave 17 individual sittings through the day.

Martine Faideau phoned from Paris to say that she and Pierre will come here to Copenhagen on Friday for two days stay with Master.

There was no evening satsangh today.

16 Jun. 76 - Wednesday

Master is in some pain today. After his bath he gave me a sitting lasting eight minutes. At the end I felt as if I was trembling all over, but there was no visible trembling. Nor could I feel any unease or other adverse sensation. But when I put my right palm on my thigh, I could feel a sort of subcutaneous vibration. This was quite intense — this inner vibration — and continued till 3:00 P.M. It subsided after this.

I gave a total of 20 individual sittings today. There was again no evening satsangh. Master said there was no need for it, people being already "full" as he put it.

I have been fasting since Monday 14th. Today is the third day of fast. I am allowed fluids and light food in the evening only. Master has been extending it day by day, and when I asked him why he did not tell me in the beginning that I would have to fast so many days, he laughed and replied that he was following Lalaji's technique in this, as in everything else that he does. It seems Lalaji had made him fast like this, one day after another, on an important occasion.

Just before going to bed Master smiled and said, "Shall I reveal it to you? There is a saint in Madras. He is very happy that you are being given the post of *Parishad*. Now look here. He is of course a saint but he has not yet lost his narrow-mindedness. He is happy because this post has been given to a person of Madras."

17 Jun. 76 - Thursday

Master well. After his bath he gave me a long sitting of 25 minutes. It was very subtle and deep. About midway through the sitting I saw myself lying stark naked near a white gleaming outcrop of rock which resembled a tombstone. I was alive, but thin, emaciated and stark naked. Just as the sitting ended, Master solemnly said, "Now by Lalaji's grace, you have been granted the status of *Parishad*." This was at 9:30 A.M. local European time, and therefore 2:00 P.M. I.S.T. Just before the sitting began, Master told me, "Look, I am telling you your own condition. There is absolutely no power grossness in you and when so much cleaning has been done and there is so much power in you too, it is now only necessary to mould it properly. Brother, this is Lalaji's work. Lalaji told me, 'I had made only you,' (meaning Babuji) and you know what I replied to Lalaji Saheb? I said, 'Saheb, I shall make one dozen persons,' and Lalaji laughingly said, 'I congratulate you!' Now look here, I can send any fool that I want to to the central region — what is there in it? But Saheb, to make a Personality is something else. I am only now able to understand how far-sighted Lalaji Saheb was. In your making too, sufficient effort had to be made. You are no doubt very capable and there is no doubt about this. During the last three days I have been looking for every minute defect inside you, and whatever I could find I have taken out." He laughed and said, "I also excited you a little but you did not know it — anger was surfacing but it did not manifest in you."

I laughed and said that for the past three days I had been noticing irritation cropping up in me, which I had been able to control, and that I therefore knew that he was doing something in me. He laughed and said, "No food today, night and day both times." I said it was OK.

After this I related to him my experience during the sitting. Explaining it Master said, "You are not a corpse but it reveals your condition. Your condition is that which I describe as the naked condition. This condition is now in you. Now you should do a lot of work."

I was also forbidden from giving any sittings today — except the four I had already given before this sitting.

18 Jun. 76 - Friday

Master well, also well rested after a good night's sleep. Udo and Magda arrived from Hamburg by car in the morning. H and his wife Inna, accompanied by H's secretary Renate Baumann, all arrived in the afternoon from Munich by air. Late in the evening Pierre Faideau and his wife Martine arrived from Paris by air. Stella Jaquerod-Davis also arrived from Etoy by train. A full house!

At 1:30 P.M. I went with Vibe to the flat of Raja Srinivasan and Leela for lunch. Left there at 2:45 P.M. and went with Vibe to her home for about 15 minutes and then got back to Mikala's house. Vibe upset by many problems of her mind — some temporary problems with "power", "liberation" etc. — also why the "Ultimate" cannot be brought down here, etc.! Problems galore. H brought lovely colour photos of Master taken at Munich by Irene Brandt Ramirez, and processed by Carlos — both abhyasis. They are sold at 60 DKr. each — a stiff price. I bought two.

19 Jun. 76 - Saturday

Master said a couple of days ago that he wanted to upgrade some preceptors to full permission — and Vibe, Thomas, Jan, Jytte, Elsebeth and Mikala were chosen for this honour and privilege! This morning Master wanted to take up their work. Originally he wanted to do it all himself, but he said Lalaji told him, "You have prepared Parthasarathi, and powers are there in him too — now take work from him! Your health is not good and you should rest." But Babuji still wanted to take up one case himself, with me observing. So he took up Thomas Mogensen first with me commenting on the various stages of the work as he did it. Master complimented me on my observation and entrusted the other five cases to me — though permission would be granted only by him. "This is the work of a very higher level — you do the work, but the full permission can only be given by the representative of the Master, Lalaji

Saheb." I remarked that on Master's behalf I had been granting provisional permission to abhyasis. Master smiled and said that that was OK, but full permission could only be granted by him as Lalaji's representative. Anyway I took up the remaining five cases one by one and prepared them. Master granted them permission as I finished with them. All six were greatly elated and happy. The work took me from 10:30 A.M. to 12:30 P.M. Master complimented me on the work done, particularly in the case of Jytte Gravesen — the last case I took up! I rested the whole afternoon. In the evening we had a meeting of all abhyasis. H spoke to them, very well indeed, and I later spoke to them for 20 minutes. Later Master's first movie film was screened for the benefit of the non-Denmark abhyasis present.

20 Jun. 76 - Sunday

Don Sabourin and Jackie left to go to Delhi via Moscow by Aeroflot. They travel on a cheap fare and so could not fly with Master on the scheduled SAS service. Renate left for Munich at 10:30, followed by H and Inna at 2:00 P.M. H appeared very moved when parting from Master. H and Inna have developed great devotion for Master and are a lovely dedicated couple. Udo and Magda left last at 5:00 P.M. to return to Hamburg in their car. At 2:00 P.M. Mikala and Palle threw a party for all present, but since the number present exceeded the food available a few, including myself, had to go without lunch! After lunch Mikala and Palle spoke briefly. There is already an emotional charge in the atmosphere at Master's impending departure, and I too felt quite moved and overcome. The group became quite thin by the evening. To bed at 11:30 P.M. Woken up by Vibe coming into the room at 12:50 A.M. She kept Master up till 2:00 A.M. with her personal problems. Very frank and fearless, the questions she asked. She is definitely a very brave, an extraordinarily brave girl. She also has a great deal of faith and confidence in Master, otherwise she would not have come to him with her questions. Master was very upset, however and annoyed too. I pacified him and put him to bed after she left at 2:00 A.M.

21 Jun. 76 - Monday

Problems of Vibe. Thomas too very upset. Mikala saw Master alone at 11:30 A.M. to confess to exactly identical problems as Vibe has! Master continues to be very angry with Vibe. Later Vibe came and surrendered to Master and promised to obey his mandate. This pacified him and restored his good humour somewhat.

Master has referred several times to preceptor Dhond Rao of Kalahasti, and the need for his correction. Master appears to be very dissatisfied with his work and attitude and indiscipline. He said he had granted Dhond Rao provisional permission only due to compulsion by Dr. Varadachari.

Vibe still puzzled, shocked and sticking to her own opinions. Master still annoyed, but as he said, "She is not changing yet," I continue to plead with her and for her with Master. Thomas really hurt and very dejected. He has been pleading with Master to forgive her. A miserable day, on the whole.

Charlotte O'Brien and companion left for Norway.

22 Jun. 76 - Tuesday

Vibe came early morning 7 A.M. and spent half an hour alone with Master. Master smiled later and said all is well between them. He said, "She is of course a good girl. But I don't understand what goes wrong now and again in these persons." Vibe also smiling and looking happy, though lost too!

We left for Kastrup airport at 9:30 A.M. About 10 abhyasis assembled there to say good-bye to Master. We left Denmark by flight SK 987 at 12 noon, 35 minutes behind schedule. Our flight arrived at Frankfurt at 13:10 hours and left at 14:00 hours on its non-stop flight to Delhi. Master referred several times to Dhond Rao and the need to correct him, and also for the need to punish him if necessary. An uneventful 7 hours 55 minutes journey to Delhi.

(END OF EUROPEAN TOUR)

23 Jun. 76 - Wednesday (Delhi)

Landed at Palam airport Delhi, at 2:30 A.M. IST. Don, Jackie, Mr. Chopra, Krishnaswamy, Sat Deo and some 25 others received Master at the airport. I was informed at Palam that Shri Dhond Rao of Kalahasti had expired about 15 days ago!! Master has been referring frequently to him — and did not seem to know that Dhond Rao was no more. Must ask Master for clarification. We drove in several cars to Mr. Chopra's house where Master is to stay the day. Don and Jackie also came. We went to bed at 4:30 A.M. — and woke up again at 5:30 A.M.! Mr. Chopra had put up a *shamiana* and there was a festival atmosphere with a lot of abhyasis present.

Master, Don, Jackie, and I left for Madras by IC 540 at 6:20 P.M. About 50 abhyasis were at Palam to see Master off. A severe thunderstorm over Hyderabad shook the plane badly for some 20 minutes before we could land there — and also delayed the flight, so that we landed at Meenambakkam only at 10:15 P.M., 40 minutes late. Master drove off to Umesh's residence. Don and Jackie go to hotel Woodlands.

24 Jun. 76 - Thursday

Master at Besant Nagar the whole day. Went to see him in the evening. He is in bed resting.

25 Jun. 76 - Friday

Master came to 'Gayathri' at 4:00 P.M. He conducted satsangh at 6:00 P.M., had dinner with us, and went back to Besant Nagar at 9:30 P.M. Clarifying his 'double' vision in Mikala's house in Copenhagen, when he saw the normal scene, with Shahjahanpur superimposed over it, he said, "Something like a different layer is created above. Look here. This is a new bit of research. In this second layer other things are seen. It is written in the *Gita* that Sanjay, from where he was sitting, was able to see the war. But as far as I can understand it there was no question of any divine vision. Today I have discovered that a second layer is formed and this is correct."

Don and Jackie shifted into our home.

26 Jun. 76 - Saturday

To Besant Nagar for one hour. Gunde Rao Nagnoor has arrived from Gulbarga to rejoin Master.

27 Jun. 76 - Sunday

Whole day (within permissible limits of 7:30 to 10:00 A.M. and evening) at Besant Nagar. Master was to take a special group satsangh at 6:00 P.M. and then dine with us at 'Gayathri', but he developed stomach pain and cancelled this at 5:30 P.M. I rushed back to Gayathri where some 250 abhyasis including Dr. V. Parthasarathi and family had assembled, to announce this. Appa took the satsangh. Then Don addressed the gathering followed by several others.

28 Jun. 76 - Monday

Master was to go to Madurai, then to Virudhunagar, and I was to go with him. This trip was cancelled at 2:00 P.M. mainly I think at Umesh's insistence! He has challenged that Master would not go — and has won! Sarvesh has been here, and stays back. His family will be called to Madras.

29 Jun. 76 - Tuesday

To Besant Nagar both morning and evening. Master better. I find he cannot tolerate more than five persons at a time in his room!

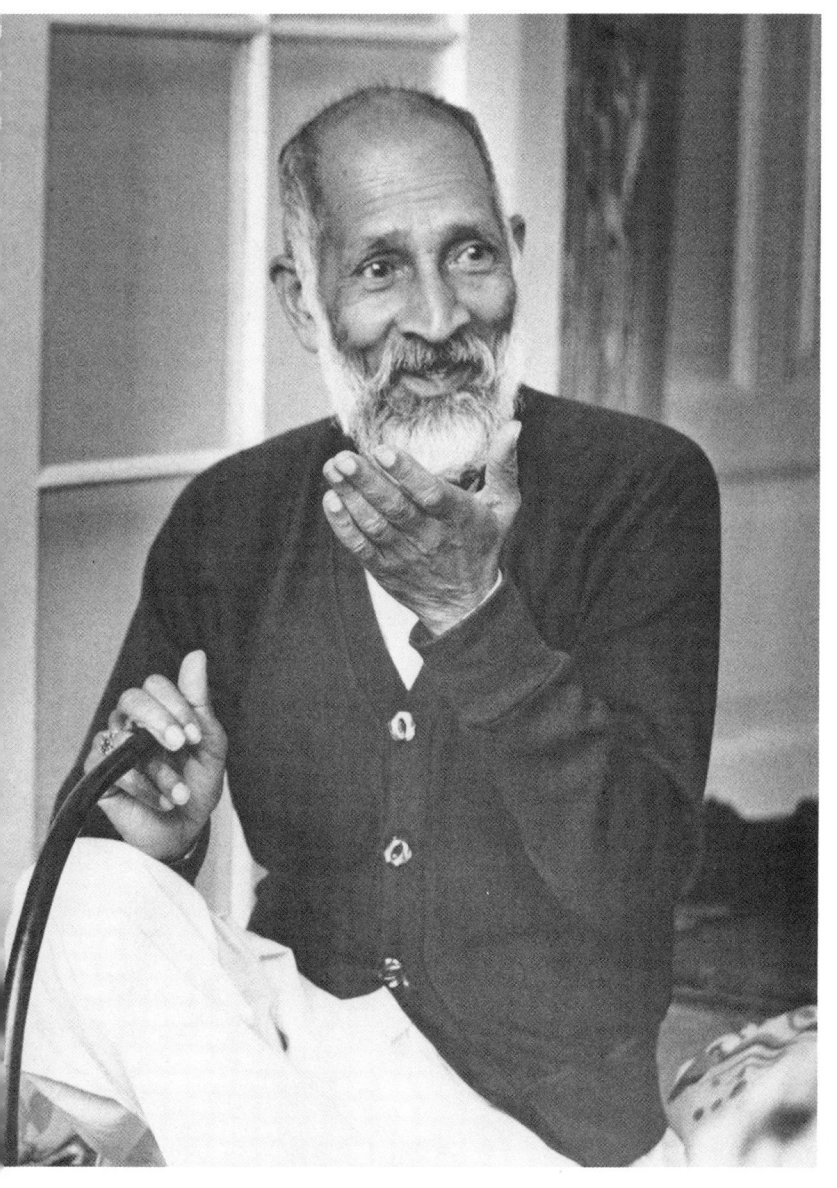

Glossary

Abhinaya: Acting, as in a theater; movements of the body, signs made by fingers, or facial expressions to denote various sentiments.

Abhyas: Practice.

Abhyasi: Aspirant; one who practices yoga in order to achieve union with God.

Agni: Fire.

Ajna Chakra (or Agya Chakra): The point located between the eyebrows. Trikuti.

Akarta: Non-doer; one who does not do.

Annamaya kosha: Physical sheath, or food sheath (matter).

Atma chakra: Heart chakra.

Avatar (or Avatara): Incarnation of a Divine soul.

Baniya: Merchant, shopkeeper; member of the Vaishya community or caste.

Baraat: Marriage procession.

Bhabhi: Elder brother's wife.

Bhagavad Gita: Divine knowledge given to Arjuna by Lord Krishna in the *Mahabharata*.

Bhajan: Chanted prayer.

Bhakti: Devotion.

Brahman (or Brahm): Creator, God.

Brahmanda (or Brahmand): Astral world. Cosmos.

Brahmanda mandal (or Brahmanda desh): Mental sphere, supra-material sphere, cosmic region; sphere where everything manifests under a subtle shape before taking place in the material world.

Brahma randhra: The point at the crown of the head.

Buddhi: Intellect.

Chela: A disciple.

Chit (or Chitta): Consciousness.

Chit-lake (or Cit-lake): Another name for Brahmanda Mandal.

Dakshinayana: The six months of the sun's southern path.

Darshan: Vision of someone's inner Reality.

Dharamsala: A hostel where spiritual pilgrims can stay free of charge.

Dhruvadhipati: Cosmic functionary below the Parishad who directs the work of the Dhruvas.

Dhruv Pad (or Dhruva): Cosmic functionary below the Dhruvadhipati who directs the work of the Vasus.

Fana: A spiritual condition; also, destroyed or sacrificed.

Geet: Song.

Gita: See *Bhagavad Gita*.

Gnanendriyas: Five senses pertaining to perception, knowledge or wisdom.

Gnani: One who has knowledge.

Guru: Master, who transmits light, knowledge; a spiritual teacher.

Guru dakshina: Offering by disciple to Guru for training received.

Guru Sthan: The place where the guru sits during satsangh.

Gyana (or Jnana): Supreme Wisdom or Knowledge leading to Realisation.

Hiranya garbha: A golden foetus; the name of Brahma the creator; a soul invested with the sukshma-sarira, or the subtle body.

Indriyas: Ten senses/organs of Indian philosophy, subdivided as jnana and karma indriyas. The former are five senses pertaining to perception, knowledge or wisdom, while the latter are five senses pertaining mainly to action.

Kaajal: A Hindu marriage ceremony performed by the groom's eldest brother's wife; also, black eye shadow.

Karmendriyas (or Karma indriyas): Organs, or senses, of action.

Khumra: Subtle form of spiritual intoxication.

Kriya: Action.

Kundalini: The power which is coiled like a serpent at the base of the spine.

Layavastha (or Laya avastha): The state of merging.

Mahamaya: The spiritual sphere where avatars come from.

Maha Parishad: The highest cosmic functionary; ruler of the universe.

Maha samadhi: The final samadhi when a saint renounces his body and enters the brighter world.

Manas: Psyche, mind.

Maya: Phenomenal appearance. It is really a power of God. All manifestation or expansion which seems illusory is the play of Maya. Illusion.

Mudras: Secret yogic exercises.

Nadi (or Naadi): The body's pulse beat; also, any tubular organ of the body.

Pandal: Tent.

Para Brahman (or Par Brahma): Indeterminate Absolute — God as the Ultimate Cause of Existence (see *Reality at Dawn*).

Parabrahmanda (or Para brahmanda): Supra-cosmic consciousness.

Para brahmanda mandal: Supra-cosmic region of the mind.

Paramanus: Subtle particles, fine particles.

Parishad: Cosmic functionary below the Maha Parishad who directs the work of the Dhruvadhipatis.

Pind: Material or gross existence, that which exists in the gross or material state.

Pind desh (or Pinda desh, or Pind pradesh, or Pinda pradesh): Material sphere; the heart region.

Prabhu-prapanna: Spiritual condition experienced as being both Master and one who has surrendered.

Prapanna: A spiritual stage; also, one who has surrendered.

Prasad (or Prasadam): Divinized food, usually sweet; an offering to Master or God.

Pucca: Ripe; complete.

Rishi: Saint; seer; one who has realized Self.

Sadhana: Spiritual practice.

Samadhi: State in which we stay attached to Reality. In Sahaj Marg the return to the original condition, which reigned in the beginning.

Sambandhi: Relation, relative; parents of bride and bridegroom.

Sankalpa (or Sankalp): An act of will.

Glossary

Sannyasa (or Sanyas): Renunciation of the world, solitary life of celibacy and asceticism.

Sannyasi (or Sannyasin): One who has renounced the world and leads a solitary life of celibacy and asceticism.

Sanstha: Spiritual tradition; organisation; group.

Shakti: Power.

Shamiana: Tent.

Shramdan: An offering of physical labour.

Siddhis: Capacity to do miracles; powers.

Sita-Phal: Custard apple, a fruit covered with small bumps.

Sooksma sharir (or Sukshma sharir, or Sookshma sharir, or Suksham sharir, or Sukshama sharir): Astral body, subtle body.

Tilak: Hindu marriage ceremony for the groom; also, pigment mark on the forehead.

Turiya: Fourth state; the other three being: Jagrat— waking state; Swapna— dream state; Sushupti— deep sleep state.

Turiya avastha: Fourth state of the soul, when it becomes one with God.

Upanayanam (or Uppanayana): Opening of the higher eye.

Uttarayana: The six months of the sun's northern path.

Vasu: Cosmic functionary below the Dhruva who conducts petty godly work in a local area.

Yaksha: A class of semi-divine beings; a living supernatural being.

Yaksha prasna: Series of questions asked by a *yaksha* to Dharma Putra in the *Mahabharata*.

Yatra: Voyage, spiritual pilgrimage.

Yoga: A system of Hindu philosophy showing means of emancipation of the soul from further migration, mainly subdivided as raja yoga and hatha yoga.

Yogi: One who practices yoga; one who achieves union with the Absolute.